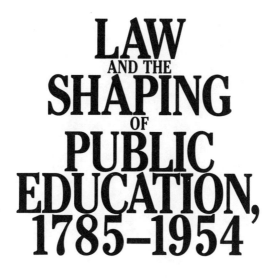

LAW
AND THE
SHAPING
OF
PUBLIC
EDUCATION,
1785–1954

LAW
AND THE
SHAPING
OF
PUBLIC
EDUCATION,
1785–1954

David Tyack
Thomas James
Aaron Benavot

The University of Wisconsin Press

Published 1987

The University of Wisconsin Press
114 North Murray Street
Madison, Wisconsin 53715

The University of Wisconsin Press, Ltd.
1 Gower Street
London WC1E 6HA, England

First printing

Printed in the United States of America

For LC CIP information see the colophon

ISBN 0-299-10880-5

For Elisabeth
dear wife, best friend, stimulating colleague

To Regina

For Ruhama
whose gentle spirit has touched mine

CONTENTS

vii

TABLES AND FIGURES

ACKNOWLEDGMENTS

We are most grateful to the Spencer Foundation and to Stanford University's sabbatical grant for supporting David Tyack's research and to the Center for the Study of Youth Development for funding the work of Thomas James and Aaron Benavot. The Center has been a superb place in which to pursue this study, and we thank colleagues there and in the School of Education for their support, interest, and criticism. Tyack also is grateful to the Rockefeller Foundation for providing a month of uninterrupted time for reflection and writing at the Villa Serbelloni.

We also wish to thank several colleagues who worked with us as research assistants. Three law students—Karen Harbeck, Susan Looper, and Michael Schlessinger—guided us through some complex legal paths and helped us in both the quantitative and doctrinal analysis of case law. Robert Lowe, coauthor of chapter 5, was imaginative and thorough in conceptualizing and researching the educational politics of Reconstruction. Jill Blackmore, Rene Fukuhara, and Arthur Hall assisted us in a variety of ways with library research and the preparation of our descriptive statistics.

Earlier versions of parts of this book have appeared as articles in *The American Historical Review, American Journal of Education, History of Education Quarterly, Law and Society Review, Pacific Historian, Teachers College Record, This Constitution*, and *School Days, Rule Days*, edited by David Kirp. We are indebted to the editors and blind reviewers of those journals for excellent suggestions for revision.

We are especially indebted by David Kirp, first for inviting Tyack to participate in a seminar on law and education under the sponsorship of Stanford's Institute for Research on Educational Finance and Governance —which was the origin of this study—and then for tough-minded criticism and excellent substantive suggestions. Carl Kaestle gave an earlier draft of the book a rigorous criticism that forced us to rethink a number of central questions. Throughout the writing and revisions Elisabeth Hansot helped us to discover our central themes and provided the right blend of stimulus and encouragement. In a series of illuminating discussions David Rogosa probed the meaning of our statistics with us. James Anderson, Stephen Arons, Larry Cuban, Don Fehrenbacher, Lawrence Friedman, Patricia Graham, Robert Gordon, John Meyer, Theodore Mitchell, Jeffrey Olson, John Richardson, John Simon, and Ann Starer gave us the benefit of their advice on part or all of the earlier versions of the book.

We thank them all and trust that readers will not tar them with the brush of our errors. With colleagues like these we have most enjoyed what James March calls "the pleasures of the process" in exploring what, for us, was a new and fascinating domain.

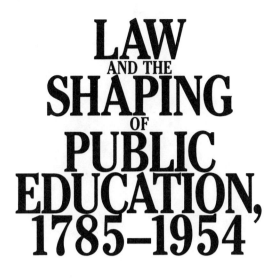

LAW
AND THE
SHAPING
OF
PUBLIC
EDUCATION,
1785–1954

Introduction

Law, says the judge as he looks down his nose,
Speaking clearly and most severely,
Law is as I've told you before,
Law is as you know I suppose,
Law is but let me explain it once more,
Law is the Law.

Yet law-abiding scholars write;
Law is neither wrong nor right,
Law is only crimes
Punished by places and by times,
Law is the clothes men wear
Anytime, anywhere,
Law is Good-morning and Good-night.[1]

W. H. Auden's "law-abiding scholars" have demystified the magisterial vision of law as a forbidding doctrinal realm guarded by robed sentinels. Law is custom, they say, it is politics, it is an intrinsic part of the economic system. Anthropologists, political scientists, sociologists, and historians have sought to link the black-letter world of judicial decisions, constitutions, and statutes with larger social, political and economic contexts. They probe how law and society interact. "The legal system, described solely in terms of formal structure and substance, is like some enchanted courtroom, petrified, immobile, under some odd, eternal spell," writes Lawrence Friedman. "What gives life and reality to the legal system is the outside, social world."[2]

The law is not a neutral instrument, enacted by impartial representatives in constitutional conventions or legislatures or interpreted by lawyers and judges in courtrooms hermetically sealed from society.

3

Law responds to demands placed on the legal system by the groups that compose society and thus provides a map of patterns of power. Law not only reflects differences of political influence and economic interest; it also expresses beliefs in systematic and binding terms, thus framing the ways in which people can make claims on government. With respect to race, for example, law can legitimate rights or declare an entire caste to be separate and inferior to the dominant group.[3]

Similarly, in recent years scholars have punctured the notion that public schools have been self-contained, consensual institutions, run by professionals for the public good and securely "above politics." Instead, they have shown that the supposed value consensus on "non-sectarian" morality and "non-partisan" civic instruction represented only part of the broad spectrum of beliefs held by the citizens of a pluralistic society and that in fact public education has reflected alignments of power in the broader polity, expressing the influence of the haves and the exclusion of the have-nots.[4]

In the last generation it has become obvious that the conjunction of law and public education has a strong political dimension. The controversies law has engendered have become front-page news. Commentators have talked about the present as an era of overregulation, of litigiousness, and of an imperial judiciary. Legal issues involving race, religion, language, gender, and cultural expression have agitated legislatures and courts. Michael A. Rebell and Arthur R. Block argue that public education is "the single area where judicial activism has had the most direct, visible, and controversial impact on Americans." But it has not only been in the courts that education law has changed. In the last generation Congress and many state legislatures have passed scores of ambitious statutes seeking to reform schooling in a variety of ways. Administrative regulations have multiplied.[5]

Amid the uproar over a supposed legal revolution in education, people sometimes forget that Americans have always used law to shape public education. They have written constitutions and statutes to build and transform public schooling. The legal system has been used to require that instruction be given only in English as well as to provide bilingual classes, to mandate Bible reading as well as to declare it unconstitutional, to inculcate monocultural Americanism as well as to offer multicultural instruction. Organizations ranging from temperance advocates to ecology militants have sought to have their views legally embedded in the curriculum. In one form or another, government has always been in the classroom.[6]

The actors in this legal drama have changed over time, and so have the purpose, scope, and intensity of legalization. One way to appraise the conflicts of recent years is to view them from the vantage point of history. Not all groups have had equal access to legislatures or courts, nor have all conflicts been defined as legal ones. The ability to define an issue as a legal question is one index of the relative power of groups. Particularly in times of social dislocation and major economic change, people may employ the law to create a real or imaginary continuity with the past, to camouflage—intentionally or unintentionally— transformations in society. Some characteristics of the legal profession— its concern with precedent, its opaque language—can make law a screen to obscure social change and to blur conflicts of value and interests.[7]

For this reason a history of the law in education needs to keep a wary eye on the political equation, on whose interests are being served and whose are not. Uproar over recent "litigiousness" may result from dominant groups perceiving that hitherto powerless groups have won new influence. Insiders tend to perceive their values and power as natural or consensual and that of outsiders as particularistic and divisive.[8]

In the tumultuous past three decades, Americans have become aware that new groups have used law to challenge the status quo in education and in much of the rest of society. There never was some supposed golden age, however, when education law was apolitical or free of intergroup conflict. The rapidity of recent legal change has clouded the fact that historically law has been Janus-faced. Law has been used by some to preserve their privileges and by others to press for redress of grievances. The legal system has expressed common political values and it has also reflected sharp conflicts between the ins and the outs. In the educational provisions of nineteenth-century state constitutions, for example, one can discover the conviction of many Americans that public schools were essential to the survival of republican institutions; in the post-Reconstruction constitutions and statutes of southern states one can also find the clear intent of racists to use law to perpetuate the caste system.[9]

Precisely because law is Janus-faced, the politics of legal change offers a special vantage point for examining the changing politics of education as legal institutions intersected with public schools. As Alexis de Tocqueville noted, political issues in the United States have a way of becoming matters of law. Constitutions help to set the rules of the political game and together with statutory law frame the structure of political institutions. Courts often are called on to interpret such rules and to regulate interactions between government and citizens.[10]

Yet public law and legal-institutional studies, once the core of what is now called political science, have suffered neglect in recent times, not least in the history of education. The understandable reaction against portraying both the legal system and schools as self-contained institutions, grounded in themselves and autonomous, has contributed to an alternate approach which has explained institutional life either as the product of broad economic or social forces or as the aggregation of decisions by individuals. In the process of attending to social context or individual motives scholars have often ignored the middle-level of analysis: how institutions organize collective life, how they modify the behavior of members, in short, their agency. James G. March and Johan P. Olsen point out that there is emerging, however, a new institutionalism:[11]

> Without denying the importance of both the social context of politics and the motives of individual actors, the new institutionalism insists on a more autonomous role for political institutions. The state is not only affected by society but also affects it. . . . Political democracy depends not only on economic and social conditions but also on the design of political institutions. The bureaucratic agency, the legislative committee, and the appellate court are arenas for contending social forces, but they are also collections of standard operating procedures and structures that define and defend interests. They are political actors in their own right.

We reject the assumptions of the older forms of institutional analysis that isolated institutions from their environmental context, but we believe that there is much to be learned from examining how the legal system shaped public schools by giving them direction and permanence as institutions. Such an approach need not ignore the relation of the larger society to these legal and educational institutions, but it pays attention to the ways in which the distinctive character of the institutions themselves filtered those societal influences. Both courts and schools were embedded in the structures of public law—constitutional and statutory; they were supposed by some to be above the hurly-burly of politics and thus accorded a special, quasi-sacred status, replete with ritual and justified by a legitimating ideology; they developed their own claims of professionalism and autonomy; and they displayed important forms of institutional continuity that made them seem solid and essential.

In this book we explore how three parts of the legal system shaped public schooling, each in interaction with the others. First, we examine how state constitutions—especially in the new states formed from the public domain—justified public education and structured its governance and finance. Second, we look at how state statutes and administrative law institutionalized the system and influenced the moral and civic content of the curriculum. And third, we use a quantitative analysis of appellate decisions in public education to examine what kinds and numbers of issues were litigated and how the courts helped to shape schooling. We explore how education law, thus broadly construed, worked together with political processes to mold the public school in the period from 1785 to 1954, before the major shifts in education law that have marked the decades since the landmark desegregation decisions of *Brown* in 1954.

Most prior scholarship on school law has focused on litigation and has taken two forms, sometimes combined. One has been a study of landmark decisions in education, usually those of the Supreme Court in the twentieth century. Another has been a pragmatic summary of legal precedents in different fields of school litigation. Such studies have been useful as delineations of doctrine and as guides for administrators and school lawyers. Our strategy and purposes are different, however, from this traditional legal research. Since our central interest is how law shaped schooling, we think a broad-angled view of the interaction of state constitutions, statutes, and court decisions will best serve our aims. In a recent appraisal of legal history, James Willard Hurst urged a broadening of the scope of research, commenting that the field "has long been inclined to put disproportionate, indeed more often than not nearly exclusive, emphasis on the activity of appellate courts" even though the "predominant body of public policy" from the 1880s on consisted of statutory and administrative law.[12]

In a study such as ours, the question arises not only of what kinds of legal evidence to employ but also what should be the focus of attention within education. We have chosen to concentrate largely on the state as our unit of analysis, although we do pay some attention to the federal government and to local districts. As we explain in Part I, in recent years educational historians have largely ignored state governments, although they were the central focus of much early

work in the field. Instead, the unit of analysis has typically been
cities, or racial or ethnic groups, or social movements, or configu-
rations of education in communities. For examining the impact of
law on schooling, however, the interaction of state systems of law
and education provides a useful and neglected focus. Our strategy of
focusing on the state, while attending to the interaction of constitutional, statutory, and quantified aggregations of appellate cases in
education, means that we have only lightly touched on other important
topics. For example, we do not deal much with continuity and change
in legal doctrine, with the comparison of case law in education and
in other legal domains, or with the implementation of state law at
the local level.

To illuminate state legal policy in education we examine two themes.
In Part I we examine how leaders used constitutional and statutory
law to build common schools and then to standardize these as state
systems. We concentrate especially on education in the new states
created by Congress from the vast public domain during the nineteenth century. We look at the tangled web of finance and control,
ranging from federal land subsidies and congressional mandates to
the tussles between centralizers and localists in the states. We also
examine how case law and bureaucratic regulations interacted with
this constitutional and statutory process of institution-building.

Our second theme, overlapping in chronology somewhat with Part I
but focusing more on the twentieth century, is the tension of majority
rule and minority rights in education law. To probe this complex
subject we present three case studies of statutory, constitutional, and
case law in Part II of the book: the attempt to provide equal public
education for blacks and whites in the South during Reconstruction
and the subsequent imposition of a caste system of schooling; the
campaigns to mandate temperance instruction, patriotic rituals and
teaching, and religion by groups that regarded themselves as moral
majorities; and a case study of Oregon's attempt in 1922 to require
all children to attend public schools.

In both parts we explore the relation between the legal institutionalization of public schools and the belief systems that undergirded
educational policy in state constitutions, statutes, and court decisions.
We analyze the search for common ground, the imposition of values
by competing ethnocultural groups, and resistance by dissenters. As
Hurst notes, legal historians—like educational historians—"have been

appraising issues of (1) consensus or want of consensus on values, (2) pluralism expressed through bargaining among interests, and (3) social and economic class dominance in legal order." Law, he points out, may express widespread agreements or may be used to manipulate a supposed consensus in the interest of powerful groups. "The real issue in appraising the social history of law," he writes, "is not to establish consensus or no consensus as the single reality, but to determine how much consensus, on what, among whom, when, and with what gains and costs to various affected interests." We explore how a widely shared republican ideology legitimated the creation of common schools, and how suppressed minorities sometimes used the legal system to achieve rights denied by local majorities. Law provides one means of illuminating the intersection between institutions and belief systems.[13]

Today, amid the furor over litigiousness and regulation, it is easy to forget both the injustices of the old legal order and the beliefs that ground the common school constitutionally in a republican political philosophy. After exploring the earlier world of education law, we will return, in the Epilogue, to suggest how the present appears from the perspective of that past.

PART I

Building Common Schools in a Nation of Republics

The foundation of our political institutions, it is well known, rests in the will of the People, and the safety of the whole super-structure, its temple and altar, daily and hourly depend upon the discreet exercise of this will. How then is this will to be corrected, chastened, subdued? By education—that education, the first rudiments of which can be acquired only in common schools.

REPORT OF U.S. HOUSE COMMITTEE ON PUBLIC LANDS, 1826

Exploring the "Primeval Forest"

James Bryce observed in 1888 that "he who would understand the changes [in] the American democracy will find far more instruction in a study of the State governments than of the Federal Constitution." So neglected was the subject, he found, that it could not even be called a field: "it is rather a primeval forest, where the vegetation is rank, and through which scarcely a trail has yet been cut." Although Bryce himself cut one such path in *The American Commonwealth,* much of the educational terrain of state government in the nineteenth century remains unexplored to this day.[1]

This is not to say that the state's role in public education has been totally neglected. It was the organizing principle of the early chronicles of state school systems and a major concern in the influential writings of Ellwood P. Cubberley. The central theme of much of this pioneer work in educational history was the progressive evolution of the power of the state to standardize public schooling, a tale of reformist battles won and further professional goals to accomplish. Critics of the Cubberleyan approach have attacked the earlier historiography for its celebratory tone, its narrowly institutional focus on matters of prime concern to educators, and its naive view of the political economy of education in the United States. In recent years historians of education have mostly bypassed state governments, although there are some important exceptions like Carl Kaestle's *Pillars of the Republic.*[2]

However tangled may be the undergrowth of state government and complex the relations of Congress to the new republics it created, it is time to reopen the types of educational questions that arose when Congress and the citizens of the territories created new states. Together they formed by law a nation of republics from the vast spaces of the continent, and their debates and actions provide useful perspective on the ideology and structure of public education.

Consider, for example, how the federal government worked with citizens to create systems of public schooling in the new states formed from the national domain. Through land grants Congress subsidized and stimulated the formation of common schools. Even Southern Congressmen committed to states' rights and opposed to federal subsidy of internal improvements believed it appropriate for the national government to underwrite schooling in the new states. By requiring territories to devise state constitutions, Congress induced leaders in new states to think systematically about how to provide public education as one among an array of institutions designed to build a republican form of government. Although the federal government initially saw its role as distributing benefits rather than regulating schools, over time Congress became more and more prescriptive about public education in its enabling acts and more careful to ensure that the land endowments were not wasted, as they had typically been in states admitted to the union in the early nineteenth century. This muted but important federal role is apparent in the history of new states as they were formed from the public domain. People who discussed the purposes of education in the Congress and in the state constitutional conventions seemed to regard the common school as the *sine qua non* of republicanism, in effect a fourth branch of government.[3]

Many conservatives regarded the public schools as the safest branch of government in a time when the stability of the American republic —or at least their favored position in it—seemed threatened. As European visitors noted, the United States lacked agencies that stiffened the structure of foreign regimes: hereditary power, an established church, a large standing army, strong executive bureaucracies, or omnipresent uniformed police. If Americans had rejected such buttresses that supported the state in other nations, what might take their place? conservatives asked. If white male suffrage was becoming nearly universal, what guarantees might there be against anarchy or despotism? One way to save republican government from the uninstructed minds and unruly wills of the people was to educate the citizens correctly—that is, to instill proper civic beliefs and mold upright individual character.[4]

This was the message of the Committee on Public Lands of the U.S. House of Representatives when it argued for federal support of schools in 1826 by declaring that the will of the people was to be "corrected, chastened, subdued" by education in the common school. School leaders thought it natural and not at all paradoxical that a government by the people must also restrain the people. John D. Pierce, Michigan's first state superintendent of public instruction, put the matter this way:[5]

However unpretending and simple in form, our government is nonetheless effective and perfect. It proceeds from the people—is supported by the people—and depends upon the people—and at the same time restrains and controls the people more effectually than the most rigid systems of despotism. But how is this political fabric to be preserved? Only by the general diffusion of knowledge. Children of every name and age must be taught the qualifications and duties of American citizens, and learn in early life the art of self-control—they must be educated. And to accomplish this object, our chief dependence must necessarily be the free school system.

While some Americans were concerned about how to protect the government from the people, others worried about how to protect citizens from their government. Those who were vigilant about threats to republican liberties and the growth of state power also turned to education to fortify citizens. Both groups could use the rhetoric of republicanism to justify the common school, but their goals were different. So, too, their means. The people who wanted to inculcate a common and conservative civic culture in children were apt to use state power to achieve their ends—to centralize supervision and finance in the state, to enact laws compelling school attendance, to press for "Americanization" of immigrants. Those who distrusted state government and feared the loss of republican liberties and opportunities were more likely to advocate decentralized control of schools and thus local adjudication of conflicts over values and practices in public education.[6]

The political ideology underlying the common school was consistent on a high level of generality—that public education was necessary to sustain republican institutions—but problematic when exposed to the competing claims of order and liberty. Children were to be taught to be loyal citizens who would perform their civic duties, yet adults were admonished to be wary of the incursion of government on their rights and liberties. Stephen Arons suggests a tension here "between an individualist worldview with its reliance on libertarian political structures and rights, and the need for cohesion and a shared worldview if the society is to be governable."[7]

Battles over educational policy in the states reflected the tension between competing views of the relations of education to the republican form of government. A central feature of state educational politics during the nineteenth century, as we shall indicate, was the tension between attempts to extend state control over education and resistance to centralized power. In education, as in other domains, citizens often sought to constrict the scope and influence of the legislative and executive branches of state government.

State governments mediated the forces emanating from the central government and from below in local communities. Placed between the federal government and the lower jurisdictions—counties, cities, townships, and districts—state governments found themselves at a vortex of struggle over the direction and pace of educational change. State leaders responded to federal authority at the crucial stage of state formation, acted as arbiters in jurisdictional arguments over which level of public authority was to decide educational questions, and reacted to demands from local communities. This conflict took place in all three branches of state government—executive, legislative, and judicial—as well as in constitutional conventions.

Citizens active in local communities in the common school crusade often turned to the legislature to write into state law the gains they had achieved locally through persuasion and the work of voluntary groups. Other citizens actively fought such centralization. There were many heated disputes in territorial constitutional conventions and in state legislatures: whether to employ state and county superintendents or to leave management to local school committees; how to finance common schools; how comprehensive the public system should be— should it include high schools and normal schools, for example; what sort of religion, if any, should find its way into the common school; whether to accommodate to differences of language and ethnicity; and whether to draw a sharp line between private and public schools, both in control and funding. Given the diversity of opinions, the conflicting pressures on legislators, it is not surprising that many of the laws they drafted appear to have been confusing and perhaps deliberately ambiguous. One of the major tasks of the courts in education cases was to construe the meaning of such vague statutes.[8]

In theory the common school was to embrace all children. Indeed, a major claim made by school promoters was that if pupils of all social classes merged in the school, the rich with the poor, a shared education would begin to erase artificial social distinctions, while people of different backgrounds would learn to understand one another. A judge in Kansas eloquently expressed this ideal of inclusiveness in a case in 1881 arguing that blacks should be admitted to white schools:[9]

> At the common schools, where both sexes and all kinds of children mingle together, we have the great world in miniature; there they may

learn human nature in all its phases, with its emotions, passions and feelings, its loves and hates, its hopes and fears, its impulses and sensibilities; there they may learn the secret springs of human actions, and the attractions and repulsions, which lend with irresistible force to particular lines of conduct. But on the other hand, persons by isolation may become strangers even in their own country; and by being strangers, will be of but little benefit either to themselves or to society. As a rule, people cannot afford to be ignorant of the society which surrounds them; and as all kinds of people must live together in the same society, it would seem to be better that all should be taught in the same schools.

A more typical court decision on the segregation of black students, however, and one that became a central precedent for the key U.S. segregation decision of *Plessy v. Ferguson* in 1896, was the conclusion reached in 1850 by the Massachusetts Supreme Court in the case of *Roberts v. City of Boston.* In that opinion the court rejected the charge that segregation "tends to create a feeling of degradation in the blacks and of prejudice and uncharitableness in the whites." It judged separate schools for blacks to be reasonable and denied that law could erase the prejudice that created the distinction in the first place. Blacks in both North and South, and Chinese in California, and other suppressed groups like Indians and Hispanics, often learned that the public school was common for whites, not for people of color.[10]

Although racial, ethnic, religious, and class conflicts—mediated, mobilized, and mollified by political parties—sometimes energized state politics of education, often powerless minorities were unable to muster the funds or the political influence to get their concerns on the political agenda or into the dockets of the courts. What was typically not on the agenda of state educational reform or was not litigated was often as significant as those questions that did emerge for political resolution in constitutional conventions, the legislatures, or the courts.

State constitutional provisions and statutes on education offer one map of the forces that shaped the development of public schools. Constitutions perform many functions. As organic law, they establish a framework of government. They can be designed both to create a stable political order and to limit the powers of government. Powerful interests use constitutions to protect privilege, and, on occasion, downcast groups use them in an attempt to reconstruct the rules that have confined them. Constitutions assert rights and buttress liberties.

They express aspirations. As ideological statements, they serve symbolic functions, and nowhere more so than in education.[11]

Education occupied a prominent place in most state constitutions, both original and revised. Those documents and Congressional enabling acts for states mirrored the relation of new states to the federal government that created them. Constitutional revision, moreover, left successive imprints of political conflict and accommodation that reveal changing attitudes toward the authority of different branches of state government. The later states, in particular, often wrote into their constitutions details of governance and finance that were usually left to statutory law in the established states. Rather than revering state constitutions as spare frameworks of government, like the federal constitution, citizens often loaded them with lengthy provisions that represented the victory of temporary political coalitions.

Nineteenth-century voters came to distrust strong government, cut back its powers and expenditures in a number of domains, and were slow to create a stable civil service and social services. Why and how did people who distrusted governmental authority nonetheless use state government as one means of creating the most extensive network of public schools in the world? Part of the answer lies in the tensions within the republican ideology itself, while part lies in the ways in which distributive policies of federal and state governments still permitted considerable local autonomy.

Often reluctant to adopt policies of *regulation* or *redistribution,* both federal and state governments were busy, however, *distributing* benefits. In the case of education, these benefits initially came mostly from the sale of federal school lands. Such subsidies were the chief source of state common school funds in the new states (supplemented, of course, by local and county taxation and sometimes by school bonds). The tension between widespread distrust of public authority and approval of distributing benefits led to a splintering of authority over public education and a tug-of-war between state control and decentralization of decision-making at lower levels. But the conflict over specific forms of governance and finance took place within a broader agreement among state leaders who assumed education to be a necessary form of internal improvement—and more than that, essential to the political fabric of the nation and its component republics.

In chapters one and two we explore these themes at the federal and state levels, probing the connections between ideological commitments, state constitutions, and political actions in public education during the nineteenth century. We also look at litigation in education and compare courts with other arenas for conflict resolution. In chapter three we look in more detail at two states, Michigan and California.

In chapter four we explore an intensified phase of institution-building beginning in the Progressive era of the early twentieth century. This represented not simply a quantitative increase in regulatory use of state power, as compared with the older pattern of distributing state benefits, but also a qualitative change in governance. Here we examine the attempts of school leaders to use state law to bureaucratize and centralize public schools according to their notions of progress and professionalism. Throughout the nineteenth century educators had sought to replace haphazard standards of teacher training and certification, supervision, and curriculum by centralized state regulation and consolidation of school districts. Except in the cities, such efforts had produced results more symbolic and scattered than actual and standardized. But from the Progressive era onwards, the administrative progressives did achieve greater success. Theirs was a top-down mode of reform that relied heavily on lobbying by professionals and the authority of expertise rather than lay participation in decision-making.

These educational reformers hoped that state-level standardization by law would not only be non-political but also non-controversial. They found, however, that citizens were quite prepared to go to court to contest new laws bureaucratizing schooling, and employees gained new standing in court to bring suits. Although they did not intend to induce more litigation by such fast-paced changes, educators found that the use of law to bureaucratize education, coupled with the growth of administrative buffers against citizen participation, made the courts a somewhat more common recourse for dissidents in the twentieth century than they had been in the nineteenth.

The stance of personal disinterestedness and professional expertise taken by the administrative progressives was politically useful, nonetheless. So successfully did educators insulate their domain from outside political pressures that by the 1950s some political scientists described public schools as classic examples of closed political systems, a claim that would have appeared implausible if not absurd at the time of the creation of state systems during the heyday of American expansion.

CHAPTER 1

Federal Influence on the Spread of Public Education, 1785–1912

Today, when people dispute federal policies in education, the first century of the American nation may appear to some to have been a golden era when public schools were a community affair. Compared to the bureaucratic school systems of the present, it may seem that the schools of the past were grassroots institutions, unconnected with federal policy or national politics. But that is not quite the case. The federal government did help to shape public education in two important ways: through its grants of public lands to the state common school funds; and through the process by which Congress and the settlers of the territories created new states from the public domain. Article 4, section 4 of the U.S. Constitution required Congress to guarantee that new states had "a Republican form of Government." Over time both national and state leaders came to articulate and readjust the linkages between the common school and the formation of new states.[1]

As the nation grew during its first century into a union of states that reached across a continent, Congress had the duty of ensuring that each territory aspiring to statehood created through its own constitution a "Republican form of Government." Since the vastness of the continent created anxiety over the coherence and stability of a republican nation of individual republics, Congress took care to ensure that the people of the new states would understand themselves to be citizens of the larger nation, sharing not only a commitment to republican rights and liberties but also an allegiance to the larger polity based on those principles. When successive states framed constitutions and joined the nation of states, it became a working assumption that public education was an essential feature of a republican government based upon the will of the people. Both by reinforcing the legitimacy of schooling and by subsidizing public education, national and state governments complemented local grassroots efforts in the spread of the American common school.[2]

The organization of public education grew more elaborate during the nation's westward expansion. State constitutional provisions on schools reflected this growing complexity. In the earlier documents, idealistic preambles and brief treatments of federal land grants seemed enough when settlers were building log schools and fledgling academies in the wilds of the Midwest. People believed in the benefits of education, but they were casual about means. By contrast, when territorial assemblies in the sparsely populated far Northwest states created constitutions in the late nineteenth century, they mandated elaborate new bureaucratic structures in their educational provisions partly in response to specific Congressional mandates and partly to emulate exemplary public school systems in the older states. In 1874 a group of 77 college presidents and city and state superintendents of schools described this process of institution-building:[3]

> As a consequence of the perpetual migration from the older sections of the country to the unoccupied Territories, there are new states in all degrees of formation, and their institutions present earlier phases of realization of the distinctive type that are presented in the mature growth of the system as it exists in the thickly-settled and older States. Thus States are to be found with little or no provision for education, but they are rudimentary forms of the American State, and are adopting, as rapidly as immigration allows them to do so, the type of educational institutions already defined as the result of American political and social ideas.

In forming public school systems in new states, the federal government played an indirect but important fiscal role that changed slowly over time. Many of the founding fathers shared a commitment, in principle, to education as a bulwark of republicanism, but neither the Articles of Confederation nor the United States Constitution mentioned education. The relation of the federal government to education in the territories and states grew incrementally, in piecemeal fashion rather than as the result of the planned educational policy characteristic of more centralized nations. Initially, the practice of granting public land as endowments for schools seems to have been more an incentive to rapid settlement than a carefully conceived federal policy in education. Before the Civil War, especially, many of the new states mismanaged and squandered the land grants.[4]

But as time went on, Congress took greater care in setting the terms for territorial government, shaping the requirements for admission in the enabling acts, approving the new constitutions, and devising greater controls over the disposition of the ever-growing amounts of federal land to stimulate improvements, including public schools, in the new societies on the frontier. Far from being an inert bystander, Congress bargained with territorial representatives over educational subsidies even in the antebellum period of relative mismanagement, and after the Civil War it increasingly wrote specific requirements about public schools into its enabling acts for new states. Altogether, Congress gave the states 77,630,000 acres for common schools, far more than the total of 21,700,000 it gave the states for universities, hospitals, asylums, and other types of public institutions under the land-grant provisions of the Morrill Act and other federal laws. By the end of the nineteenth century, most states west of the Mississippi River were receiving more than 10 percent of all their school revenues from income from those grants.[5]

Congress exerted its greatest influence on public education through its role in the forming of new states. Other Congressional efforts to influence the common school largely foundered. When Congress finally established a federal department of education in 1867, encouraged by the hopes of Radical Republicans that Congress could shape education in the conquered South, the new administrative office had only a tiny staff, an austere budget, and feeble powers. It scarcely realized the hopes of its founders. Likewise, Congressional bills to award large cash grants to states for developing common schools repeatedly failed to pass during the nineteenth century. Both foreign and American commentators have characterized public education in the United States as the quintessentially decentralized system in which local initiative and minimal state control were the rule and federal influence almost nonexistent. They were only partly right. Despite the failures of other forms of federal regulation and subsidy, and despite the strong traditions of localism that persisted in education, the federal government did help to shape public education as the nation formed new internal republics, expanding from east to west from the Ordinance of 1785 to the admission of Arizona and New Mexico in 1912.[6]

Republican Values and the Creation of Common Schools

The lack of educational provisions in the federal constitution did not mean that national leaders were uninterested in education during the revolutionary generation. Many of the key political spokesmen of the time were deeply concerned about education as a guarantor of ordered liberty. Thomas Jefferson wrote to his friend George Wythe, "Preach, my dear Sir, a crusade against ignorance; establish and improve the law for educating the common people." On another occasion, Jefferson had written, "I know no safe depository of the ultimate powers of the society but the people themselves; and if we think them not enlightened enough to exercise their control with a wholesome discretion, the remedy is not to take it from them, but to inform their discretion by education." John Adams, James Madison, and other central actors in the creation of the new republic made similar pleas for an expanded commitment to learning as a safeguard for the republic. "In proportion as the structure of government gives force to public opinion," warned George Washington in his Farewell Address as president of the United States, "it is essential that public opinion should be enlightened."[7]

After the American Revolution, some commentators on the relation between education and politics—for example, Jefferson, Benjamin Rush, and Noah Webster—believed that without a transformed educational system, the old pre-revolutionary attitudes and relationships would prevail in the new nation. Jefferson wanted to create public primary schools to make loyal citizens of the younger generation and secondary schools and colleges to train leaders. "The business of education has acquired a new complexion by the independence of our country," Benjamin Rush wrote in 1786. "The form of government we have assumed," he continued, "has created a new class of duties to every American." Rush thought it necessary to establish "nurseries of wise and good men," a system of education from common schools through a federal university that would prepare a governmental elite, to ensure the survival of the republic. Webster called for an "Association of American Patriots for the Formation of an American Character," strove to promote uniformity of language, and devised a "Federal Catechism" to teach republican principles to school children. He declared that[8]

In our American republics, where government is in the hands of the people, knowledge should be universally diffused by means of public schools. Of such consequence is it to society that the people who make laws should be well informed that I conceive no legislature can be justified in neglecting proper establishments for this purpose.

A number of educational theorists during the revolutionary generation confronted the republican challenge—one might say paradox— of how to combine order and liberty, patriotism and freedom. On the one hand, they were determined to preserve the individual rights and liberties for which they had fought. On the other, they wanted to make sure that people felt part of a larger polity to which they owed a common loyalty, rather than continuing to give their primary allegiances to family, class, sect, ethnic group, or region and locality. Education—civic as well as intellectual—seemed an ideal instrument to turn people with diverse loyalties into citizens of a new entity—the republican state—while at the same time training them to be alert to their rights, liberties, and responsibilities.[9]

Undergirding the connection between faith in education—in the diffusion of knowledge—and the political and economic and moral common good was a web of assumptions. One was the belief that in a government depending on the will of the people, the citizens must be properly instructed so that they could, in turn, instruct their government in an orderly way. Donald S. Lutz has shown how central in the political theory of the early state constitutions were the notions of consent and instruction in expressing popular will. In practical terms, the state legislatures through majority rule constituted the active will of the governed; legislators were expected to represent not special factions but "the interests of the entire community." Frequent elections were designed to make sure that they did express that common good. To supplement this, the early constitutions provided avenues for citizens "to give instructions to their representatives" through petitions and other means of influence and redress. Lutz comments that "the people did press their demands vigorously and often, whether their state constitutions urged them to or not."[10]

There were, then, specific channels through which Americans sought to realize the common good by way of the political process. An underlying principle was that well-educated leaders would perceive the common weal, and that when they did not, they could be instructed by citizens who were educated to recognize their rights and responsibilities. In 1822 an advocate of such a link between republicanism and education, Governor Dewitt Clinton of New York, argued that "the first duty of a state is to render its citizens virtuous by intellectual instruction and moral discipline, by enlightening their minds, purifying their hearts, and teaching them their rights and their obligations." This argument might well be regarded as an educational theory of the state, though any idealism along these lines must be tempered by a clear recognition of the ethnic and class biases of the political elite, its willingness, perhaps unwittingly as much as purposefully, to use newly constructed notions of the public interest and the common good to favor some people's interests over others.[11]

Conflicting interest groups at both the federal and state levels gave rise to political parties that construed the common good in quite different ways. In public education, nevertheless, leaders aimed to keep alive the dream of a consensual polity that sought the common weal because it was educated to do so. Herein lay the appeal of a system of common schools that would somehow exist above politics, nonpartisan and nonsectarian. That ideology surfaced repeatedly in state constitutional debates and educational provisions, in the speeches of politicians and school leaders, and in the textbooks children read in school. People as diverse politically as Thomas Jefferson, Noah Webster, Benjamin Rush, and Joseph Story hoped that by teaching the "science of government" (a different "science" for Jefferson than for Story) to the rising generation, conflicts might be averted, the republic made permanent, and the interests of all people served.[12]

Fresh from his battles with President Jackson and the errant troop of Democrats, Judge Story told a group of New England educators that in a properly taught class on government a youth "may learn enough to guard himself against the insidious wiles of the demagogue [few in his audience would have failed to identify his target as "King Andrew"] and the artful appeals of the courtier, and the visionary speculations of the enthusiast, although he may not be able to solve many of the transcendental problems in political philosophy." It was not only practicable but essential to "teach the science of government as a branch of popular education." A free republic was the most complicated form of government known to humanity; but its principles "admit of a simple enunciation, and may be brought within the comprehension of the most common minds." In the schools only "the principles of government should be . . . taught, and not the creeds or dogmas of any party." No doubt Story believed that was possible, but textbooks for schools written by Yankee conservatives like himself taught a political philosophy that other Americans thought partisan. Even Jefferson, who wrote eloquently on intellectual freedom, wanted Virginians to learn his own version of the science of government. Nevertheless, leaders of many persuasions could subscribe to Story's admonition that "the American republic, above all others, demands from every citizen unceasing vigilance and exertion, since we have deliberately dispensed with every guard against danger or ruin, except the intelligence and virtue of the people themselves."[13]

Leaders differed, however, on the institutional forms that education should take. Some, like Rush and Jefferson, developed systematic and symmetrical plans for distinctively public schooling that would be imbued with republican principles. As the nineteenth century progressed, especially during the common school movement of mid-century, these ideas were increasingly institutionalized until public education became the mainstream of schooling. Other leaders in the early national era, however, thought of education as a diffuse public good and were eclectic about the means of instruction.[14]

In the early national period the latter, more eclectic, group of leaders had more influence on educational practice than did those who called for elaborate state systems. The development of schooling in the first half-century of the nation did not follow the neat blueprints of public school systems that would be uniform, free, republican in orientation, and controlled by the state. As Carl Kaestle has shown, schools of that period in the settled states were rarely organized into coherent state systems; they continued to reflect differences of class, religion, and ethnicity; the lines between public and private were seldom sharply drawn; and the "public" schools were largely governed and financed at the local level, especially in rural areas, with little control by the state. This non-system, however, produced relatively high levels of literacy and school attendance. By the 1820s a large proportion of school-aged children were enrolled in some kind of school, at least in the older sections of the North.[15]

Some of the constitutions of the original 13 states suggested that the common good might be realized through a combination of diverse educational institutions. The line between "public" and "private" was often obscure or unimportant in these documents. Through such institutions Americans might realize both private and public aims. No one put this argument in more influential language than John Adams in the Massachusetts Constitution of 1780. Adams' educational preamble was echoed in the lofty rhetoric of the Northwest Ordinance and in a number of other state constitutions (it was copied almost verbatim into New Hampshire's constitution in 1784). He wrote:[16]

> Wisdom and knowledge, as well as virtue, diffused generally among the body of the people, being necessary for the preservation of their rights and liberties... it shall be the duty of legislatures and magistrates . . . to cherish the interests of literature and the sciences, and all seminaries of them... to countenance and inculcate the principles of humanity and general benevolence, public and private charity, industry and frugality, honesty and punctuality in their dealings, sincerity, good humor, and all social affections and generous sentiments among the people.

One reason why Americans of the early national period were relatively casual about institutional means in education, seeking to realize Adams' catalogue of civic and religious virtues in diverse ways, is that there was no sharp distinction in their thinking between private interest and the public good. Willi Paul Adams notes that in the generation following 1776, political writers spoke frequently about "the public good" or "the general happiness of the People" and that this concept informed the writing of state constitutions in those years before the emergence of a developed party system. He writes that these constitutions "did not reach a definition of the common good that resolved the ambiguities inherent in the concept as it was developed in the decade prior to 1776. The common good and the sum of private interests were seen as synonymous, and the possibility of conflict between them was belittled." Many Americans shared, he argues, a belief "that individual interests, clearly recognized and openly promoted, could be reconciled in the context of an expanding economy." An ambiguous metaphor in a pamphlet of 1777 shows how internal improvements might contribute to the common weal rather than simply enriching the few, though the failure of such endeavors might lead to common hardship as well: "Public good is, as it were, a common bank, in which every individual has his respective share; and consequently whatever damage that sustains, the individuals unavoidably partake of that calamity."[17]

The expansion of the nation westward and the formation of new states placed a strain on the faith that the diffusion of "wisdom and knowledge, as well as virtue" could be entrusted to a variety of institutions, as they had been in settled states in the East. As Robert H. Wiebe has observed, leaders worried about how a nation could retain republican coherence and stability if dispersed across a huge continent. They wondered how to master the problem of size and how to "define a republican relationship between America's new leaders at the top and a dispersed, diverse population at its base." If the "diffusion of knowledge" was to be the key to building character and virtue, which in turn would preserve individual rights and liberties, then the means must be potent, universal, and predictable in their effect.[18]

The national government, facing the reality of a polity ever-expanding across vast spaces, gradually began to structure land and school policies that favored the growth of common school systems as the central form of republican education. As a result, the educational blueprints of republican theorists like Rush were more consistently represented in the educational policies evolving in the new states of the west, in intergovernmental relations between the Congress and the settlers of the territories, than in the educational practices of the older states during the early national period.

In 1826 the U.S. House committee on public lands—which urged unsuccessfully that half the proceeds of sale of the public domain go to common schools—argued that the citizens of all states had a direct interest in the schooling of all citizens. Education, it claimed, "has directly in view the improvement of the minds and morals of the present generation, and of generations to come. It contemplates giving additional stability to the government, and drawing round the republic new and stronger bonds of union. We are, indeed, a peculiar people." That peculiarity, which defined the republic, came from a freedom that needed to be disciplined by instruction, from a religious tolerance and liberty of conscience that was "chiefly the result of education," and from governmental and legal principles such as representative institutions and trial by jury that depended upon the educated will of the people. In advocating federal aid for education in the states the committee hoped to create greater loyalty to the Union, but it sought as well to prompt "a just emulation" between the states in "the glorious purpose of training up the young mind in the way of knowledge and morals."[19]

The framing of state constitutions, as well as the debates over their acceptance in Congress, reveals ways of thinking about education that were national in scope. In the California constitutional convention of 1849, for example, a delegate quoted the view of U.S. Secretary of the Treasury Robert J. Walker that "each state is deeply interested in the welfare of every other; for the representatives of the whole regulate by their votes the measures of the Union, which must be the more happy and prosperous in proportion as its councils are guided by more enlightened views, resulting from the more universal diffusion of light, and knowledge and education." Delegates to such constitutional conventions in the territories also had many parochial attitudes about education, but the republican ideology they expressed was common to most states and referred to the nation as well as to the individual states that formed the whole.[20]

Such sentiments resonated again and again in the state constitutional conventions, especially in the North and West and in the Reconstruction conventions in the South. Delegates disagreed about many matters concerning education—about taxation, how far governance should be centralized, about the administration of land grants, and much more. Attitudes differed between members of different parties and between constitution-makers in different regions. Men who considered themselves "good republicans" could and did display racist attitudes, could and did display religious and ethnic intolerance. But on the value of diffusing knowledge through public schools there was substantial agreement, except in the prewar South. Over and over again, men would rise in conventions to dissent after prefacing their remarks with the comment that no one could be a firmer friend of public schools.[21]

At first states had considerable latitude in deciding how to dispose of land grants and what kinds of schools might be eligible for funds. But after the war, Republicans in Congress laid down specifications for public schools in a republic. In the enabling acts of 1889, paving the way for the admission of Montana, North Dakota, South Dakota, and Washington as states, Congress demanded that the new states have free, non-sectarian public schools as a prerequisite of statehood.

"Provisions shall be made," said these acts, "for the establishment and maintenance of systems of public schools, which shall be open to all the children of said states and free from sectarian control." Prior to that time Congress had assumed that the states would create common schools—without them the land grants would not have made sense—but it had not yet made the establishment of schools an explicit requirement.[22]

One sign of the ideological appeal of common schools in nineteenth-century political life is the prevalence of hortatory preambles or other rhetorical clauses in the sections of state constitutions dealing with education. With the exception of language in the declarations of rights, no other sections contained so much exhortation to virtue or justificatory prose. Sections on the legislative branch did not extol the virtues of representative government, nor those on the judiciary the glories of justice. Clauses on suffrage, militia, corporations, revenue, and divisions of the executive branch were plain and businesslike. In contrast, the high-flown justifications of the common school declared public education to be a shared value, like those embedded in the declarations of rights, a common good above the squabbles of political party or sect. Indeed, in 1802 Ohio embedded its statement of educational purpose in its general declaration of natural rights, including the right to worship God according to conscience and the right of open access to all educational institutions supported by federal land grants.[23]

At least 17 states adopted preambles on the political and moral purposes of schooling in their constitutions. In part this copying may be regarded as an obligatory bow towards the patron, Congress, an acknowledgement of the purpose of the rich land endowment the new states received (most of the constitutions with such language were in new western and southern states). More important, the frequency of reference to education's link with the stability of republics and the survival of liberty suggests that belief in common schooling was an article of political faith in nineteenth-century America. North Dakota put the case in these words in 1889:[24]

A high degree of intelligence, patriotism, integrity and morality on the part of every voter in a government by the people being necessary in order to insure the continuance of that government and the prosperity and happiness of the people, the legislative assembly shall make provision for the establishment and maintenance of a system of public schools which shall be open to all children of the State of North Dakota and free from sectarian control. This legislative requirement shall be irrevocable without the consent of the United States and the people of North Dakota.

The last clause indicates that the delegates recognized not only a state interest in education but a national one as well. Like the bill of rights, the common school was becoming "irrevocable," an inalienable guarantee of the republican form of government. Both the Florida Reconstruction constitution of 1868 and Washington's constitution of 1889 declared it the "paramount duty of the state" to educate all children."[25]

Congress as Patron of Public Education

The story of Congress as patron of the common school begins in 1785 with a surveyor's document that specified how lines should "be measured with a chain . . . plainly marked by chaps on the trees, and exactly described on a plat, whereon shall be noted . . . all mines, salt-springs, salt-licks, and mill-seats." The document indicated how land should be divided into townships of 36 square miles and subdivided into 36 lots. In businesslike fashion it established the terms of the deed between the United States and its contractors, the citizens buying lands in the western territory. One clause, buried in the legal boilerplate, linked the congressional Ordinance of 1785 to education: "There shall be reserved the lot No. 16, of every township, for the maintenance of public schools, within the said township." This was the origin of the federal government's active involvement in promoting public schools as a form of internal improvement, one that had crucial ideological and practical dimensions.[26]

Two years later Congress passed another ordinance, this one for governance of the territory northwest of the Ohio River. The Northwest Ordinance of 1787 specified a plan for a governor, general assembly, and courts for each territory to be created from that immense wilderness, and, most important, the procedure whereby each might become a state. Between the existing states of the Confederation and the new ones the ordinance proclaimed a compact that prohibited slavery, guaranteed religious freedom and basic legal rights like those later embodied in the Bill of Rights, and included a famous clause: "Religion, morality, and knowledge, being necessary to good government and the happiness of mankind, schools and the means of education shall forever be encouraged."[27]

Looking backward, one might be tempted to view these two ordinances as evidence that Congress had a vision of the future of public education and of the federal responsibility in constructing that future. The facts are otherwise. There were men in Congress with novel ideas about the role of education in a republic—Thomas Jefferson for one—but the initiative for the land grants arose elsewhere. Jefferson had a year before drafted an ordinance for governing the Northwest without once mentioning education. Most scholars agree that the sponsors of the educational provisions were Massachusetts men who wished to persuade fellow Yankees to buy lands and migrate to the West.[28]

Heirs of the Puritan biblical commonwealth, these Massachusetts men looked to the past more than to the future for inspiration. For over a century New Englanders had included land grants for education when they carved new townships out of the wilderness in chunks measuring six square miles each. Such subsidies for schools and religion reassured people that they could recreate familiar institutions and compact settlements when they moved inland. The educational provision of the Ordinance of 1787 echoed the Massachusetts Constitution of 1780, and that, in turn, captured something of the flavor of the Puritan biblical commonwealth of the seventeenth century. As successive generations of Americans undertook their errands into the wilderness, they were determined to carry with them the civilizing institutions they had known in more settled communities.[29]

In the early stages of negotiations between land buyers and Congress, grants for schools seemed more a bargaining chip than a fixed entitlement for novel republican purposes. The nation was deeply in debt in the late 1780s. Congress wanted to sell lands and to find ways to reimburse Revolutionary soldiers. If land buyers wanted school subsidies, that was part of the contract in a buyers' market. But if they did not, the federal government felt free to omit land grants for schools, as it did in some of its acts for selling land in the Northwest during the 1790s.[30]

Bargaining also shaped the formation of new states through congressional enabling acts, state constitutions, and acts admitting the state to the union. In order to gain section 16 for schools and certain other lands to support public services, Ohio negotiators had to agree in 1802 not to tax for five years the lands that the federal government sold to settlers. Congress wanted this quid pro quo to induce settlers to buy lands and to swell the treasury. In its early years the federal government was not a patron of schooling as a matter of settled principle, however much its leaders might share the common belief that enlightenment was essential in a republic. It was in later years, especially during and after the common school movement of the middle of the nineteenth century, that Congress not only supported public school systems as a fixed policy but also took an interest in the specific forms that schooling should take in the new states.[31]

As Daniel Feller has noted, the federal government was able to influence state and local institutions through its land policies in ways that it could not do directly through tax expenditures or regulations. Through these land policies it was able to shape "developmental priorities in a diverse and rapidly expanding Union." Control of the public domain gave Congress an opportunity to "govern directly, raise a revenue, and create new states. Financially and administratively, the public domain was the government's greatest asset and offered it the opportunity to test and expand its powers." Neither the Articles of Confederation nor the U.S. Constitution gave Congress authority to underwrite schools, but as Feller writes, "the school grants quickly became embedded in federal land policy and furnished a plausible precedent" for continuing subsidies. Indeed, "the Western states looked to Washington to supply the facilities for education they could not afford themselves. They asked federal aid not as a favor but as simple justice, an obligation inseparable from federal control of the public domain."[32]

There were, of course, many groups competing to influence federal land policies: settlers, squatters, veterans, eastern economic interests, state governments, townships, and political parties that used land policies to capture votes. Democrats often wanted to preempt public lands for sale for certain kinds of purchasers prior to open sales, favoring settlers intending to create small farms. Whigs, by contrast, tended to prefer less restrictive forms of sale and then distribution of revenues to states for internal improvements. Congress responded to both kinds of demands, offering benefits to certain groups while it also made broader grants for transportation, education, and other forms of large-scale improvement.[33]

As the national debt turned to a treasury surplus, territorial settlers came increasingly to regard land grants for education as an entitlement, not a bargaining chip. The negotiable question about federal land then became *how much* instead of *whether*, and the tracts ceded to the states grew steadily over the years. In the 1840s the Secretary of the Treasury and the federal land commissioner both suggested that new states should receive more than the one section 16. In 1848 Congress approved the policy of reserving two lots, 16 and 36, for schools when it established the territorial government of Oregon. In 1850 California was the first state to receive both sections, amounting to 5.5 percent of the public domain in the state. The desert states of Utah, Arizona, and New Mexico—where much of the land had little value—each received four sections. Congress also appropriated certain other lands—saline and swamplands, in particular—for use in stimulating internal improvements, including education. In 1841 it passed an act that granted 500,000 acres each to eight states, later extended to a total of 19 states, to be used also for internal improvements. A majority of these states devoted part or all of the income from these lands to schools. As we shall point out, some states squandered the income from land grants, while others husbanded them. But in almost every new state the federal land grants primed the pump of state school finance and led to greater state regulation of common schools.[34]

From a reluctant beginning, Congress became more and more generous in granting land to the new states, regarding land grants as an entitlement for public education. It also granted money, though rarely prescribing that it be used only for schools. One form of cash donation was an award of a certain percent of proceeds from the sale of U.S. lands within the borders of the new states, ranging from three percent to ten percent, with most states receiving five percent. Twelve states, all of them West of the Mississippi except Wisconsin, decreed in their constitutions that income from this source should flow to the common school fund.[35]

Eastern states that were not carved out of the public domain, and hence did not receive federal land grants for schools, protested that the Western states enjoyed an unfair advantage. Several of these older states petitioned Congress for redress. They claimed that the common domain belonged to all the states; therefore, all were entitled to benefit from its sale by receiving subsidies for education and other internal improvements. Maryland, for example, proposed in 1821 that older states without public lands deserved a share of land income to establish their own school funds. Politicians in these Eastern states, some of them hard pressed to support expanding school systems, saw the federal land largesse as an important source of revenue to which they had no access.[36]

In 1826 the Committee on Public Lands of the House of Representatives investigated "the expediency of appropriating a portion of the nett [*sic*] annual proceeds of the sales and entries of the public lands exclusively for the support of Common Schools" and distributing the money to all the states according to the number of Representatives. In an eloquent report written by a Connecticut congressman, the committee recommended that one-half of all the income from the public lands be invested in a federal school fund and the interest apportioned among all the states, to be used only for common schools "in such manner as the Legislature of each State may, by law, direct." The House did not take action on this, nor did the Senate approve similar suggestions that Congress establish a permanent fund for education and internal improvements. The issue stirred sectional controversy and raised difficult constitutional issues regarding states rights and tricky questions of land law.[37]

When a Massachusetts congressman proposed in 1829 that the House establish a standing committee on education, his resolution produced strong debate and a vote of 156 to 52 to table the motion. Such steps toward general subsidy of schooling by the federal government and assertion of the federal interest in education aroused vehement opposition among congressmen, particularly Southerners who supported states' rights. Most of these opponents, however, believed that grants to new states were different, for they promoted settlement and raised the value of lands in the public domain. Even the states rights stalwart Senator John C. Calhoun of South Carolina supported land grants for education until 1848. As Daniel J. Elazar points out, strict constructionists drew a distinction between land grants to new

states and money grants to all states for education, but federal donations of land to the new states were, in reality, grants-in-aid for schools.
Advocates justified these land grants as a way to develop the national
domain, as a form of patriotic salesmanship, but they also praised aid
to public education as serving a common good. Commitment to the
republican ideology of the common school coexisted comfortably
with the desire to use the federal land bounty to support public
education.[38]

The common school was a favored form of internal improvement.
Party conflicts in Congress over banking, internal improvements, and
the distribution of the federal surplus had consequences for public
education. The resolution of these conflicts involved loans or grants
to the states, indirectly aiding the schools even though the initiative in
how to use the funds was left to the states. In 1837 Congress distributed surplus federal revenue to the states in the form of loans which
were never recalled. All but four of the states used income from part
or all of this "loan" to support common schools, indicating the high
priority which states placed on education. In 1834 Senator Henry
Clay shepherded through Congress a bill that appropriated some of
the profits from federal lands to the states for education and internal
improvements. This bill was vetoed by Jackson, but the distribution
of the surplus funds in 1837 and similar later dispensations in the
1840s accomplished many of Clay's purposes of using the federal
money for internal improvements. The bank deposits and surplus
revenues stimulated educational systems even in New Hampshire,
known for its strong traditions of local control.[39]

Another significant source of federal support for education, though
also distributed without direction about how to spend the money, was
reimbursement to the states for costs of raising troops or for claims
they pressed for wartime damages. Virginia is a case in point. In 1816
that state received from the federal government $1,210,550 as recom-
pense for expenses in the War of 1812. It added that large sum to its
"Literary Fund," the mainstay of support for its common schools
down to 1870. In 1861 the Congress levied a tax of $20 million to
support the Civil War. In 1891 it voted to return this money to the
states. Several states placed these funds in their common school
endowments.[40]

Federal aid to public education in the nineteenth century did not
adhere to any rational model of finance and governance with clear

allocation of powers between the different levels of government. The movement of money and power reflected shifting political factions, ideological formulations, and economic conditions. Poor record-keeping of intergovernmental transfers makes it impossible to trace exactly how much federal assistance, whether in land or money, actually reached the states for school purposes. In a study published in 1911, Fletcher H. Swift estimated that the federal grants to the original capital of state school funds totalled over 77 million acres and over $13 million (not counting certain sources, such as percentage grants from the sale of public lands in new states). The sources and amounts of state appropriations to common school funds, even harder to estimate, constituted only a fraction of the federal donation.[41]

What was the relative importance of these endowments called "common school funds"? In 1885-86, when it cost, on average, $15.40 per year to instruct each pupil, the interest on these permanent funds and rent from school lands together contributed about six percent of total school expenditures. The proportion increased when the better endowed states of the West entered the Union. State taxes accounted for about 18 percent, local taxes for 70, and "other sources" (unspecified) for about 7. As the U.S. Commissioner noted, however, inaccuracies in reporting and ambiguities in categories made such breakdowns approximate at best. No doubt much of the federal contribution was obscured by pouring it directly into state and local coffers without adequate records.[42]

Dollars and acres tell only part of the story of federal influence. Equally important is the evolving system of management of the grants and the ways in which the federal government, territories, and states interacted as new states emerged from the public domain. The federal Commissioner of Public Lands and his staff became important actors in school finance. In 1847, for example, the Commissioner issued elaborate instructions on how school lands should be selected and sold, specifying their size, the avoidance of preempted properties, and the way they should be registered. The Commissioner also rendered decisions on disputed claims. The state and federal courts also became deeply involved in the school lands, not surprisingly since land law was a major branch of litigation, in education as in other legal domains. Elazar describes the management of federal grants for schools as one of evolving cooperative federalism between the states and the federal government. Indeed, the history differs sharply by time and place, and it illustrates the complexity of relationships between the levels of governance in American education.[43]

The state side of the story of management of land grants was often a sorry tale of wasted resources, corruption, embezzlement, lost records, and general incompetence, especially in the years before 1850. Only slowly did Congress and the states learn how to conserve the proceeds of the school lands and money grants awarded to new states by the federal government. Much income was lost through incompetence, lands sold for piddling sums, records and deeds lost, debts unpaid, and interest uncollected. In hard times—depressions, panics, and the Civil War, especially—the common school fund was an easy target for misappropriation, notwithstanding the litany of pious phrases in state constitutions that insisted that the endowments were to be "sacred," "irreducible," "perpetual," and "inviolable." Although state governments during the nineteenth century may have been inefficient and poorly organized, they frequently showed great alacrity when responding to special interests. Even when school funds were invested in good faith, they often evaporated when banks crashed or favorite internal improvements turned out to be failures. Swift estimated that the total sums lost by the states exceeded $36 million.[44]

The story of state management of the public lands is not an unmitigated tale of gloom, however. In his history of constitution-making in the far Northwest, John D. Hicks showed how Westerners, learning from past mistakes, creatively conserved and used the school lands for the common good. And the prospect of funding schools from the federal largesse encouraged many constitution-writers to plan optimistically for the kind of schooling their states would one day need.[45]

The Ordinance of 1785 gave section 16 to *townships* for the support of schools. This general provision left open many questions that agitated the politics of school lands and entered the courts of law throughout the nineteenth century. Were the lands to be sold or leased? Which level of government—federal, state, county, and local—had what kind of responsibility over the disposition of school lands? Should the income from the lands be used in the early stages of settlement, when the need was presumably greatest, or should the lands or income be held in trust for the future? At different times and places these questions generated quite different answers.

The first of the new states admitted in the nineteenth century, Ohio, illustrated the diversity of responses to the question of who should control the school funds. The enabling act passed by Congress in 1802 vested ownership and control of the funds in the townships. When Ohioans pressured Congress the following year to grant additional lands for areas of the state not covered by the enabling act, Congress vested control of the newly granted lands in the state, not the township. Ohio then delegated responsibility back to the local communities, as did several other early states. In some other states it was the counties, instead, that received and administered the funds from federal lands.[46]

Problems arose from this decentralization. In some townships the school lands, by the luck of the surveyor's transit, were valuable, while in others they were worthless. Without a higher authority to balance the distribution of income, some districts were favored and others cheated. Another problem was that officials in townships or counties often lacked the ability or motivation to keep appropriate records, and sometimes they did not even care to realize profits. They could easily be swayed by squatters on the school lands or local speculators. In Missouri, 49 of 81 counties reported losses in the common school fund resulting from insufficient security for notes, insolvent parties to contracts, absconding debtors, and inefficient or corrupt officals.[47]

Some school leaders hoped that state administration of the school lands would solve these problems. Under the influence of two Yankees— John D. Pierce and Isaac Crary—who dreamed of creating a centralized system of education, Michigan proposed a different plan when it entered the Union in 1835. The income from public lands would go not to the townships in which schools were located but to the state for central administration and distribution. Congress accepted the departure from previous practice, perhaps because Crary was in Washington to lobby for the constitution he had helped to write. But this precedent did not decide the question immediately, for states like Florida, Arkansas, and California, admitted after Michigan, still retained the township system. It was not until Minnesota was admitted in 1858 that the remaining states and Congress agreed that the state should be the recipient and administrator of money accruing from school lands. The fear of local mismanagement was a prod toward greater centralization in educational governance and finance, though states proved as capable of squandering funds as were counties and townships.[48]

The gradual evolution toward state control of federal land grants for schools was more the result of incremental learning from experience than it was the outcome of far-sighted educational policy. Partly because of a strong commitment to states' rights in the period before the Civil War, Congress was loath to control the management of education grants, even when states were abusing the terms under which they received federal funds. In Illinois, for example, where the Constitution of 1818 failed to stipulate that the income from school lands should be used for schools, townships and the legislature diverted funds intended for schools to other purposes in the 1820s to avoid raising taxes. State officials refused to make the required reports to the U.S. Treasury. In retaliation, the federal government cut off payments. Congress resolved the dispute in a way to warm the hearts of the advocates of states' rights: it repealed the requirement that states make reports.[49]

Besides the locus of control, other matters had to be worked out through experience. One was whether to lease or sell the school lands. In theory, the income from school lands was to be held in trust for the development of common schools. In practice, the sheer abundance of land in the territories and new states was an obstacle to realizing substantial profits, whether from leases or sales of the school sections. At first, states like Ohio, Indiana, and Illinois tried the strategy of leasing land (this had been customary when title to the land was vested in the federal government during territorial times). Managed by township officials, leasing proved to be almost totally ineffectual, even when renters were given long-term leases, for settlers were not eager to work hard improving land they did not own. In the late 1820s, recognizing the failure of that strategy, the three states petitioned Congress to allow them to sell the lands instead. This became the conventional way of raising school revenue from the lands thereafter.[50]

Growing consensus on the sale rather than the renting of school land left open the questions of how rapidly it should be sold and at what price. A key issue here was balancing the desire to realize short-term profits on the school lands, so that the first and second generations of settlers could have common schools immediately, against the needs of future generations of children whose interests might be served better by holding the lands in public trust as their value increased. The matter was not easily resolved. Americans wanted the national domain to be settled right away, and prompt establishment of school systems seemed to advance that purpose. Economic development—a concomitant of land sales—would provide a tax base for later generations, and it could plausibly be argued that the most critical need for pump-priming and stimulating school formation came early in a state's economic history. Yet haste did produce waste, and the opportunities for embezzlement were monumental. Until the second half of the nineteenth century, Congress gave little definitive guidance on this matter.[51]

Individual states varied in the choices they made about the price and rate of land sales. Among states east of the Mississippi, Michigan made the boldest attempt to weigh the interests of posterity in the balance. There the legislature, under the guidance and encouragement of the first state superintendent, John Pierce, agreed that the minimum price for school land should be eight dollars per acre—a respectable sum when much land was going for $1.25. For a time the plan worked well, but the Panic of 1837 and the overextended state budget together scuttled Pierce's attempt to establish a munificent common school fund. As in other states, legislators came under pressure from citizens who had bought school lands when times were flush and who sought relief when the economy soured.[52]

Profiting from the mistakes of Eastern states, leaders in several states west of the Mississippi became more judicious in selling their school lands. The governor of Minnesota pointed out that in Wisconsin speculators gobbled up prime land at $1.25 per acre, and in other states greed and haste squandered a potential endowment. In its constitution of 1857 Minnesota provided that all school lands should be sold but that it should be done in stages, with the most valuable lands sold first: one-third in two years, one-third in five years, the rest within ten years. Similarly, General William H. H. Beadle, appointed superintendent of public education in Dakota territory in 1869, became an expert on how to enhance the income from school lands for the common school fund. He was convinced that only by setting a minimum of ten dollars per acre, and embedding that provision in the state constitution, would South Dakota realize full benefit from the federal endowment.[53]

In the last quarter of the nineteenth century, Congress itself began to set the terms for the sale of school lands. In its enabling acts it typically called for the school lands to be "disposed of at public sale," set terms for leases, and sometimes fixed minimum prices per acre: $2.50 for Colorado (1875) and $10.00 for the six Western states admitted to the Union in 1889 and 1890. In this region, moreover, state officials found it necessary to dicker with the federal land offices over which lands—especially those containing minerals—belonged to the state and which to the national government. Thus it was that the federal government came to participate more and more in the administration of the school lands. Congress also specified from 1889 onwards that the proceeds of the land grants should be safely invested in a permanent school fund and used only for nonsectarian institutions under state control.[54]

The existence of federally supported state school funds hastened centralization of power by the states in American education. The state designated lawful uses of the funds and could require compliance by local districts to state education laws as a condition for receiving aid from the school fund. The most common uses of the funds were for teachers' salaries, schoolhouses and their care, and newly mandated services such as teacher institutes. States imposed requirements for participation in the funds, including the submission of statistical reports, the raising of local taxes, the hiring of only certified teachers, and the holding of school sessions for the term set by law.[55]

This centralization of power was a long-term process, and schooling in 1900 was a far different enterprise from that of 1800. But underlying the institutional changes, the tangled web of federal-state-local finance and governance, was a set of beliefs linking republican values and the common schools, beliefs that the educational theorists of the revolutionary generation might have recognized. Education was becoming a fourth branch of state government, and the federal government had played a part in that history.

CHAPTER 2

Education as a Fourth Branch of State Government: Nineteenth Century

To numerous European observers, familiar with governments on the continent, the United States appeared to be almost stateless. Alexis de Tocqueville thought the sovereignty of the people so complete that goverment became virtually indistinguishable from society:[1]

> there society governs itself for itself.... The nation participates in the making of its laws by the choice of its legislators, and in the execution of them by the choice of the agents of the executive government; it may almost be said to govern itself, so feeble and so restricted is the share left to the administration, so little do the authorities forget their popular origin and the power from which they emanate.

Although citizens confined the power of government, they politicized all domains of life, said Tocqueville—commerce, social reform, religion, and even everyday conversation, in which an American, "if he should chance to become warm in the discussion,... will say 'Gentlemen' to the person with whom he is conversing" as if he were giving a political speech.[2]

Citizens organized much of this intense political activity through political parties. These organizations were private, but they were potent in their effect on state governments. Fierce loyalties attached families and ethnocultural groups to parties. As the constitutions of new states and revisions of older constitutions broadened the suffrage, a high proportion of white male citizens voted in elections from the Jacksonian period to the end of the century, mobilized by these active political parties.[3]

State constitutions during the nineteenth century demonstrate, however, a curious phenomenon. Even though the suffrage of white males was democratized to an unprecedented degree, Americans revealed in their constitutions a growing distrust of the very agencies of government they were continuously revising in their conventions. The delegates who fought over extension of the suffrage, reapportionment of representation, election or appointment of officials, and other changes in state governments reflected sharp conflicts between parties and classes or interest groups. They argued not only about who should control the state government but also over its proper scope and powers. Those who sought to revise state constitutions believed that experience could teach citizens how to perfect the republican form of government. State constitutions attracted little of the reverence accorded the federal constitution. The intensity of popular fear of public authority ebbed and flowed, but distrust of strong government was a salient theme of the first century of political history of the American states.[4]

Partly because of this distrust of government, the severe restrictions citizens placed upon legislatures, and the haphazard quality of many state administrative departments, American state governments were slow to develop consistent and well-implemented policies. In comparison with many European nations, America lacked continuity and expertise in its civil service and lagged in providing social services. Indeed, in the United States some functions performed by public agencies in other nations were delegated to private groups.[5]

But public education was in some respects an exception to what has been called "the weakened spring of government" in the United States. Under state aegis and operating legally under the framework provided by state constitutions, though decentralized in control, American public schools outpaced public schools in other nations in enrollments and in expenditures per pupil. To a greater degree than in other social services, citizens agreed that education should be a public function.[6]

This does not mean that citizens agreed on how to govern and finance public schools nor that American public education was uniform. They argued in constitutional conventions, in legislatures, in elections, in local communities, and in the courts about the legal framework that should govern public education. Some people—many of them defined as outsiders—lacked the power even to get their concerns on the agenda or, like many Catholics, decided to abandon unavailing combat to form their own schools.

Although public education was controversial and diverse, it nonetheless formed in certain ways a fourth branch of state government, dependent on the other branches but standing in a special relation to the polity. The republican theory of education focused on the individual as the key to political stability and schooling as the means of shaping the citizen. The educated character and tamed will of the individual was the foundation of civic virtue, a small *imperium* in the larger *imperio* of the state, a better guarantee of lawful behavior than regiments of constables. An unrestrained individualism was corrosive, but a schooled individual would recognize the bonds of obligation that make society cohere. This view of the political function of schooling, represented in the Protestant-republican ideology that fueled the common school movement and part of a larger millennial conception of the destiny of the nation, envisaged public school systems as a force distinct from political parties and the kaleidoscopic change characteristic of many other governmental institutions.[7]

Public education was different in other ways as well. It had by far the largest number of employees and the biggest budget of any activity of government in peacetime. Public schools arose in almost every type of community, the most geographically dispersed of any public service. Sooner or later all but a small fraction of children found their way into these institutions. Hundreds of thousands of citizens served as locally elected school board members, the most numerous category of public officials. The structures of control of schools formed a tangled and overlapping web of federal, state, county, and local governance and finance.

The Distrust of Strong Government

If one were to focus only on public education in examining state governments in the nineteenth century, one might conclude that Americans were distrustful of state regulation of schooling, niggardly in providing funds for public schools, contentious about means, and inconsistent in educational policy. But seen in the broader perspective of the development of state government in the nineteenth century, state school systems represented a less ambiguous commitment than found in many abortive reforms, a more universal and costly public service than any other in a time when government delegated many functions to private agencies, and an institution that citizens were willing to entrust to public authority in an era when distrust of government was rife.

During the revolutionary generation, the framers of state governments feared a strong executive branch because of their experiences with the agents of the Crown. Legislatures, by contrast, enjoyed popular legitimacy as the defenders of the liberties and powers of the people, and they received broad charters of authority. In 1788 only two states gave governors the veto power. As we have mentioned, in the political thought and practice of the first generation after 1776 the doctrines of consent and instruction linked the people with their legislators. Ideally, legislators spoke for the people, and the people spoke through their petitions to their representatives. In this sense, the process of governing was one of mutual education between the people and their representatives.[8]

As time went on, state legislatures lost much of their legitimacy, and the executive branch and the courts gained new power to nullify their acts. By the end of the nineteenth century only two states lacked a governor's veto, while state supreme courts acquired substantial authority to declare laws unconstitutional. Especially from the 1840s onward, Americans grew disillusioned with legislators even though they were elected by an ever-growing proportion of male white citizens.[9]

There were many reasons—some conflicting—for this delegitimization. Some attacked legislators for being fiscally irresponsible and for plunging states into debt to promote banks, canals, and other institutions designed to accelerate economic growth. Such complaints were especially frequent in the depression years following the panics of 1837 and 1873. The aggregate debt of American states soared from $12,790,726 in 1825 to $203,777,728 in 1842. Most in the red were the states that had subsidized extensive internal improvements through underwriting construction and trading companies and banks. Many of these enterprises failed, while in some cases speculators reaped profits but left states heavily in debt. A number of states repudiated their obligations, and 31 wrote provisions into their constitutions forbidding legislatures to give or lend the public credit of the state to any person or organization, municipal or private. Judge Thomas I. Cooley thus described the chain of events that led to public disillusionment with state-sponsored internal improvements:[10]

> A catalogue of these [evils] would include the squandering of the public domain; the enrichment of schemers whose policy it has been, first, to obtain all they can by fair promises, and then avoid as far and

as long as possible the fulfilment of the promises; the corruption of legislation; the loss of State credit; great public debts recklessly contracted for moneys often recklessly expended; public discontent because the enterprises fostered from the public treasury and on the pretense of public benefit are not believed to be managed in the public interest; and, finally, great financial panic, collapse, and disaster.

Even when they were not directly subsidizing corporations, as in the schemes for internal improvements, legislators distributed other important benefits like charters, favorable tax treatment, and rights-of-way. Some critics portrayed legislators as corrupt officials selling influence to the highest bidder or as agents of powerful corporations, such as railroads. In California, for example, members of the Workingman's Party sought to rewrite the constitution to weaken both the government and the hold of the elites who had used it to further their own ends. Commenting on constitutional clauses designed to prevent favoritism toward special interests, Bryce wrote that "one feels. . . . as if the legislature was a rabbit seeking to issue from its burrow to ravage the crops wherever it could, and the people of the State were obliged to close every exit." On the other hand, some capitalists feared that state governments would cripple companies by punitive legislation. Whether objections came from the right or the left of the political spectrum, citizens questioned the ways state governments had become intertwined with the economy.[11]

State taxation was another bone of popular contention with legislatures. The delegates who wrote educational provisions in state constitutions were well aware of this popular resistance to taxes and hoped that the stimulus and bounty of federal land grants would mitigate opposition to publicly supported schools. The forms of taxation were various, but the chief one was the property tax. In theory, assessments were to be equalized, and both real and personal property were to be taxed. In practice, gross inequalities of assessment were the rule, and real estate bore the heaviest burden, partly because it was less easy to hide from the collector than personal and intangible forms of wealth. Farmers complained that they were hard hit by taxes while businessmen dealing in corporate property were escaping a proportional burden. From all over the country came reports of massive tax-dodging. In West Virginia, the tax commission reported that the only people who seemed to pay taxes on "invisible property" were "a few conspicuously conscientious citizens"—chiefly widows, executors, and guardi-

ans of the insane and infants; "schrewd traders" paid little, whatever
their wealth. In many of the new and revised constitutions after the
Civil War, angry citizens attempted to correct these inequities and to
equalize the burden by taxing corporations like banks and railroads,
but they met with only limited success.[12]

Another way to revolt against taxation was to limit state expenditures,
a strategy that became common in the second half of the nineteenth
century. By 1882, only seven states spent more than $2 million annually.
In constitutional conventions delegates often argued about how much
to pay state officials and sometimes wrote low salaries into constitutions. Parsimony was the rule in the legislatures of Illinois, Iowa, and
Wisconsin in the late nineteenth century, writes Ballard C. Campbell:
"Beset by criticism about the inequities in the revenue system, yet
constrained by public fears of new taxes and unnecessary expenditures, lawmakers endeavored to confine spending to the meager resources raised by traditional means." School finance often suffered
from such penny-pinching. Speakers in constitutional conventions
often referred to the resistance of citizens, especially in cash-poor
rural districts, to paying taxes for schools, whether they were levied
by the state or by local districts. A delegate in Michigan's convention
of 1850, for example, spoke of New York's attempt to raise district
taxes as "an apple of discord." Although almost all the speakers were
in favor of free schools in principle, the pro-school coalition splintered
when it came to deciding who was to pay the bills. In California's
convention of 1879 delegates debated whether to cut costs of public
education by abolishing state and county superintendents, whom one
man condemned as "mere parasites" who go about to schools "asking
some few silly questions." Post-Reconstruction constitutions in the
South frequently cut the allowable mills of school taxes in an attempt
to economize.[13]

Disenchanted—often for different reasons—with their state governments, citizens used constitutions as a way to correct abuses or to
protect against the power of special interests. Between 1864 and 1879
alone, there were 37 new constitutions and many amendments. These
charters grew notably longer and more prescriptive, sometimes resem-
bling prolix legislative codes more than austere frames of government. One common device for limiting the damage that lawmakers
could do was to permit the legislature to meet only every other year,
and then only for a short time. Another was to limit subjects on which

they could legislate (forbidding special laws for particular communities, persons, or companies, for example). As a result of such restrictions, the number of bills passed and the amount of money spent by states dropped in the 1870s.[14]

A common tactic was to settle disputed issues in the constitution itself—taxation of corporations or the pay of government officials, for instance—in order to preempt statutes on those subjects. Framers of constitutions frequently forbad states or lower jurisdictions to incur debt or to raise taxes beyond a certain level. Especially in the later Western constitutions, as we have shown, delegates wrote elaborate provisions on the sale of federal land in order to prevent the squandering of funds that had often occurred in states in the Middle West.[15]

The result of all these restrictions was a severe limitation on the powers of legislators and the discretion of elected officials. Inflated constitutions became emblems of citizens' distrust of their own governments. The *reductio ad absurdum* of this disenchantment with legislatures was a resolution proposed by a delegate to the 1879 California convention: "There shall be no Legislature convened from and after the adoption of this Constitution, . . . and any person who shall be guilty of suggesting that a Legislature shall be held, shall be punished as a felon without benefit of clergy."[16]

Bryce once asked the governor of a state in the Far West how he got along with his legislature. "I won't say they are bad men," he replied, "but the pleasantest sight of the year to me is when at the end of the session I see their coat tails go round the street corner." As the century progressed, almost all governors gained the power to veto legislation— sometimes also to veto line items—but unless they were powerful in the state political party, and were members of the same party as both houses in the legislature (which was often not the case), they typically lacked strong influence over the policy of state governments.[17]

The executive branches of the states also lacked the cohesion found in the federal cabinet appointed by the President. State constitutions reflected the Jacksonian aspiration of direct popular control of public officials. In almost every state the key officials—lieutenant governor, secretary of state, treasurer, controller, and superintendent of schools— were elected by the people. These state officers often belonged to different parties. Their independent bailiwicks were limited in powers and insulated from each other by the specialization of their policy concerns. Bryce observed:[18]

These officials, even the highest of them who correspond to the cabinet officers in the National government, are either mere clerks, performing work, such as that of receiving and paying out State moneys, strictly defined by statute, and usually checked by other officials, or else are in the nature of commissioners of inquiry, who may inspect and report, but take no independent action of importance. Policy does not lie within their province; even in executive details their discretion is confined within narrow limits.

State superintendents of public instruction exemplified this limited formal power. They distributed money to districts from the common school fund, collected statistics, prepared annual reports, and gave speeches to arouse greater enthusiasm for the latest improvements in schooling. There were a number of superintendents—like Horace Mann of Massachusetts, or John Pierce of Michigan, or John Swett of California—who parlayed such limited functions into real influence, but even the most eminent superintendents had little power to regulate education.[19]

High turnover of state legislators and officials undermined continuity in state government. The legislators were overwhelmingly first-termers, new to the job. From 1820 to 1860 in New York, even the speaker of the assembly had an average of only 2.53 years of prior legislative experience. The committees that channelled legislation were typically recreated from freshmen every two years for the brief tenure of the legislature. Hastily entered into the legislative hopper, often poorly drawn, and frequently requiring judicial interpretation, laws tended to reflect the local outlooks of legislators more than well-considered state policy. Elected executive officials received small salaries, as did assemblymen, and they often rotated out of office at election time. Like the legislatures, the administrative branches of state government enjoyed little continuity of personnel during the nineteenth century. State bureaucracies were small and mostly clerical in function. They lacked the professional standing achieved by the civil service in many other nations. What continuity there was in state governments came largely from the structures laid down in state constitutions and the coordination provided by state-level political parties.[20]

The international contrast is illuminating. Compared to several European regimes, some of them autocratic like Bismarck's Prussia, American federal and state governments were late in creating an expert civil service and in providing social services and social insurance (such as workingmen's compensation and retirement benefits). Ann S. Orlov and Theda Skocpol argue that it took more than the development of urban industrialism, congruent values, or working class demands to create these new state services; it also required a particular configuration of political leadership that was lacking in the United States. It was not only social demands from the outside that shaped the welfare state, they write, but also " 'political supply' by state and party managers." In the nineteenth century, American political parties and governments failed to develop coherent programs for social services—with the exception of public education —and lacked the skilled civil service needed to administer them.[21]

In contrast to the expansion of general public social spending in Europe, American governments legally confirmed and expanded the power of private groups to conduct major functions of public life. Distrustful of police and standing armies, Americans nevertheless deputized citizens to act with public authority in times of civic turmoil. Slow to provide child welfare service, governments vested private charitable agencies with official powers to care for children. Reluctant to provide direct public relief to the poor, legislatures subsidized private (often religious) associations that assisted the downtrodden. In the cities, private political machines, such as Boss Tweed's in New York, funnelled aid selectively to the immigrant poor.[22]

One result was a privatization of functions that in Europe became for better or worse a part of the state apparatus. Far more than European nations, governments in the United States entrusted the task of correcting inequities to voluntary groups and to the operation of the market, believing that charity was the way to help the afflicted and that poverty was a temporary misfortune to be corrected through general economic growth and individual effort. Complementing this private power over social services was a growing concentration of private control over the economy and a disinclination of governments to regulate business effectively.[23]

"Americans had long displayed a split political personality," observes Campbell; "they revered representative government but remained cynical about the intentions of elected officials. Hence, the same political ethos that nurtured the short session—a virtual obsession with some lawmakers—also supported state legislatures that collectively enacted thousands of authoritative decisions each decade. . . ." This ambivalence complicates the analysis of public attitudes towards state power; it was not simply a tale of distrust. Numerous studies of state governments have shown that citizens wanted state governments to promote economic development, even though they might distrust the motives of legislators. Willing to spend in good times, citizens would often condemn costly ventures in bad times.[24]

Whigs, Democrats, and Republicans all engaged in distributing benefits such as charters or grants for railroads or canals, though Democrats often differed in the manner in which they allocated largesse and sometimes opposed a state role in internal improvements. The parties also tended to respond differently to ethnocultural demands to pass or oppose laws regulating liquor, lotteries, observance of the sabbath, and compulsory school attendance. Assemblymen of all political persuasions also introduced thousands of "private bills" sought by local constituents and local governments; according to Bryce, such "measures of a local and special nature" outnumbered more general private or administrative laws, despite prohibitions in state constitutions.[25]

Much of state politics, then, could be understood as "the arena for the clash of innumerable and transitory interest groups," writes Gerald Grob. Within a general ethos of distrust of government, such groups wanted to use the state to promote economic and social development without harsh taxation. "State governments," he observes, "were engaged in anything but systematic policy formation. Most legislatures, on the contrary, seemed to view as their primary function the task of processing individual and group demands that involved the distribution of resources, privileges, and favors." As a result—and contrasting with modernizing European nations—the American political system did not "centralize and rationalize authority nor did its political institutions become structurally differentiated." Typically, legislatures lacked the data needed for systematic policymaking and the skilled civil service required to implement legislative decisions. In Michigan a House committee complained in 1841 about the dearth of information about public schools:[26]

> The *returns* give us a few statistics. . . . But of the *real* character of these schools, and their success, nothing, literally nothing, is known. . . . Beyond the limits of each man's district or neighborhood, nothing is known, either to the people or to the legislature. The legislature cannot act *intelligibly* upon the subject, because they do not have the necessary information.

Grob argues that in social legislation states acted chiefly after being prodded by individual activists. Because of the lack of continuity in state governments, "each succeeding legislature discussed the problem in a virtual vacuum; there was little realization that past actions had created an institutional framework that would have a marked influence on current decisions." Even when industrial states like Massachusetts and New York created regulatory welfare commissions to provide more continuous and effective programs, the result, he argues, was to diminish state authority:[27]

> Although most of these boards subsequently evolved into elaborate bureaucratic structures, they were at the time of their founding given a mandate to introduce greater efficiency and rationality into public welfare, and ultimately to dismantle the public welfare apparatus. In other words, the reaction of many states to welfare and dependency-related problems was simply to establish a structure that would terminate public responsibility. Since the political system had always existed on a base of distrust of power and authority, the negative response of many states was neither unpredictable nor surprising.

In one domain of social policy, however, a strong and evolving sense of governmental responsibility gradually emerged, even though people argued about the form it should take. Public education was this anomaly. By the middle of the nineteenth century, education had become one public service widely accepted in the North as a proper function of public agencies. Advocates of spending for public schooling portrayed the common school as the great preemptive social service, the public good that made other forms of social spending less necessary if not superfluous. Parsimonious citizens advocated less taxation and less county and state supervision, but few denied the value of common schools.

The magnitude of the collaborative achievement of states, the federal government, and local districts becomes clear when one compares schooling in the United States with that in other industrializing nations. During the latter half of the nineteenth century, the United States outpaced European countries in the proportion of its school-aged population who attended school. Americans paid more per pupil for schooling than other industrialized nations, including England, France, and Germany.[28]

A salient feature of nineteenth-century educational history was a sharpening legal line between public and private in education that contrasted with the blurring of that line in the privatization of social services in other domains. One sign of this distinction was an increasing tendency in state constitutions to forbid public funds to sectarian schools and to ban sectarian teaching in common schools. The proportion of American children attending private schools fell sharply during the nineteenth century as private schools—especially charity schools serving poor children, and local academies—came increasingly under public aegis. The ratio of public expenditures to total costs of education—including all levels of schooling—rose from 47 percent in 1850 to 79 percent in 1890. By that date over 90 percent of children in rural elementary schools were attending public institutions, while students attending private schools were becoming concentrated in Catholic schools, especially in large cities. Public subsidies to private schools—traditional in the years before the Civil War, and in most English-speaking nations in the twentieth century—dropped sharply after the war. While many other public services in the United States were meager, and often privatized, education became the largest part of the public sector in a period marked by distrust of government.[29]

Diversity and Conflict within a Framework of Republican Values

As we suggested in chapter 1, the educational clauses of constitutions of new states admitted to the Union reveal much about the purpose and structure of public schools. From the early years of the nineteenth century, three types of clauses appear with great frequency: ones dealing with purpose, typically statements of republican ideology; statements about the disposition of federal land grants; and provisions to establish state school funds. These suggest how two zones of agreement—republican ideology and the value of distributing profits from land to stimulate common schooling—worked together to hasten the spread of public schooling and to legitimize the educational role of state government in the process. Under the prodding of lay school reformers and professional educators, states learned to use their common school funds to stimulate local communities to build schools and as levers to secure compliance with state regulations. Although the first steps toward state control were halting, meager, and contested, they helped to persuade Americans to accept education as a proper function of the state.

A second observation is that from the 1850s onward states increasingly began to provide rudimentary structures of state authority—superintendents, state boards, state taxes, and provisions for nonsectarian instruction (differentiating public from private)—in their constitutions. As we shall suggest, states emulated one another as they established systems of public education, thereby creating some degree of standardization from coast to coast. In addition, constitutional provisions for schools became more detailed and bureaucratic toward the end of the nineteenth century.

Traditions of localism remained strong, nonetheless, and the centralizers had great difficulty securing compliance with state law. To stress elements of consensus and forces leading towards centralization is not to deny diversity and conflict, for education was a domain in which growing agreement over purpose coexisted with sharp disagreement over means.

Table 2.1 summarizes the educational provisions of the initial constitutions of states admitted from 1792 (Kentucky) to 1912 (New Mexico). We also include the educational provisions of key Reconstruction constitutions since they represented a sharp and deliberate departure from Southern constitutional tradition, which is discussed in detail in chapter five, and revealed salient trends in the growth of state authority.[30]

Almost all constitutions of the new states contained provisions concerning federal land grants and the establishment of a state school fund. Most of them also had statements about the purposes of public education. When one reads these clauses, two points converge: the writers of the constitutions saw a strong ideological connection between an educated citizenry and the success of a republican form of government; and they believed that funds derived from the sale of federal lands should stimulate the creation of schools. Although citizens were often reluctant to tax themselves, not surprisingly they welcomed federal subsidies for common schools, for land grants seemed to be a free good derived from an apparently inexhaustible public domain and earmarked for an institution well designed to serve a political common good.[31]

In constitutional conventions and in the documents themselves, citizens talked about education as a non-politicized common good that was essential to the survival of republicanism. Consider this impassioned moment of concord amid the jousting of Whigs and

TABLE 2.1
State Constitutional Provisions for Public Education

	STATE SUPT.	STATE BOARD	COUNTY SUPT.	LAND GRANTS	SCHOOL FUND	STATE TAXES	NON-SECT	PUR-POSE
1792 Kentucky								
1796 Tennessee								
1802 Ohio				X				X
1812 Louisiana								
1816 Indiana				X	X			X
1817 Mississippi								X
1818 Illinois								
1819 Alabama				X	X			X
1819 Maine								X
1820 Missouri				X	X			X
1835 Michigan	X			X	X			X
1836 Arkansas				X				X
1838 Florida				X	X			
1842 Rhode Island					X			X
1846 Iowa	X			X	X			X
1848 Wisconsin	X			X	X		X	
1849 California	X			X	X			X
1855 Kansas	X			X	X		X	
1857 Minnesota				X	X	X		X
1857 Oregon	X			X	X			
1863 W. Virginia	X			X	X	X		X
1864 Nevada	X			X	X	X	X	X
1866–67 Nebraska					X		X	
1867 Alabama	X	X		X	X	X		
1867 Maryland					X	X		
1868 Arkansas	X			X	X	X	X	X
1868 Florida	X	X		X	X	X		X
1868 Georgia	X					X		
1868 Louisiana	X			X	X	X		
1868 Mississippi	X	X	X	X	X	X	X	X
1868 N. Carolina	X	X		X	X	X		X
1868 S. Carolina	X	X	X	X	X	X	X	
1868 Texas	X			X	X	X		
1870 Virginia	X	X	X	X	X	X		
1876 Colorado	X	X	X	X	X		X	
1889 Idaho	X	X		X	X		X	X
1889 Montana	X	X	X	X	X	X	X	
1889 N. Dakota	X		X	X	X		X	X
1889 S. Dakota	X	X	X	X	X		X	X
1889 Washington	X			X	X	X	X	X
1889 Wyoming	X	X		X	X	X	X	
1895 Utah	X	X		X	X		X	
1907 Oklahoma	X	X	X	X	X		X	
1912 Arizona	X	X	X	X	X	X	X	
1912 New Mexico	X	X	X	X	X	X	X	

Democrats in the 1847 Illinois convention: "As the soul rises into immortality when the body falls into decay and perishes, so does the cause of education rise in splendor and grandeur above all party schemes and factions." Education was no more a domain "above politics" in the nineteenth century than it is today, but members of different political factions in the North, at least, were mostly committed to education as a matter of principle even while they argued at length about such matters as taxation, textbooks, state and county superintendents, and how to distribute common school funds.

It was rare for a delegate to make a cynical reference to high rhetoric about public schools, as did one Michigan politician in the constitutional convention of 1850 when he complained about "electioneering efforts about the blessings of education, etc., which seemed...rather out of place; designed for home consumption rather than any particular benefit of those who heard it."[32]

Citizens forming new states typically adopted what was familiar in the states from which they had emigrated, or in the case of the Reconstruction constitutions, they borrowed models of schooling from the North. Legal structures for public schooling tended to converge over time, as new states adopted the latest forms of organization found in the pattern states they emulated and as older states revised constitutions and created new codes of school law. Almost all the new western states wrote clauses into their constitutions to establish common school funds. Public education was one form of internal improvement on which there was substantial consensus, except in the slave South. In theory the common school funds were designed to preserve and distribute the proceeds from the sale of federal land grants, although as we have said, many states left a sorry record of mismanagement and corruption.

In general, the latest constitutions contained more bureaucratic detail and less republican rhetoric, suggesting that as schooling became more institutionalized, structure became more urgent than philosophy. Whereas the eight new state constitutions written between 1841–60 contained an average of 6.3 educational provisions, the seven approved by Congress between 1881–1900 had an average of 14.0. As John G. Richardson has observed, these later constitutions often contained elaborate blueprints of their own version of the one best system, creating bureaucracies even while there were sometimes only a few thousand schoolchildren within state borders.[33]

Table 2.1 shows convergence in state constitutions on the kinds of educational provisions included. Beginning with Michigan in 1835, most state constitutions created a state superintendent of public instruction (or some similar title). From the 1860s onward, most new constitutions also provided for a state board of education, for state taxes for schools, and for county superintendents. A few constitutions included provisions for compulsory attendance, while a larger number specified the length of the school term. The view across time which table 2.1 provides indicates increasing state control over education in the constitutions of new states, particularly during the decades following the Civil War.

Constitutional provisions on education in new states offer only one glimpse into the legal structure of public schooling, however. As a rule, the established state governments in the older northern states relied more heavily on legislation than on constitutional revisions to shape schooling, whereas delegates to constitutional conventions in western territories and during Reconstruction put more detail into their constitutions. Thus a complete picture of the legal framework for public education needs to include statutory law. To supplement the over-time perspective in table 2.1, table 2.2 provides a comprehensive view of the constitutional and statutory framework for public education at one point in time, 1885–86.

Table 2.2 shows that both new and old states tended to provide, by 1885–86, similar legal structures to shape educational governance and finance (although there were regional and urban-rural differences which we shall discuss in a moment). Nearly all of the states provided legally for a state superintendent, local school trustees, a public school fund, local (county or township) school taxes, teacher certification, and a defined school age. Recognizing the importance of improving the skills of teachers, 34 states specified the qualifications of teachers and created teacher institutes (or short training sessions); 28 took the more expensive route of building normal schools. Thirty-four states also prescribed school subjects and 31 decided by law who should select textbooks. Twenty-two made special provisions for what was then called "defective" pupils (for example, blind, deaf, mute, truant, and delinquent children and youth), while 23 provided for a school census.

It would, of course, be incorrect to imply that similarity of legal frameworks between states meant homogeneity of actual practice.

TABLE 2.2

**Number of States with Constitutional and Statutory Provisions
for Public Education, 1885–86**

(Percent of all states with each provision in parentheses)

State Boards of Education	26 (68)	*Qualifications of Teachers*	34 (89)
(of which:)		(Specific qualifications:)	
Ex-officio membership	17	Pass test	33
Ex-officio and appointed	8	Moral character	18
Ex-officio and elected	1	Minimum age (16 to 20)	4
State School Superintendents	38 (100)	*Normal Schools*	28 (74)
(of which:)		*Teacher Institutes*	34 (89)
Elected	22		
Appointed	12	*Compulsory*	
Elected by legislature	3	*School Attendance*	15 (39)
Principal of normal school	1	*Prescribed School Subjects*	34 (89)
County Superintendents	27 (71)	*Determination of Textbooks*	31 (82)
(of which:)		(of which:)	
Elected	16	State	14
Appointed	7	County	5
Other	4	Local	9
		Other	3
Local School Trustees	34 (89)		
(of which:)		*Schooling for "Defectives"*	22 (58)
Elected	28		
Appointed	4	*Segregation of Pupils*	23 (60)
Other	2	(of which:)	
		Mandatory	15
Public School Fund	37 (97)	Permissible	2
		Forbidden	6
State School Tax	26 (68)		
Local or County School Tax	37 (97)	*Legal School Age of Pupils*	37 (97)
Teacher Certification	38 (100)	*Provision of School Census*	25 (66)
State only	2		
Combined state-county	20		
Combined state-district	3		
Normal school diploma	11		
County only	10		
District only	2		

SOURCE: "Summary of Constitutional and Legal Provisions Relating to Education in the Several States and Territories," in U.S. Commissioner of Education, *Report for 1885–86* (Washington, D.C., 1887), 47–214.

States differed greatly in their geography, demography, economy, historical tradition, and political culture. In some respects lawmakers chose to organize public schools in ways adapted to the peculiar character or values of each state. Fifteen states, for example, required segregation of the races in public schools, while six forbad it. Seven states made English the mandatory language of instruction, while New Mexico tried to create a bilingual educational system in its constitution of 1912. Historical traditions and patterns of settlement gave prominence to county governance and finance of education in the thinly populated states of the South and Midwest and Far West, while in the urban states of the Northeast counties were less important. The newer states were far more likely to have elected educational officials above the district level than were the older eastern ones.[34]

Differences in the structure of state systems tells only part of the story of the great diversity in American public education. Isolating several important variables in the development of school systems, table 2.3 demonstrates the large regional differences in attendance rates, ratios of children to adults, taxable wealth, and expenditures in 1885–86, the year treated in table 2.2. Such variables as these profoundly influenced what states could do in education. The deep South, the statistics show, was in many respects almost a separate country: so poor, and with so many children in proportion to productive adults, that with the best of legal frameworks for schooling, and without the curse of racial supremacy, it would still have lagged far behind the rest of the country.

TABLE 2.3

Regional Differences in Dependency Ratios, Taxable Property, Average Attendance, and School Expenditures

CENSUS DIVISION	RATIO AGE GROUP 6-14 TO TOTAL POPULATION	VALUE TAX PROPERTY AGE GROUP 6-14	AVERAGE ATTENDANCE AGE GROUP 6-14 (%)	EXPENDITURES PER CAPITA AGE GROUP 6-14
N. Atlantic	17	$3,382	75	$10.94
S. Atlantic	21	1,037	53	3.52
S. Central	22	605	49	—
N. Central	19	1,808	76	11.41
Western	16	3,446	71	15.83

SOURCE: U.S. Commissioner of Education, *Report for 1885–86* (Washington, D.C.: GPO, 1887), 20.

Besides regional differences, a major dividing line in American education was the urban-rural division within states. Urban schools typically had older and better trained teachers, longer school terms, more elaborate curricula, much higher per-pupil costs, and more bureaucratic organization than did rural schools. Urban school districts typically were far in advance of state laws in systematizing schooling; the campaign to use state law to standardize public education was aimed largely at one-room schools and often was spearheaded by school leaders from urban districts (this topic will be further explored in chapters 3 and 4).[35]

Although constitutional provisions and statutes governing education became more similar, complex, and prescriptive by the latter half of the nineteenth century, still in most parts of the country state control of schools was rudimentary and often haphazard. Many Americans were not certain that they really needed state boards and superintendents. For the most part, the Democrats were more opposed to centralized governments than were Whigs and Republicans. Citizens tried to economize by appointing various state officers—governors, secretaries of state, auditors, superintendents of schools, and others—as ex-officio members of state boards of education. As table 2.2 shows, state boards in 1885–86 were almost all composed of ex-officio members. Citizens apparently assumed that state officers with other duties were not too busy to dispose of education along with their other assignments. This was normally a safe assumption, for state boards generally performed few functions beyond managing and disbursing funds.[36]

Superintendents of public instruction were almost all elected officials who served relatively short terms of two to four years. Only two states specified in their constitutions that state superintendents should have had school experience. State superintendents had little formal power to compel observance of laws when local people disagreed. Some of the state superintendents effectively used relatively small official powers with considerable effect, however, to exhort, instruct, and coax citizens to improve the public schools. In many states, superintendents rallied teachers and local supporters of the schools into lobbies that effectively pressured state legislatures. Nonetheless, a superintendent of schools in a large city like New York might have far more power to regulate education for more children than did most state superintendents. As late as 1890, the median size of state departments of education was only two—the superintendent and a helper. The range, however, was large, indicating considerable variation in the extent of bureaucratization at the state level.[37]

Actual influence of the various levels of government often differed sharply from the formal distribution of authority. Initially, the new states carved out of the public land were the creatures of the federal government; counties, cities, townships, and school districts were artifacts of the states. The influence of the federal or state governments on public education was diffuse, however, throughout most of the century. Public hostility to centralization of power, weak federal and state bureaucracies, executive turnover, splintered administrations, and court review of legislation—to say nothing of the weaknesses of the legislatures themselves—all combined to attenuate the influence of federal and state governments on the county and local governments. Even in the Congress and state assemblies, legislators often saw themselves as representatives of their particular district rather than as designers of a broader program.[38]

Everyday decision making in public education, as in many other public affairs, was largely in the hands of local officials, both lay trustees and professional leaders. The sum of the budgets and staffs of local and county governments was far bigger than the total employees and funds on the federal or state levels. The largest enterprise of local government was public education, comprising hundreds of thousands of paid teachers and administrators and lay trustees.[39]

Attempts to centralize state control in the latter half of the nineteenth century led to conflict between the layers of government. In the early stages of most state school systems, trustees in small school districts usually were able to decide whom to hire, what kind of school to build and where, how long to keep it open (with some guidance from the state), how much to tax locally to supplement funds coming from the state, and what textbooks to use and what subjects to teach. Local trustees hired the teachers and chose the textbooks they wanted. In a number of cities, paid superintendents, acting as agents of school boards, issued complex regulations about curriculum, attendance, the grading and sequence of instruction, and the employment of teachers. As table 2.2 shows, by 1885–86 most states were delegating duties like certifying teachers or deciding which textbooks to use to county boards and superintendents or to state agencies. State laws on compulsory school attendance and instruction only in English especially provoked controversy (notably in Illinois and Wisconsin in 1889–90, when those state legislatures passed laws requiring compulsory attendance in schools taught in English).[40]

Disputes over the locus of control and over ethnocultural politics peppered the politics of education at state and local levels. Citizens cribbed and confined the direct power their state governments could exert, partly from a belief in local autonomy and partly from fear of what unconstrained state governments might do. But on the necessity of state-sponsored schooling in a republic and on the benefit of distributing funds to stimulate the growth of common schools there was substantial agreement.

Just as federal land grants primed the pump for state systems of public education, so the state school funds gave incentives to local communities to create schools. In the early stages of institution-building, local and state school promoters worked together in a social movement that was decentralized but which also used the sanctions of state law to persuade, entice, and finally to coerce local people to establish public education. At first, state government could do little save provide meager state funds, a rationale, and an institutional model to local districts. But even such relatively limited contributions helped produce in education "a release of energy" in the common school movement. Thus voluntary groups and persuasive leaders at the local level worked together with the growth of state authority to expand public education. But this process produced conflicts, and Americans turned to courts and other agencies to resolve their disputes.

Courts and Other Arbiters of Educational Conflict

A widow in Currie, Nevada, reached the end of her patience with the chairman of the school board. The schoolhouse, she believed, was on her land, and she made up her mind that she was going to turn it into a washhouse. It was time to get a court order. She took the morning train to Elko to fetch the sheriff to eject the trespassers. When the sheriff arrived on the afternoon train, there was no sign of the schoolhouse, not even the foundation stones or the fence that had surrounded it. As soon as the morning train had rounded the bend, local residents had assembled teams of draft horses, put the school-house on skids, and moved it a quarter of a mile to some railroad property, where the teacher and the pupils commenced again their regular lessons. The sheriff could find no one who had ever seen the schoolhouse on the old lot.[41]

Americans had many ways of settling disputes about their common schools. One of these was going to court—the strategy unsuccessfully attempted by the widow in Currie. As school governance and finance developed during the nineteenth century, overlapping authorities and obscure allocation of responsibility in public education gave rise to litigation. As we have shown, many Americans were reluctant to assert centralized control because they feared strong government, while others sought greater standardization of schools, particularly from the state level. One result of this political conflict was an ambiguous compromise in school governance and finance, in which legislative, executive, and judicial powers were intertwined. To complicate the picture still further, each level of school government—federal, state, county, township, and district—had differing constitutional and statutory responsibilities, sometimes conflicting. In examining this phase when the framework of school law was often jerry-built and even deliberately ambiguous—an era which lasted in most states at least until the turn of the twentieth century—we explore how court decisions gradually clarified the character of authority in a decentralized system, largely in a pragmatic, case-by-case manner.[42]

Only certain kinds of conflict over public schools entered the courts, for there were many other ways to resolve disputes over education. We are interested in how often citizens went to the courts to settle educational disputes, what were the litigated issues, and what sorts of conflicts rarely showed up in the dockets of judges. We then wish to turn these facts into puzzles and to offer tentative explanations.

To answer questions like these requires a foray into territory largely uncharted by writers on school law. Traditional legal research has focused on landmark decisions or has provided summaries of legal precedents and legal doctrines in different fields of school litigation. Both of these are useful. Studies that focus on major constitutional decisions are a fascinating part of U.S. intellectual history and illuminate changing ideologies about the role of schooling in society. Landmark decisions are politically important as well, for not all legal decisions are born equal: one *Plessy v. Ferguson* justifying racial segregation or one *Brown v. Board of Education* outlawing it in assigning pupils to public schools may serve as a major ratification of caste or a challenge to it, outweighing countless other cases in political importance and doctrinal precedent. Serving a practical purpose, textbooks inform school lawyers and educators about what they must and cannot do.[43]

Our questions, however, require a different strategy of research from that employed in studies of landmark decisions and textbooks on school law. We are concerned with the whole universe of cases dealing with public education during the nineteenth century. For our purposes the most useful and comprehensive source is the legal digest series compiled by the West Publishing Company. Under the category "Schools and School Districts" the West lawyer-editors digested substantially all the recorded appellate cases bearing on public education. The West digests offer some special advantages, given our purposes: they are the most comprehensive digests of appellate cases available for long time periods and for the nation as a whole; and the taxonomy of cases remained relatively constant, permitting comparison across decades. There are some problems and cautions, however, to bear in mind in using the digests to map educational litigation: one never knows how well appellate cases approximated the volume of trial court cases; and because of disparate structures and legal cultures in different parts of the country, there may be considerable variation in the likelihood of appeals. In the Appendix to this book we discuss in greater detail our rationale for using the digests, their advantages and limitations, and the procedures we used in constructing our tables. We also provide summary tables that compare litigation over longer periods of time.[44]

Using this comprehensive source of reported cases, we estimate the absolute numbers of reported decisions in school law during the nineteenth century, the rates of litigation when standardized by population, the types of questions that were contested in courts, and how these variables differed over time. We then suggest some possible explanations of the puzzles these data reveal: why were there so few cases? What were alternative methods of settling disputes? Why did people bring certain kinds of issues to the courts and fail to litigate others? We deal in later chapters with a related question: whom did the legal system serve, and whom did it neglect or even oppress?

Table 2.4 shows nineteenth-century trends in the numbers of reported appellate cases in state and federal courts under Schools and School Districts and in rates of litigation adjusted for population (we do not include cases involving higher education). These education cases formed a very small proportion of all reported litigation: only 3,286 out of a total of about 500,000 cases reported up to 1896.

TABLE 2.4

Volume of Educational Cases and Litigation Rates in State Appellate and Federal Courts during the Nineteenth Century Estimated in Ten-Year Intervals

	Estimated Volume of Educational Cases Litigated in Court System			Average Annual Rate of Educational Litigation per Million Population		
TEN-YEAR INTERVAL	STATE APPELLATE	FEDERAL	TOTAL	STATE APPELLATE	FEDERAL	TOTAL
Before 1836	112	0	112	.83	.000	.83
1837–46	187	0	187	1.03	.000	1.03
1847–56	263	1	264	1.07	.004	1.08
1857–66	365	2	367	1.13	.006	1.14
1867–76	518	3	521	1.25	.007	1.26
1877–86	787	12	799	1.51	.021	1.54
1887–96	1,020	16	1,036	1.58	.025	1.61
Totals	3,252	34	3,286			

SOURCE: See Appendix.

Table 2.4 reveals a very low rate of reported cases in education per capita. Yearly litigation rates grew slowly from .83 per million people per year before 1836 to 1.61 in the decade 1887–96. This is consistent with the generally low rates of public law cases, perhaps because people generally regarded the courts as a place to settle disputes—often financial—between private parties. But taken together, the low proportion of reported appellate cases on school law and the miniscule rates of litigation per capita still suggest a puzzle: why did such a major institution as the public school system generate so few appellate cases? In the nineteenth century public education was the largest employer and had the largest budget of any part of the public sector (save in wartime); it affected daily more people than any other public institution; it potentially touched on the deepest questions of human values. Both in direct economic interests and in normative terms, then, public education was an arena fraught with potential conflict, and it was certainly prominent on the agenda of constitutional and statutory law.[45]

There are several ways of interpreting the scarcity of appellate decisions in public education. One may have been the aversiveness of the court system to the average citizen: its costs in time and money, its delays, its technical and impersonal processes. Another may have been the fact that unpopular laws that relied on ordinary citizens for enforcement were often ignored, rather than challenged in court. This was often the case with compulsory attendance statutes, for example. Although almost all states outside the South had passed such laws by 1896, the West Century Digest reported only two cases for the nineteenth century. A school official in Nevada suggested why: in the rural sections of his state the compulsory law "is a dead letter," he wrote, "and will remain so as long as the initiative for the enforcement is in the hands of the trustees. They simply will not swear out warrants for the arrest of their neighbors."[46]

Another dampener of litigation may have been the set of cultural beliefs that justified the common school. Many of the promoters of public schooling saw public education as a quasi-sacred institution, a domain in which litigation seemed out of place. In this public philosophy of education, the schools were almost an establishment of a Protestant-republican civil religion. By contrast, groups or individuals who stood outside this Protestant-republican consensus may have thought that they stood little chance to redress their grievances in local courts. On some issues like the legality of Bible reading the judges themselves seemed often to wonder why citizens wished to challenge a self-evident civic necessity in court.[47]

Thus cloaked in consensus, the schools would have seemed to most Americans to pose few issues for litigation, save in the conventional categories of the common law (like contracts) or specific issues in public law, like conflicts of authority over governance and finance. In any event, litigants rarely questioned in any fundamental way the principles that underlay the system. Judges, sharing that civil religion, were in general highly deferential to the professional prerogatives of educators—for example, in disciplining pupils or deciding what should be taught—and eloquent in defending the necessity of public schools. The courts were bulwarks of the system.[48]

Finally, Americans had other means of settling disputes in education that were simpler, less costly, and seemed more appropriate than going to court. County and state superintendents of education often had official authority to adjudicate disputes, as well as the informal ability to resolve controversies as they arose. States sometimes encouraged or required citizens to take their disputes first to such officials to settle before turning to the courts. In 1822, for example, the New York State legislature gave the state superintendent authority to hear controversies that arose over public education. Between then and 1913 state superintendents rendered over 12,000 official opinions. Elected county and state superintendents had a vested interest in mediating disputes to the satisfaction of the majority of those who elected them (although they sometimes complained that the local officials ignored their decisions). Just as the growth of debt collection agencies diminished the role of courts in debt cases, such appeals processes probably dampened litigation, especially in view of the costs of appeals.[49]

Local citizens also could—and did, in large numbers—go to the legislatures to obtain special laws adapted to their local needs. They could ask their representative to introduce special bills that enabled them to change the rules for electing school directors, to change school boundaries, to alter bonds or taxes, build schoolhouses, and to accomplish many other purposes. Legislators often held parochial views of their duty that predisposed them to look first to local interests. In Ohio, as a fairly typical example, the legislature passed hundreds of such special acts serving the needs of individual districts. This was cheaper and simpler than going to court. Citizens could also throw the legislative rascals out when assemblymen passed laws they did not like, as happened in Wisconsin and Michigan when the states passed laws in 1889 banning the teaching of foreign languages in elementary schools.[50]

There were still other ways to change school policies. Discontented citizens could elect new local school trustees who agreed with them about where to place a new school or whom to hire as teacher. They could take a dispute to a respected member of their community to mediate. Dissidents could take matters into their own hands. In Currie, Nevada, as we have seen, local citizens, aided by their draft horses, simply moved a disputed schoolhouse (a practice common elsewhere).[51]

If they were members of a deeply alienated minority—for example Catholics in a district in which students were forced to read the King James Bible—they might withdraw their children and send them to church schools. Exit from the system was one means of resolving disputes, but costly. Often the burden of creating alternative school systems fell on persons least able to pay, as in the case of immigrant Catholic working class families.[52]

Both the disinclination to go to court and the existence of alternative ways to resolve or avoid conflicts probably contributed to the low rate of educational litigation throughout the nineteenth and most of the twentieth century. But these low rates of litigation are only one part of the picture. What were the kinds of issues that did turn up in court? Table 2.5 breaks down the nineteenth century cases according to the major categories in the West Centennial Digest.

From the data in table 2.5 we can suggest some generalizations about the character of litigation. First, the great majority of court cases in education seemed to fit into standard categories of the common law (land law, contracts, torts) and of public law (taxation, statutory interpretation, public personnel issues). Judges and lawyers had ample precedents from other domains of law for deciding such questions. The compilers of the West Century Digest, eager to employ the categories most familiar to practicing lawyers, did not need to create many new basic classifications (like pupil discipline, curriculum, or separate schools for blacks) specific to education. This is not surprising, for public schools resembled small businesses: they owned land, made contracts, bought supplies, hired employees. At the same time, they were public agencies created by the states, and bound by statutes and constitutional provisions, thus fitting the rubrics common in public law more generally.

Second, the great bulk of cases fit into the twin categories of finance and governance. Finance issues are generally included in categories 5, 6, and parts of 2. Governance issues are found mainly in categories 3, 4, and 7. We estimate that issues involving finance and governance may account for some three-quarters of all cases until 1896.

Third, it appears that it often took a specific motive—often a monetary one—to drive people into court. Note, for example, the large proportion of cases under contracts, liability, debt, and taxation.

Finally, despite some fluctuations, there appears to be considerable consistency over time in the proportions of cases in the different categories.

We have included cases on private schools for comparative purposes. The proportion of cases involving non-public schools was far smaller than the percentage of the population attending such institu-

TABLE 2.5

Percent Distribution of School Law Cases by Major Legal Categories for the Nineteenth Century (1810–96)

	1810–46	1847–56	1857–66	1867–76	1877–86	1887–96
1. Private School Cases	6.4	3.4	1.4	1.3	1.5	1.3
Public School Cases:						
2. Establishment & Regulation of School Lands & Funds	4.3	9.8	5.7	7.3	7.9	6.8
3. Creation, Alteration, and Dissolution of School Districts	13.0	11.7	18.0	17.5	14.0	15.6
4. Government, Officers, and District Meetings	24.1	22.3	18.3	18.0	19.0	18.6
5. District Property, Contracts, and Liabilities	7.4	9.5	11.4	12.3	10.9	11.2
6. District Debt, Securities, and Taxation	27.1	24.2	22.6	24.0	24.0	23.0
7. Claims and Actions against School Districts	5.7	4.5	5.4	2.7	4.1	3.0
8. Teachers: Employment, Tenure, Discharge, & Compensation	10.4	10.2	12.5	10.4	12.3	12.8
9. Pupils, Conduct, and Discipline of Schools	1.7	4.2	4.6	6.5	6.3	7.7
Totals	100.0	100.0	100.0	100.0	100.0	100.0
Estimated Number of Cases	(299)	(264)	(367)	(521)	(799)	(1036)

SOURCE: See Appendix.

tions (roughly 10–15 percent from about 1890). One reason may be that about 70 percent of pupils in such schools were in Catholic institutions in which other methods of settling disputes than going to court were common (church law and the sacred authority of prelates, for example). Another may be that people discontented with private schools embraced a remedy common in the market sector—they took their business elsewhere.[53]

Much litigation over finance and governance involved ambiguities about public authority. Some concerned the federal government. A number of legal questions, for example, arose from federal grants of school lands and other subsidies stemming from the Northwest Ordinances of 1785 and 1787 and later congressional legislation. These endowments, regulated by state constitutions and statutes, created lively litigation about who was to rent or sell school lands; whether the proceeds were to go to townships, counties, or states; how the funds were to be distributed and spent; and whether the proceeds were illegally diverted to other uses.[54]

Many more issues concerned state laws. In the nineteenth century, the standard view was that under the Tenth Amendment to the U.S. Constitution education was a function left to the states. Thus, legally, all subordinate levels of educational governance—counties, townships, and districts—were creatures of state constitutions or statutes. State constitutions sometimes conflicted with state statutes on school law, however, and it was often unclear how powers had been allocated among the different levels and branches of government. In part this ambiguity resulted from ambivalence over centralization versus decentralization of authority and in part from sloppy draftsmanship by amateur and part-time legislators.[55]

Most issues in school law treated by the United States Supreme Court during the nineteenth century seem trivial by twentieth century standards. Five of the seven education cases it decided concerned questions like whether funds generated by the sale of school lands should revert to the township in which they originated in Indiana; whether a special Nebraska law empowering a district to levy bonds was legal; whether a farmer had to pay city taxes for schools when his land was annexed to Pittsburgh; whether school bonds issued in excess of a constitutional limit had to be honored; and whether a school trustee had illegally incurred a debt of $772.50. These were hardly landmark constitutional cases, but they were important to the litigants, and they involved questions that were important to money markets and school finance.[56]

Although the federal, state, and county governments were all part of the complicated network of school finance and governance, everyday decision-making about education was highly decentralized, usually down to the individual district. As the nineteenth century advanced, states prescribed increasingly complicated regulations about the procedures such districts should follow in making binding decisions: when trustee elections and annual meetings should be held, how district boundaries should be determined, how to allot school funds and raise taxes, how to obligate the district legally in making contracts or hiring certified teachers, and many other matters.[57]

Laws on such procedures probably had a double effect: they channeled local conflicts into prescribed methods of settling disputes; and when these routines were violated, they gave the losers a means of redress in the courts. The potential for conflict at the local level was high. It was no trivial matter in a cash-poor rural district to decide who was to obtain a contract to provide firewood or to teach, where the school was to be located, or how much to tax the farmers. The law thus could be seen as a fence—"Good fences make good neighbors" —and a doorway into the courts if necessary, although knowledge of the law in the local community might prevent litigation.[58]

There is some evidence that many lay trustees and teachers knew school law, although some state superintendents complained that local officials either did not know or chose to ignore school regulations (perhaps what mattered was whether the local citizens were more interested in using the laws for their own purposes or in voiding unpopular ones through neglect). In his study of rural schools in the Midwest, Wayne Fuller found that many district officials went by the book in running district meetings and kept the painstaking records required by law. A Minnesota superintendent of schools commented that citizens there knew more about education law than about any other kind—except perhaps the fish and game laws. Knowledge of school law was often a part of the examinations teachers took to win certificates and was stressed in the teacher institutes. In Colorado, school law was a required part of the school curriculum for all pupils.[59]

In Nebraska in 1877 the official pamphlet on school laws bore this message in bold letters on its back cover:

THIS VOLUME IS PUBLIC PROPERTY!

It is to be kept in the custody of the school officers, and produced by them at all meetings of the district, for consultation by the voters. . . .

The state superintendent who issued the pamphlet appended footnotes to the more controversial or obscure provisions to prevent "the burden of a voluminous correspondence" from school officers requesting clarifications of the law.[60]

In this public philosophy of schooling, the law was not so much the esoteric domain of the lawyer as it was a guide accessible to all patrons, a way of resolving conflicts among them about procedures or substantive questions without recourse to the courts. In 1851 a writer of popular manuals on civics and law estimated that as many as one-fourth of all white male citizens might be called on at some time to serve in a public office—the most numerous of which were positions as school trustees—and he claimed that "full that proportion of citizens have time and means to make themselves acquainted with the organic law of the republic." School patrons and trustees could use their knowledge of the law to protest the procedures used when votes went against their wishes, either by calling state regulations to the attention of the district voters or, if need be, by going to court. Court decisions sometimes revolved, for example, on such issues as whether the trustees posted notices properly, whether the district school meeting took place on the state-appointed day, or whether it was held in a school building or a church.[61]

Local decision-makers also chose sometimes to ignore the legal framework rather than to invoke it to win a point or mediate local conflicts. Many school trustees were more responsive to what they thought the local people wanted and believed than they were to state laws. Although statutes and constitutions increasingly distinguished between public and private education as the nineteenth century progressed, local school trustees continued to ignore the lines between the two in many parts of the country. Many districts ran a free "public" school on funds from the state (usually derived from the federal land grants) until the cash ran out, then charged the parents tuition if they wanted their children to continue. Often free and tuition schools operated in the same building. In many places nuns taught with public funding and instructed in the Catholic religion; urban political machines sometimes deliberately blurred the public-private distinction to please their constituents. People winked at other laws if local people were agreed on their violation, as in Wisconsin where many schools were illegally taught in German or French in the 1860s and 1870s. State superintendents lamented in the 1880s that new compulsory attendance laws were dead letters wherever people wanted to ignore them. In the South whites routinely violated constitutions and statutes that pledged equal schooling for blacks.[62]

A frequent source of controversy in local districts, in constitutional conventions, in legislatures, and in the courts was the proper scope of the "common school system." Many citizens, especially those who wanted low taxes, fought the expansion of the system beyond the minimal provision of a teacher, a building, and a short term. As local patrons debated "necessary appendages," cases reached the courts that questioned the purchase of globes and maps for one-room schools. Delegates in constitutional conventions, legislators, and individual plaintiffs argued against the inclusion of high schools, kindergartens, and normal schools as part of the system of public education. They contested the teaching of music, foreign languages, Latin and Greek, and other additions to the curriculum. The courts typically upheld these elaborations of public education, as in the celebrated Kalamazoo case in Michigan in 1874, which argued that that the common school system could include high schools.[63]

If constitutional and statutory law interacted with litigation as people established school systems, it is reasonable to expect that rates of school litigation would rise during the early stages of school formation and then decline as governance and finance became more routinized and as legal precedents became set. Laws provided a framework of governance and finance, but one that was often ambiguous in details that mattered to citizens in local districts. The courts provided a means of clarifying the meaning of laws and of resolving disputes that arose as educational leaders and state legislators attempted to structure the educational system through statutes. To provide a partial test of this idea that litigation rose and fell as schools became institutionalized, we regrouped data on litigation by region, as shown in figure 2.1.

Figure 2.1 shows rates of educational litigation during the nineteenth century for different regions of the country, grouped roughly according to the periods in which common school reformers created legal structures for public schools like compulsory attendance legislation and school legal codes. Figure 2.1 partially confirms this expectation that litigation accompanied the legal establishment of common schools. Note the pattern of a rise in litigation followed by drops in New England, the East North Central States, and Western states admitted before 1875. Litigation rates in the Western states admitted after 1875 climbed dramatically towards the end of the nineteenth century. The South showed the lowest rates of reported court cases, but litigation began to rise there after public school systems expanded

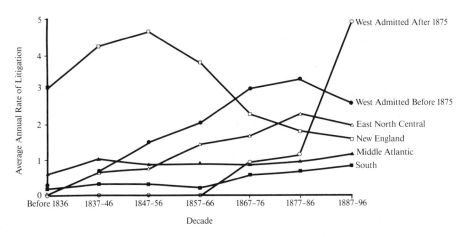

Figure 2.1. Regional breakdown of rates of educational litigation in the nineteenth century

Notes to Figure 2.1:

Region of Country	States Included	Mean Year of Compulsory Attendance Legislation	Range of Years
New England	Maine, Vt., N.H., Conn., Mass., R.I.	1870.0	1852–1883
Middle Atlantic	N.Y., Penn., N.J., Del., Va., Md., W.Va.	1894.0	1874–1908
South	Ala., Miss., Ark., La., Tex., Fla., Ga., Tenn., S.C., N.C., Okl.	1912.0	1905-1918
East North Central	Ohio, Ind., Kent., Mich., Ill., Wisc.	1881.4	1871–1897
West Before 1875	Minn., Iowa, Mo., Kan., Neb., Cal., Ore., Nev.	1877.3	1873–1905
West After 1875	N.D., S.D., Colo., Idaho, Mont., Utah, Wyo., Wash.	1882.8	1871–1890

after the Civil War. Rates of litigation in the Middle Atlantic States slowly increased during the entire period but were relatively low in comparison with other states. One reason is that several of those states tried to settle disputes within the educational system, by appeals to the county and state superintendents. Taken as a whole, the graph suggests a rough correlation across time between legislation establishing school systems and challenges in the courts.[64]

Local conflicts and ambiguities in the public law governing the schools seem to have been a major cause of litigation during the nineteenth century, but in the twentieth century the character both of the schools and of litigation underwent important changes. In later chapters we will analyze those new developments. We will also inquire about people who rarely found their way into the courts and rarely had an opportunity to shape the agenda of schools as a fourth branch of government.

CHAPTER 3

Law and State School Policy: Case Studies of Michigan and California, 1835–1900

The two men sat on a log on a hill overlooking the new settlement of Marshall, discussing the future of public education in Michigan. John D. Pierce was a minister sent into the wilderness by the American Home Missionary Society; Isaac I. Crary was a young lawyer about to embark on a distinguished political career. A newly translated version of Victor Cousin's report on the Prussian system of education had recently come into their hands. From that description of centralized schooling in an autocratic state and from ideas they had brought with them from their native New England, they developed a blueprint for education in Michigan, the new republic that would emerge from a territorial constitutional convention in 1835. As chairman of the convention's committee on education and Michigan's first representative to Congress, Crary would soon work skillfully to enact their vision into constitutional law. As the state's first Superintendent of Public Instruction, Pierce would soon be responsible for drafting school statutes and seeking to translate them into practice in settled townships and new communities.[1]

In the midst of the gold rush of 1849, fifteen years later, delegates met in Monterey to frame a state constitution for California. The president of the convention, Robert Semple, spoke to his colleagues in terms that Pierce and Crary might have used. Education, he argued,

> is the foundation of our republican institutions; the school system suits the genius and spirit of our form of government. If the people are to govern themselves they should be qualified to do it; they must be educated; they must educate their children; they must provide for means for the diffusion of knowledge and progress of enlightened principles.

Semple had opened the convention by asking the delegates to "prove to the world that California has not been settled entirely by unintelligent and unlettered men." One way of demonstrating that, he believed, was to draw a clear plan for an effective system of common schools. He and the other delegates assumed that enormous federal grants of land would amply endow California's public schools. Semple argued that the state school funds should be equitably allotted to each school district so that every child could have an equal opportunity to gain a common school education. In practice, however, state government in California attended only haphazardly to public education during the 1850s, provided minimal funding, and left the governance of schools to local bodies, both private and public. In this early period, which educator John Swett called the "protozoic" phase of public schooling in California, the state lacked leadership in public education of the sort exemplified by Pierce and Crary in Michigan.[2]

In states across the nation, leaders like Pierce, Crary, and Semple sought to use constitutions and statutes to build legal frameworks for state school systems. It would be misleading, of course, to suggest that state law was responsible for creating public education. The actual history of schooling in new states like Michigan and California is more variegated and lines of development more subtle. Haphazardly at first, amid the other challenges facing pioneer settlements and rapidly developing towns and cities, citizens constructed schools both collectively under public aegis and through private initiatives. As in states to the east, public authorities and private groups—often religious denominations—worked together to create educational institutions in piecemeal fashion to serve local needs. The pace of school building differed greatly depending on density of settlement and the local campaigns of common school crusaders. State government often seemed remote and the reach and impact of its laws problematic.

In Michigan and California citizens disagreed about how far and how fast their elected legislators and officials should go in using the authority of the state to mandate, support, and regulate public schooling. Prodded initially by the need to rationalize the distribution of federal land grants, the newly formed states experimented with legal frameworks to govern a system of public education across communities of all kinds. Constitutional revisions and statutes in both states treated such issues as school finance, teacher certification, textbook selection, compulsory attendance, and the racial composition of schools. The process differed in the two states and in neither was one of linear evolution from less to more state control. The legalization of public education was hardly a steady march of pedagogical progress.

We examine the ebb and flow of centralized state power in Michigan and California as reformers sought to use the authority of the state to build common school systems during the nineteenth century and as others challenged them. The comprehensive vision of the school founders in Michigan, expressed in the Constitution of 1835, collided with the the Panic of 1837 that sliced revenues from land grants. Corrupt state politicians and entrepreneurs plunged the state into deep debt. Local officials sometimes sabotaged state policies. Even friends of the common school were forced to compromise their hopes when faced with the powerful demand for retrenchment in state finance and power in the Constitution of 1850. In California, reformers fumbled with symbolic and unenforceable provisions for schools in the first decade of statehood, moved toward greater state control in the next generation, and then fought a rear-guard action against those who sought a return to a decentralized system antithetical to the quest for professionalization and bureaucratization.

The educational reformers in Michigan and California—people like Pierce and John Swett—were convinced that their kind of common school was essential to the survival of the republic. They had trouble imagining a principled opposition to the educational means they espoused. Without proper state laws, they believed, the "educational rights" of children would remain unrealized and the rising generation would be diminished as citizens and producers of wealth. Despite the eloquence of these and other advocates, the means they chose were not self-evident as moral axioms to many other citizens. The state could compel, but many thought that republican liberty was safe only in a minimal state. The state must rule, but in a republic, state authority was based upon the consent of the governed, and about educational governance and finance the polity was divided. In these two states most citizens were agreed that some form of common schooling was essential to preserve the republic—but what sort of education, and under which form of control?

Dreams and Realities: Michigan in the Early Years

As they built their educational castle in the sky that warm afternoon in Marshall, Pierce and Crary agreed on several principles that were new to state constitutions but that would be widely imitated in the future. They believed that education "should make a distinct branch of the government, and that the constitution ought to provide for an officer who should have this whole matter in charge and thus keep its importance perpetually before the public mind." They borrowed this concept of a superintendent of public instruction from Cousin's description of the Prussian Minister of Public Instruction. They thought that federal land endowments, if properly managed and equitably distributed, could support a unified state system that reached from primary schools through the university. Instead of granting the proceeds from the sale of school lands to the townships in which they lay—which had been the case in previous states carved from the public domain—they advocated state control and distribution of the common school fund. They sought to stimulate local communities to build schools and to penalize them if they did not. One way to accomplish this was to grant state aid only to communities that kept schools open for at least three months each year.[3]

Earlier leaders of the territory had anticipated some of these ideas. In 1817 the governing body of the territory adopted an act for "the Catholepistemiad, or University, of Michigania," pedantic in its language but far-sighted in its principles: that schooling should be tax-supported, complete and coordinated, and cheap and available to all, regardless of ability to pay. Lewis Cass, who was Governor from 1813 to 1831, was a Yankee who fully shared the republican conviction that "public opinion, to be safe, must be enlightened." Under his guidance, and with some assent from settlers from New York and New England who were pouring into the wilderness, the legislative council passed laws in the 1820s reminiscent of the Puritan laws of the 1640s. The law of 1829, for example, called on townships of different sizes to establish various types of schools, demanded that parents send their children to them, and established a superintendent of schools to administer the land funds. Settlers did not take kindly to taxation for schools, however, and an escape clause in the law—that two-thirds of the citizens in a township could vote to nullify the law—essentially destroyed its effect. Apparently no one stepped forward to take on the job of superintendent for the munificent sum of $25 per year.[4]

It was one thing to dream, another to build. While leaders designed towns and schools, settlers faced the daily grind of clearing land, building houses, making roads, and plowing fields. Pierce recalled:[5]

Outside of Monroe and Detroit we had no cities and villages. True, we had a great many on paper, but they were yet to be built. So, also, churches and schoolhouses—they existed only on printed plats, like the blacksmith's shop. A traveller inquired for such a place; he was told he would find one at Marshall village. He went on and on till, out of all patience, he asked a settler where he would find said shop. "Oh," said the man, "you are in the shop now, but the anvil is back seven miles on a stump."

In 1835, when the convention met, the typical school on the frontier was made of rough logs, heated by a fireplace or box stove, with slab seats and desks, and miscellaneous books brought West by the pioneer families. A young woman might be paid eight dollars a month to teach in summer, while in the winter a man might be persuaded to teach for double that amount. Parents typically paid the teachers' wages and boarded them in their cabins. In the more settled communities private schools, many of them religious in inspiration, gained a foothold. To most settlers, there was little difference between "public" and "private" schools.[6]

When the 89 delegates elected by the frontiersmen met in Detroit in 1835 to frame a constitution, they adopted a constitution based on familiar principles "of popular sovereignty, political equality, and individual liberties." The delegates were heavily Democratic in party allegiance, but more sympathetic to state action in promoting internal improvements than Democrats in many other places. Half of them were farmers and the rest mostly small businessmen or professionals. Most members had little prior political experience or knowledge of constitutional law. The constitution they adopted, writes Harold M. Dorr, was "relatively free from substantive and procedural restrictions designed to limit the scope of legislative powers." It provided for the appointment rather than the election of all state administrators and judges. As a general framework vesting broad powers in the legislature, the constitution authorized the state to fund internal improvements and set the stage for an activist government.[7]

The education provisions proposed by Crary's committee fit this activist conception of government. The delegates accepted his report with scarcely any debate, despite the novelty of several of his proposals. No prior constitution had included a separate office of state superintendent of public instruction appointed by the governor. None had provided that the common school fund created from the sale of

public lands should be "appropriated to the support of schools throughout the state" rather than returned to the townships where they were
located. And no previous constitution had contained a clause saying
that a school district might forfeit its share of the school fund if it
failed to maintain a school for at least three months per year.[8]

The constitution became prologue to the continuing teamwork of
Crary and Pierce. Elected to the U.S. House of Representatives, Crary
stopped on his way to Washington to visit the new Governor and
urged him to appoint Pierce as superintendent. Once in the capital,
Crary quietly shepherded through Congress the new plan to vest the
school funds in the state. The Michigan legislature passed an act
requiring Pierce to "submit a plan for the organization and support
of primary schools" and a plan for disposing of the million acres of
school and university lands. This Pierce did in 1837, after a trip to the
East in which he conferred with educators who were spearheading
the common school crusade in other states.[9]

Pierce's program of educational reform for Michigan blended diverse
and seemingly contradictory elements: republican purposes and Prussian means, exhortation to local citizens to do their educational duty
coupled with threats of fund cut-offs if they did not, appeals to
religious principles alongside a decrying of sectarianism, a desire for
state-imposed standards yet a glorification of local initiative. Holding
such ideas in an optimistic if somewhat illogical unity of purpose,
Pierce was hardly atypical. Many other common school reformers
did the same, blending the exhortation of the missionary with the
proto-bureaucratic mentality of the state functionary, the desire for
compulsory socialization of children together with the rhetoric of
American individualism.

In Pierce's view, only common schools were "truly republican" in
character; private schools were divisive. Since only public schools
could accomplish the political purposes of education, schooling was
an essential function of the state. Indeed, education was so crucial to
the survival of the republic that schooling should be compulsory for
all children between the ages of five and seventeen for at least three
months per year. Able teachers were so essential to the success of the
common school that the state might set minimum salaries for male
and female teachers and refuse to pay districts from the common
school fund if they did not pay those amounts.[10]

The design Pierce proposed to the Michigan legislature for primary education combined the carrots of republican ideology and state fiscal support with the stick of forfeiture of state aid for noncomplying districts. The public lands would, he believed, create an ample source of income, and grants to local districts of a dollar or more per year per child would "infallibly secure the interest of the great mass of the people in the welfare of the public schools." The system depended on local officers fit for their duties and prepared to carry out the law; he advocated reducing the number of these school board members to avoid confusion and neglect. Local districts should raise local taxes equivalent to the sums distributed by the state.[11]

Pierce offered his plan to the legislature at the end of a boom period of optimism about using the powers of state government and of expansion in the economy. The population of the state almost doubled between 1834 and 1837, and land sales in 1836 exceeded those in its entire previous history. The state began three railroads and one canal, chartered dozens of banks, and engaged in numerous other ventures. Seen in this context, the ambitious attempts to create a vast school fund and to found a public school system were part of a larger enthusiasm for state-sponsored internal improvements. The legislature enacted the main body of Pierce's recommendations, approving his plans for governance and finance but not those for compulsory attendance or minimum salaries for teachers.[12]

In the early stages of his work as superintendent, Pierce sold large tracts of land at auction for good prices. He publicized the new laws through newspapers and urged communities to comply. The stimulus of state aid induced many communities, both new and old, to organize districts and to hire teachers for the required school term of three months. The number of pupils enrolled in 1839 was six times those listed in 1837. Pierce edited a professional journal and encouraged morale-boosting conventions of teachers and "friends of education," using the familiar missionary techniques of the educational revival to arouse enthusiasm at the grass roots. At the same time, his blueprint for educational reform called for tightening the screws of state control as well.[13]

When the Panic of 1837 hit Michigan, however, money troubles afflicted the schools, and the legislature cut back on its initial decisive legislation. People who bought school lands at high prices begged for and won relief in the form of delayed payments and lower prices, thereby slashing the common school fund. State finances were in calamitous disrepair after the collapse of state-subsidized internal improvements. The legislature "borrowed" the common school fund to pay its debts.[14]

Not only did school income from federal land grants decline sharply, but the legislature also cut back on matching county taxes. It changed the rules for voting on school construction from a simple majority to a two-thirds vote, and it legalized the practice of charging parents rate-bills (or tuition) if public funds ran out. Such changes undermined the goal of free schools, or education supported entirely by public funds and open to all. And, in a blow to those who sought greater state control over local districts, the legislature decreed that the state should distribute the common school fund to local districts even if local officials failed to send in reports or neglected their other duties. So much for Prussia. State aid was an entitlement not subject to the supervision of the superintendent, provided that people kept schools open three months a year.[15]

A mood far different from that of 1835 pervaded the convention of 1850 called to rewrite the Michigan constitution. Boosterism during the birth of the state had led to catastrophic debt and failed "internal improvements" during the depression years that ensued; distrust of state government mushroomed in hard times. The keynotes of the 1850 convention were economy in state government and restriction of its authority. The constitution made state administrative offices (including the superintendency) elective for a term of only two years, banned the use of state funds or credit for most forms of internal improvements (the main exception was public roads), denied special incorporation, and hemmed in the discretion of the legislature with numerous restrictive provisions. The advocates of state control and finance in education were fighting a holding action, hoping to find compromises that would preserve some of the gains they had won so easily fifteen years before.[16]

Amid great skepticism about the use of public authority, education still retained its privileged ideological position as bastion of republicanism. No one questioned whether the state should be in the business of education, though the delegates argued vehemently about how it should be financed and how prominent should be the role of the state in comparison with that of the local districts. Pierce and Crary were among the 100 delegates, and they were joined by many other eloquent advocates of common schooling. A merchant, E. S. Moore, summarized the arguments that by 1850 had become commonplace: that "every holder of property has a direct interest, in a pecuniary point of view, in educating the masses" since ignorance led to vice and crime and since "intelligent labor is doubly . . . productive"; the common school discovered and developed talent "that had otherwise laid forever buried in the obscurity of poverty" and was thus a practical demonstration of the principle that "all men are born free and equal"; and the perpetuation of the state depended on educated citizens. Unlike many of his fellow delegates, Moore believed that only a general tax, providing free schools from levies on the property of all, was adequate to the task.[17]

Moore thought that if citizens were willing to support common schooling through taxation, this commitment could lead them to see the public interest in a variety of other domains:[18]

> as men come to understand the doctrine upon which the right to tax them is based . . . they will discover also that they have in many other respects mutual interests; and so, public spirit, so necessary to general improvement, will be more and more promoted.

Thus public schooling was doubly a common good, essential for the civic socialization of children but also valuable because it led adults to adopt a broader conception of the public interest.

One delegate estimated that in all the convention there were not six men opposed to *free* schools, and even those less ardent than the reformers typically spoke of their commitment to the principles that undergirded the common school. Most of the debates—which were often sophisticated and cogent—concerned not ends but money. Some delegates reminded their fellows that the convention had been called to cut down expenses, not increase them. One member suggested that a way to economize was to abolish the "sinecure" of the superintendency and to assign his functions to the secretary of state. This proposal was withdrawn after a protest from Pierce:[19]

> It has been said . . . that the office of Superintendent has been "a sinecure." From my own personal experience . . . I may say it is not so. During that time I visited every organized county in the State, and drew up all the laws passed during that period in relation to common schools. In my first report I advocated that system which the State should adopt, that is, the free school system.

Why is it, I would ask, that Prussia stands at the head of education in Europe? For the simple reason that she has a Minister of Public Instruction to superintend and foster everything relating to the education of her people.

The key disagreements focused on school finance and governance, the familiar question of how far taxation and control of schools should be centralized. A number of the members showed themselves to be knowledgable about taxation in New York and New England and took a cosmopolitan view of the questions of finance. Others talked more about the experience of their own districts and sought to represent the interests of their constituents. Delegates from thinly settled or established communities, for example, argued with each other about the unequal incidence of taxes in the different kinds of districts and disputed whether the state should penalize districts that failed to meet state standards. Largely agreed on the principle of creating free schools, but divided on the way to accomplish that purpose, the delegates compromised. They wrote into the constitution that the legislature should create a free school system within five years. One man, unhappy with this solution, compared the foot-draggers to tipplers hiding their bottles at a temperance lecture.[20]

Michigan's constitutional conventions in 1867 and 1908 later showed the same disputing over means within a larger consensus over purposes that characterized state educational policy to 1850. Delegates disagreed over how long the required school term should be and how to pay for the system of common schools. They quarreled over whether attendance should be compulsory ("We do not live in Prussia," complained one member of the convention of 1867). They disputed how much state and county educational bureaucracy was necessary. But on the need for common schools to maintain a republican form of government there were few dissenters, perhaps because the common school ideology was broad and ambiguous enough to paper over contradictions. Into the constitution of 1908 the delegates inserted a clause that Governor Cass would have recognized in 1813: "Religion, morality, and knowledge, being necessary to good government and the happiness of mankind, schools and the means of education shall be forever encouraged."[21]

California: Setting the Ground Rules for a State System

Over most of its territory California lacked strong community traditions of public schooling rooted in the past, as had existed in New England prior to the common school movement of the 1830s and 1840s. In its first decade of statehood California also lacked leaders of the caliber of Pierce and Crary. As in many other states, however, citizens in constitutional conventions, in the legislature, and in the public school system debated how fast and far the state should go in disseminating and requiring educational standards set by the leading systems of the state, mostly those in cities. Thus the making and unmaking of state laws and constitutional provisions became a prominent form of educational leadership, and state government became a point of leverage for expanding schooling beyond major centers of population.

Throughout the nineteenth century, cities and larger towns led the rest of the state in building schools, employing teachers, and improving the means of instruction. San Francisco set up its first school board during the year before the Constitutional Convention of 1849. "In this protozoic period of development the people in the centers of population were in a state of school evolution far in advance of state legislation," later wrote John Swett, California's most renowned state superintendent.[22]

The cities also provided many of the leaders in state politics of education. Several school officials from San Francisco—Swett, Henry Bolander, and Ira Hoitt—were elected to the state superintendency. Often such men had more real power in urban bureaucracies than in the top state office. Even the most famous state superintendents like Swett had few official duties save for clerical tasks, exhorting local officials, and lobbying the legislature. Minor functionaries with an abundant sense of mission, they spent much of their time recording and encouraging local progress, and they pressed for legislation to professionalize teaching and to standardize instruction. They appealed repeatedly to the legislature to authorize more generous funding of schools through taxes at the state, county, and local levels. Working within a severely constrained zone of state power, school officials in the state capital and in local communities collaborated in a joint venture of institution-building in which state law provided a framework of minimum requirements and gave local districts fiscal incentives to comply with these standards.[23]

The powers of the state in education coalesced initially around the disposition of federal lands. By the time California became a state in 1850, Congress was granting sections 16 and 36 of each 36-section township in public lands, or twice the allotment granted to earlier new states, for the support of public schools. California received, in addition, a special grant of 500,000 acres from Congress under an act passed in 1841. After some debate about using the proceeds to support state government as well as schools, the Constitutional Convention of 1849 decided to retain the proceeds of land sales exclusively for common schools. The delegates believed that this revenue would so richly endow the schools that neither they nor the first session of the state legislature saw any need to raise taxes for that purpose.[24]

Mostly copying Iowa's constitution of three years before, Article IX of the new constitution directed the legislature to "encourage, by all suitable means, the promotion of intellectual, scientific, moral, and agricultural improvement." It called for a state superintendent elected by the people, a common school fund derived from the sale of public lands, and the subsequent passage of laws ensuring that schools would be open at least three months a year for children in the state.[25]

For many years, however, the public lands remained largely unsurveyed and unsold. The legislature did not enact its first school law until 1851, and then only grudgingly. The measure lacked any means of raising revenue for schools. In the following year the first state superintendent of public instruction, Judge John G. Marvin, persuaded the legislature to make a direct appropriation of $50,000 for schools. The rich endowment of lands, which he figured would be more than five million acres when it was surveyed, had not yet produced any revenue. The legislative appropriation declined in the next two years. It appeared for a time that the legislature was backing out of any commitment to provide funds for common schools. Not only was there no common school movement in the state to put pressure on lawmakers, but the elected school leader carried little weight within the Democratic Party, which controlled the state government.[26]

As David Ferris has shown in his study of Marvin, the position of state superintendent of public instruction was part-time and politically expendable. After his election, Marvin spent as much time outside of the capital as in it, mostly on business and in Indian wars. When it came time to make the second annual report, he requested information from local officials and travelled around the state gathering information, but could locate only 20 public schools and 12 religious schools in California. These schools combined had only 3,893 students in attendance, or about 22 percent of the 17,821 children of legal school age in the state. San Francisco alone had seven school districts and 2,282 children enrolled, funded through a local school tax. Without San Francisco and half a dozen other towns, the state had no school system. Writing some years later about the development of schooling in the West, A D. Mayo said of these years that "the common school in California was virtually in the condition of an unnaturalized foreign visitor."[27]

But Judge Marvin experienced one triumph in his term as state superintendent, and it was a legal one. This was fitting for a man who studied with Joseph Story at Harvard Law School, had a promising legal career, and came around Cape Horn to seek a new life and fortune in California. Realizing the inadequacies of the state's first school law of the previous year, he worked with the legislature in producing the school law of 1852, "An Act to Establish a System of Common Schools." This law created a state board of education and set the terms for electing local boards of education throughout the state. Composed of the governor, the state superintendent of public instruction, and the surveyor general, the board did little more in the early years than arrange for the apportionment of revenues from public lands, but it initiated a form of governance at the state level that could be elaborated—and soon was in the regulation of curriculum. The new law also required the examination of teachers and authorized the state superintendent to sponsor yearly meetings of all school teachers in California for mutual encouragement and professional education.[28]

The legislature confronted the problem of how to finance schools since the federal land grants were not producing the large revenues predicted during the constitutional convention. Thus legislators passed a temporary state property tax and empowered counties and cities to raise taxes themselves through similar means for schools. The state tax, five cents per $100 of assessed valuation of property, failed to produce much revenue because the state left the determination of assessed valuation to localities. This policy opened the way for drastic under-assessment and diminished revenues. Nevertheless, the enactment of taxation, meager as it may have been at the outset, did commit the state to supporting the institution for which it had created the constitutional and legal framework. During the rest of the nineteenth century, no state superintendent allowed the lawmakers to forget this precedent or its implications as the educational needs of the state continued to grow.[29]

The school law of 1852 also specified intermediate levels of administration below the state and above the local school district. The local constable became the school census marshall, charged with gathering statistics required by the state. The county assessor became the *ex officio* county superintendent of schools. It could be argued, along the lines of Daniel Webster's famous comparison of education with the police power of the state, that these appointments added authority to the expansion of education by integrating state leadership with local administration. The reality was far less impressive than such an argument might suggest. In accordance with Swett's later characterization of "protozoic" development in state law, the state merely added another title to existing local officials in the more developed communities. Like the state superintendent, these local officials—even if they wanted to cooperate—usually wielded little power except to entreat, remind, and reproach.[30]

At Judge Marvin's urging, the legislature decided to allow public funding of private and religious schools. This incorporated them, however ambiguously, in the fledgling common school system, thereby broadening the base of public support for state aid. In the 1850s the concept of "public" was flexible in both law and practice. A school became public by virtue of receiving support through the government, even though its form of governance and its ways of selecting students may have been fully private under the law. At the time, it was expedient for the legislature, controlled by the Democratic Party, to enact this policy. Religious bodies controlled a sizeable portion of the operating schools in the state, and some of the "public schools" had only recently been private schools run by ministers. Like public schools, religious schools were expanding to meet the demand of new immigrants, many of whom were Democrats and Catholics. Without these schools in the tally, the state's "system of common schools" would have been meager indeed, and with them included the sponsors of religious schools—like the Catholics—could become part of a pro-school coalition in partisan politics.[31]

Immediately the policy backfired by arousing controversy that undermined the legitimacy of the public system and inflamed sectarian feelings. From pulpit and podium, in newpapers and pamphlets, the state's pioneer citizens debated the proper limits of "public" education. The school law of 1852 included a prohibition against the use of religious books in schools, but it did not ban public funding of schools operating under religious auspices. By common understanding, at least among Protestants, the curricular prohibition did not include the Bible itself, which local school trustees generally expected would be used for moral instruction. Directed at catechisms and other religious curricula, the restriction on religious books offended Catholics, who in that year received a warning from the First Plenary Council of Baltimore about "the proselytizing influence of the public schools." In a set of orders written for clergy in 1854, Archbishop Alemany of San Francisco declared Catholic independence from the religious prohibitions in the law.[32]

The public funding of religious schools in California lasted only until 1855 when it succumbed to determined anti-Catholic proponents of nonsectarian schooling. The controversy over the funding of religious schools demonstrated how the state could seek to enlist religious groups as allies in garnering support for public education but then exclude them from its benefits when protest arose. For those who insisted upon religious instruction, and who were incorporated and then excluded, the shifting legal mandates had profound consequences. When the legislature repealed public funding of religious schools, Catholics mobilized to protect and expand their schools. Archbishop Alemany moved ahead immediately to set up a religious community, later St. Mary's College, to prepare Catholic teachers.[33]

Despite this religious imbroglio, the state was able to establish certain ground rules for public education during the next twenty years, even though some points of law remained ambiguous. It defined the responsibilities and limited powers of the state superintendent, state board of education, county superintendents, school census marshalls, and local school trustees. It specified by law the level of control for school resources (state and local), hiring (local) and examination (state, county, and local) of teachers, and selection of required textbooks (state).[34]

During the 1860s California moved toward centralized certification of teachers. First it set up its own board of examination alongside county and local boards, and then in 1866 the law forced cities and districts to honor the "State Life Diplomas" even if teachers had not been examined and approved by county and local boards. The state also created its first normal school for the training of teachers in 1862.[35]

California also began to straighten out school finance. It finally sold its school lands in the 1860s. Unfortunately, the legislature had arranged over the years for local authorities to sell much of the land at low prices with poor and often questionable accounting. Then, diverting education funds to pay for other expenses of state government, the legislature had endowed the school fund partly with devalued state script instead of actual land revenues. Such subterfuges made state funding of education dependent on legislative appropriations during an era when the lawmakers were more inclined to spend money expanding the state's private corporations, especially railroads, than its public schools. Since the common school fund was not munificent, state superintendents lobbied to increase taxation for schools at every level of government—state, county, and local.[36]

By 1867, despite ardent economizers in the legislature, the laws on taxation began to take systematic form. They required local districts to levy taxes to maintain public schools at least five months each year. They set a required minimum level of school taxes per schoolchild for counties. They secured the state's common school fund as a permanent investment yielding interest for the schools. They abolished the rate bills formerly charged to parents for sending their children to school ("FREE SCHOOLS AT LAST," the state superintendent wrote in his Biennial Report of 1866–67). The new laws also secured a state tax levy on property sufficient to complement the interest on the common school fund and maintain a consistent base of yearly state funding for schooling.[37]

Educational historians have tended to account for this accelerated pace of public school legislation by celebrating the pioneering energy of John Swett, who served as state superintendent during the Civil War and its aftermath. Swett's personal leadership was important, but it needs to be understood within the political alignments of the period. The southern part of the state came close to separating from northern California during the 1860s. After more than a decade of Democratic control in the governorship, the legislature, and the state superintendency, Swett rode into office on the Union/Republican ticket. Partly through his prodding, the legislature passed the most comprehensive school bills of the nineteenth century in 1864 and 1866. California exemplified the changes in political culture described by Morton Keller: American government in general experienced a significant, though fleeting, surge of authority after the Union won the war.[38]

As part of this wave of activism, the legislative record of the 1860s in public education represented a virtual Reconstruction Act for the still inchoate public school system of the state. In crucial spheres of educational policy, the state began to supplant incorporated cities as the prime mover and shaper of public schooling under the law. The state increasingly centralized textbook selection and required local districts and counties to tax their citizens for schools. Laws passed during the war mandated instruction in U.S. history and demanded loyalty oaths from all teachers in the state. Swett celebrated the new uniformity of textbooks, remarking that "we have a course of study, established by law, by means of which teachers are enabled to pursue an intelligent system of instruction, in spite of the prejudices of parents who are too ignorant to comprehend the purpose of a school."[39]

During the 1860s the legislature also took a special interest in the training and certification of teachers. It stiffened licensing requirements, supported normal schools, and increased the yearly appropriations for statewide teacher institutes under the direction of the state superintendent of public instruction. Together, these policies stimulated the professionalization of teaching in California and advanced Swett's hope that teachers might be protected by law from capricious control by local authorities. In one of his speeches, Swett noted that California was the first state in the Union where "teachers have gained the legal right to be examined exclusively by members of their own profession." He took pleasure in the fact that this development was praised by Henry Barnard's *American Journal of Education.* "In no state," Swett exulted, "is the authority of the teacher so well established and defined by law."[40]

One agency of state influence over local districts was a state-funded educational journal, *The California Teacher,* that was sent to teachers and local school trustees throughout the state. In editing this magazine Swett built upon a tradition established by his predecessor as state superintendent, Andrew J. Moulder, whose *Commentaries on the School Law* guided local school authorities on legal issues. "The

School Law does not recognize a township as such," Moulder had advised in his commentaries, asserting that state legal authority superceded local in school matters. *The California Teacher* continued this tradition in a tone that was magisterial, occasionally peremptory. "If you have not already adopted the state series of text-books it is your duty to make the change at once," it instructed local school trustees. Failure to respond to the law would mean loss of funds apportioned by the state, "and the State Superintendent is determined to enforce it."[41]

Through the official journal, Swett forcefully stated the case for more state school support. "Public schools are synonymous with taxation; they represent taxation, and the sooner the 'common people' understand this democratic-republican doctrine the better for the State, the better for property, the better for mankind, the better for the nation." Writing during the cresting of governmental authority shortly after the Civil War, Swett claimed that the common school was a creature of the state and essential to its survival. "There is altogether too much of this whining about taxation for the support of schools," wrote Swett in the same article in 1866.[42]

> Where would the nation have been today but for public schools? Who fought our battles in the last war, but the men who were drilled into patriots in public schools supported by taxation? . . . The public schools are the educators of the working men and women of the nation, and they are the producers of all the wealth which is protected by law. The schools mold the characters of the men whose will, expressed through the ballot-box, makes and unmakes constitutions, and breathes life into the laws.

School advocates like Swett looked to the state to expand and regulate public schools and believed that the educational system would revert to chaos if the legal structure were weakened. Echoing Swett, one supporter in San Francisco reminded citizens of their special destiny as Californians "The extraordinary position of this State before the world, calls for and solicits the most rapid progress in human knowledge." California should "hasten to become the *wisest,* or else, if ignorance prevail, it may be menaced soon to become the poorest." The urgency of tone of the supporters of centralization implied formidable opposition to the expansion of state authority in education. Those dissenters would soon gain the upper hand. In 1866 the legislature considered, and almost passed, a law that would have lowered the legal school age. Even as the legislature enacted most of the new proposals to stimulate school expansion during the term of Swett, a determined resistance took a different view of the creation of universal policy for schools. More likely to be rural and Democrat, more interested in keeping state expenditures down and maximizing local control, opponents to state-directed school expansion tended to view the law as authoritarian, an encroachment upon natural liberty, rather than a progressive influence upon local affairs.[43]

Swett lost his bid for reelection in 1867, defeated by the Democrat he had opposed at the beginning of the Civil War. O. P. Fitzgerald, a Methodist minister, waged an aggressive campaign, taking aim at Swett's Unitarianism, insinuating that his liberalism would bring students of different races into the same classrooms, and decrying the erosion of Christian and moral instruction in the public schools. Swett had written in his last report that "school officers and teachers should manifest a tender regard for the religious scruples of both Jew and Gentile, Protestant and Catholic, and hold the schools free from any violation of the great principles guaranteed by the National and State Constitutions, that every man be free to worship God as he pleases...It is left for the home, the Sunday-school, and the church, to teach forms of religious faith and worship."[44]

Swett's civic and statist view of education had helped to accelerate the expansion of education in the state, but his liberal outlook and his urge to professionalize teaching had offended many. While Fitzgerald agreed with much of Swett's program and also sought uniformity, his rhetoric and policies harmonized with the traditional values and localist political outlook of district school trustees. As school law continued to expand in the following decades, state authority began to take a form quite different from the patterns of centralization and coherent leadership that one might have anticipated from the experience of the 1860s.

Forging the Minimal State

By the early 1870s, California's school laws had established several rules that defined state powers over public schooling. Laws required the state and districts to tax property to support the schools. Revenues from these taxes and from the common school fund could not be used for private or religious schools. The state selected textbooks, and the credentials of teachers trained in state normal schools had to be honored locally. In 1874 the legislature passed a statute that mandated compulsory school attendance. But these matters were not settled. During a crucial decade from the mid-1870s to the mid-1880s, with the Constitutional Convention of 1878–79 at the center, dissenters sought to undo the work of the reformers by redefining the scope of state action in education.

The law on compulsory school attendance illustrates the ambiguity of state authority in the nineteenth century and differences of opinion between the political parties. Riding the wave of their victory in the state elections, Republican legislators passed the state's first compulsory attendance law in 1874. It required at least 12 weeks of schooling for every child in the state. California became the twelfth state to pass such a law, considered to be a prime reform of the day in education. It was accompanied in the same year by a law setting a yearly commitment of seven dollars per pupil in state funding, which would automatically be figured into the legislature's annual tax bill so that the necessary revenues would be generated.[45]

As a legal norm, compulsory schooling carried the state into the control of individual lives. Henry Bolander, a San Francisco educator who became the new state superintendent the year the compulsory attendance law was passed, explained its rationale: if one admits that "education forms the only secure foundation and bulwark of a *republican* form of government," that "universality of education becomes thus of vital importance to the State," and that the state must "provide all the facilities necessary to enable every child to acquire at least a common school education," then "we are forced to the conclusion that it is not only the privilege, but the duty of the State, to compel every parent to bestow upon his children at least the education which the State places within his reach." Under this reasoning the state must not only provide the means of education but also force parents to send their children to school.[46]

Many Democrats rejected this argument. O. P. Fitzgerald, a Democratic superintendent of schools, strongly opposed a compulsory attendance law because he favored local traditions and family choice in such matters. "Children may be brought to school by the constable and bayonet in the despotic governments of the Old World," Fitzgerald wrote in 1871, "but in this free country we have faith in, and rely upon reason, persuasion and argument."[47]

The theory behind compulsory attendance laws introduced new assumptions about the authority of the state in education. One was that the child had "educational rights" that must be protected by the state and could not be denied by parents. Another was that those rights were synonymous with attendance at an institution operating within the legal definition of a school. A third was that the individual child now had a firmer legal standing before the state in demanding eduational services from jurisdictions below the state level. Finally, once the state had compelled universal school attendance, it committed itself to defining more precisely the legal status of the child in school. Eventually this would lead to distinct standards of attendance, student grouping (age, sex, race, ability), evaluation, punishment, and promotion.[48]

In practice, however, these new meanings emerged only slowly in the years after California passed its first compulsory attendance law in 1874, for the statute had little impact. When John Swett wrote his *History of the Public School System of California,* his summary of school legislation did not even include the law. In the "Errata" at the end of the book appears the following note:[49]

OMISSION.

In the section on legislation, 1874, on page 65, no mention is made of the Compulsory Education Bill passed during that year; but as the law has proved a dead letter, the omission is of little consequence.

Many years later, James M. Guinn, one of the state's pioneer educators and superintendent of schools in Los Angeles, told a teachers' institute how state authority appeared from the bottom up in local communities. "There was a fatal defect in the law's enforcement," he recounted in 1909. "Some one had to swear to a complaint against the delinquent parent and have him haled before a judge and punished. It was easier and safer to let the delinquent parent's progeny go unschooled than get yourself hated and possibly hurt." Guinn was describing a situation that was widespread in nineteenth century America. He recalled one incident to drive home his point:[50]

I never heard of but one attempt at enforcement and that was up in the Tulare country. A justice of the peace had a grouch against a neighbor who was neglecting his duty to his family. So the judge haled his neighbor before him and fined him a hundred dollars. The irate parent refused to pay, whipped the judge and went unwhipped of justice himself. The law remained on the statute books in a state of innocuous desuetude for a decade or two and then was wiped off for a better one.

School enrollment figures for the state confirm Guinn's view. From the 1850s to 1875, enrollments of legal school-age children climbed from just over 20 percent to almost 77 percent, counting students in both public and private schools. From 1875 to 1905 the percentage went up only five percent more to roughly 82 percent of the eligible children in the state (although of course the absolute numbers rose sharply as the population increased). This hovering of enrollment levels after the enactment of the 1874 law suggests that the state's "system of common schools" had already reached a plateau of expansion in the decade after the Civil War when it drew about three out of four children of school age. The compulsory attendance statute appears to have had little impact on enrollments. California's experience was typical of other states. Writing in 1889, the U.S. Commissioner of Education reviewed the lack of progress in creating effective compulsory attendance across the nation. In state after state officals bewailed local indifference, inadequate school facilities, and laws too imprecise or unpopular to enforce. The levelling of enrollments in the 1880s was a national phenomenon. The proportion of children enrolled in school in California did not change dramatically until after the turn of the twentieth century, when new forms of regulation and administration were enacted into law.[51]

What, then, *did* the compulsory attendance law do? The answer is more complex than the enrollment picture might suggest, for the law reflected subtle changes in attitude toward state authority that appeared in other domains of educational policy. For example, the principle of rights inherent in compulsory education raised questions about race and about segregation of pupils. Assemblyman Jabez Franklin Cowdery thought that compulsory attendance logically entailed desegregation. "No law can be passed compelling parents to educate their children so long as our school laws remain as they are," he told the legislature in January of 1874. "If compulsory education is to prevail, then all schools must be thrown open to every child." Cowdery saw compulsory education pointing toward a new and universal standard for grouping children in school. "In educational matters merit, not color, should be the test."[52]

The following month the Supreme Court of California demonstrated that it thought otherwise. In *Ward v. Flood,* a case in which a black sought admission to an all-white public school in San Francisco, the court did recognize the right of the child to an education and the duty of the state to provide it, citing the equal protection of the law as guaranteed by the Fourteenth Amendment to the U.S. Constitution. But the court also ruled that it was no violation of rights to provide that education in separate schools. Thus, if compulsory education suggested a basis for educational rights in a universal system of common schooling, it still did not mean that all children had a right to attend the same common schools. Although San Francisco passed an ordinance the following year admitting blacks into the city's public schools, the "separate but equal" doctrine, later affirmed by the U.S. Supreme Court in *Plessy v. Ferguson,* remained the official policy of the state, particularly for the Chinese, until after World War II.[53]

Legal decisions on segregation by race created a rationale for differentiating institutions that provided the same level of educational services but to different categories of students. This development was not lost on Cowdery in his speech to the legislature, for he saw that where "color" was the standard, "merit" would be peripheral. Under California's third state superintendent, Andrew J. Moulder, a Virginian and Lecompton Democrat, racial classification had meant exclusion from white schools but access to public funds if local white citizens did not object. Under his successor during the Civil War, John Swett, the law on race changed to require districts to provide education for children from racial minorities if their parents petitioned for it, and attendance in regular public schools for racial minorities unless a majority of local white citizens petitioned to keep them out. With the return of the Democrats to controlling positions in state government the law was again changed to permit separate schools on the basis of race if local jurisdictions chose to establish them. Finally, with the passage of the compulsory attendance law and the state supreme court's decision in *Ward v. Flood,* the state required local districts to educate all children but allowed separate schools for that purpose. These changes showed that laws governing classification of pupils could fundamentally differentiate school opportunities even when education was theoretically universal and compulsory.[54]

Another test of state authority in the 1870s was the issue of textbook selection. This question mixed finance (who should win lucrative

contracts?), ideology (what values should be taught?), and governance (what level of the school system should decide which books to
use?). Here, too, the creation of a legal norm supporting compulsory
attendance had an impact on the meaning of other school laws, even
while local practice made the attendance law itself a dead letter. If
the state had the authority to compel attendance and regulate taxation, teacher training, and textbook selection, then in time it might
seek to control what was taught.

Controversy over textbooks agitated state politics for fifteen years.
The conflict migrated from the state board of education to the legislature, state supreme court, the constitutional convention, and back to
the people again in a referendum amending the new constitution of
1879. During these years the test of state authority was the question
whether the law in education should centralize or disperse the control of schools, change or conserve cultural aims, and modernize or
retain the traditional curriculum. And complicating these cultural
conflicts were charges and counter-charges of graft because of the
size of the contract and the power of the textbook lobby.

In 1870 the state board of education made a change in the curriculum, replacing a recent series of cosmopolitan textbooks with the
pietistic McGuffey Readers, which were immensely popular among
local school trustees but were considered anachronistic and inferior
by many educators in the state's leading districts. O. P. Fitzgerald,
state superintendent at the time, favored these traditional readers. He
opposed compulsion in attendance laws, but he sought a compulsory
curriculum. Under his rule, parents would retain the authority to
decide whether their children attended school, but once the children
entered a public school they would encounter a state-mandated curriculum. Fitzgerald's position on textbooks reveals the ambivalent
nature of the opposition to compulsory attendance. This conservative
minister-turned-educator showed that the universalism of state law
could be harnessed to an orthodox past as well as to a professionally
designed future. He thought the common education of the people
should be voluntary but fixed in its values, and that the government
should strive to improve institutions of higher education for training
teachers and well educated citizens.[55]

In 1870 the legislature passed a law ending the exemption of incorporated cities from the state's textbook law. This, together with the
mandating of the McGuffey readers, angered the educators of San

Francisco, who had been accustomed to taking a lead in devising curriculum. They, and most earlier state officials, had considered state selection of textbooks appropriate for developing districts but not for the metropolis. People in outlying communities resented both the cosmopolitan values and the favored position of San Francisco. When Fitzgerald justified the imposition of the McGuffey Readers and the ending of San Francisco's exemption from state textbook adoption, he used much the same language of universalism that Swett and others had adapted from the common school movement. "In California, we have had too much special legislation in school matters," wrote Fitzgerald in *The California Teacher.* "Every little town wishes to become an *imperium in imperio,* and our statute book is made plethoric with special acts, embracing provisions in many instances already comprehended in the general school law of the State, and in others conflicting therewith." He added that mandating textbooks was necessary because "in a new country, with a shifting population like ours, the advantages of uniformity are peculiarly great."[56]

The battle had just begun. In 1872 the legislature reinstated the exemption of incorporated cities from the uniform series of textbooks selected by the state. In 1874, the year of the compulsory attendance law, another law retained the exemption for San Francisco—politically the most powerful jurisdiction in the state—but forced all other incorporated cities to accept the mandated textbooks. Clearly, this was an issue at center stage in the politics of education, particularly when the state was developing a stronger legal sanction for school attendance. That summer, state superintendent Bolander called for bids on new textbooks to be made the following January. When the opening day came in the first week of 1875, the board of education dumped the McGuffey Readers and selected the Pacific Coast Readers published by San Francisco's A. L. Bancroft Company, plus a number of other replacements for texts in various school subjects. The board immediately ordered the new textbooks but was stopped by an injunction from a district court judge.[57]

Cries of corruption arose along with protests at the loss of the traditional McGuffey series. In April the state supreme court nullified the state board decision because the board had been required to give six months' notice before making any change. When the board reopened bids in June, a county judge issued an injunction against reviewing them. Finally in December of 1875 the legislature intervened directly and passed a law instructing the board to keep using the old text-books, including the McGuffey Readers. The result of all this in-fighting at the capital was that San Francisco continued to use whatever cosmopolitan series of textbooks it chose, while the rest of the state used McGuffey's and the other textbooks prescribed under the regime of Fitzgerald. Subsequent bills in the legislature that tried to change this arrangement either failed to pass or were vetoed by the governor.[58]

This was not the end of the story, however. The political fracas had been severe enough to put the issue of textbooks on the agenda for the constitutional convention of 1878–79. It became a major plank of the Workingman's Party, which had mobilized as a third party to revamp government in the state. To the Workingmen's Party and other groups opposed to centralized power and corruption in government and in business, the textbook lobby and the imposition of state-sanctioned values were both anathema. In the convention they advocated state support of textbooks but not state control and the potential boodle and mind control that came with it.

The constitutional convention of 1878–79 reflected conflicts aroused by the prior decade of social and political upheaval and the economic turmoil and suffering caused by the Panic of 1873. The educational demands of the Workingmen and other dissatisfied groups were part of a larger agenda of reform designed to regulate big corporations, to break up land monopolies, equalize taxation, and to fight corruption and special privilege in government. The list of detailed grievances that found their way into the new constitution became in effect a compendium of reform legislation.[59]

The Workingmen and their allies were not satisfied with the educational progress of the state, but their criticisms were different from those of professional educators like Swett. They wanted compulsory free schooling, racial exclusivity, nonsectarian instruction, and greater attention to the dignity of work—but they wanted all of these things at less cost to the taxpayer, and they wanted to dismantle what they regarded as superfluous state bureaucracy in the process. "Retrenchment was their cue, when they came to the cultural needs of the state," wrote Carl Swisher in his study of political alignments in the convention.[60]

Like the Workingmen, farmers protested what they saw as the white-collar bias of public education. An investigating committee of the Golden State Grange two years before the convention complained that it had "learned of no instance in which, by a common school education, has a child in California been given such an *industrial* training as enabled it to make a livelihood." Schools were coaxing the children off their parents' land and causing them to migrate to the cities, the investigating committee complained. "Nothing taught in the schools makes prominent or interesting to the children the business of carrying on the farms on which their parents are at work," continued the report, which recommended pruning the curriculum to "some practical knowledge of nature and its laws; of moral truths and the business affairs of life." Furthermore, said the Grange, the system cost far too much.[61]

Workingmen, farmers, and other delegates to the convention had quite different agendas, but many of them were agreed on the need to trim down the state bureaucracy and to retrench in government expenditures. In the convention these strands of discontent about educational expansion coincided with the desire of large property owners and businessmen to restrict public services in order to hold down the cost of government.

When submitted to the people, the Constitution of 1879 was approved by a narrow majority and the education article became law. It maintained the state's commitment to free and universal nonsectarian public education, but it diminished direct state authority over public schools. County and city boards became the chief agents of certification and textbook selection. State money could go only to primary and grammar schools, not to high schools and other new institutions such as technical and evening schools. Discrimination against the Chinese, proclaimed as enemies of the state by the constitution, remained a fixed policy, but its meaning as educational policy remained a matter of local discretion and judicial interpretation. The constitution also prohibited the legislature from enacting special school laws for local jurisdictions, and those jurisdictions were prohibited from spending more than their actual tax revenues and bonded indebtedness under law.[62]

The provisions of the new constitution shocked the state's leading educators. The *Pacific School and Home Journal,* based in San Francisco, attacked the proposed constitution as "the most iniquitous and barbarous measure ever proposed for the government of an enlightened community." The journal's editor, a teacher, pointed out that the document would abolish the uniform course of study and state selection of textbooks, expunge the state board of education and state board of examination altogether, stunt the development of high schools by making them ineligible for state aid, and destroy the teaching profession by eliminating state certification. The state superintendent would become a petty clerk, the county superintendents mere "pothouse politicians" making money hand over fist. "Every thinking teacher knows that if the standard of qualifications to obtain certificates is lowered," wrote James Denham, one of the pioneer educators of San Francisco and a former city city superintendent, "our profession will be overrun by an indigent class of illiterate tramps, who will teach for any price to obtain board and living." The same issue of the journal reported a mass meeting of San Francisco's schoolteachers on April 22, 1879, in which John Swett characterized the constitutional provisions as "a studied and deliberate insult to every teacher in the State." In another editorial dealing directly with the controversy over state authority in selecting textbooks, the journal castigated the convention delegates. "We pity the *ignoramuses* that they did not know more of educational matters than to make the egregious blunder of charging the State Board of Education with any dereliction of duty or abuse of public trust."[63]

The power of the state over local districts continued to be a contested legal issue. "The legal status of the teacher," lamented John Swett in 1880, "is strictly in accordance with the popular fallacy that anybody who can, in any way, get a certificate is fit to keep school." In that year the legislature passed a special law establishing a separate salary schedule for teachers in cities because of the higher cost of living there. The state supreme court struck it down, citing the constitution's restriction of legislative power to pass special laws for managing local schools. Early in the following decade the court reaffirmed, in *Kennedy v. Miller,* that state laws controlled local laws, noting that the constitution directed the legislature to set up a "system of common schools" for the state. "The term 'system' itself," reasoned the court, "imports a unity of purpose as well as an entirety of operation, and the direction to the legislature to provide 'a' system of common schools means one system which shall be applicable to all the common schools within the State."[64]

Despite the court's assertion of state authority over the system of public education, the contests over centralization had diminished much of the state power won by educational reformers in the 1860s and 1870s. Beset by conflict and indecision, barraged by rapidly shifting laws, many state leaders sought a low profile for state regulation and influence over the local districts. The fundamental legal rules remained in place—the state did continue to require local districts to provide public schools and continued to support them with public funds—and this enabled the system to persist and grow. But those who wanted to preserve traditional values and local autonomy successfully resisted much of the campaign to create the "one system" under state auspices to which the supreme court referred.

Again the issue of textbooks was an instructive example of the seesaw battle between state and local control. In 1884, after several years of agitation from educators, a state senator from San Francisco introduced a constitutional amendment to centralize the selection, printing, and distribution of textbooks. Educators now switched sides and opposed the amendment, largely because of the provision to have the state itself print the textbooks. This meant, educators argued, that the state would not be selecting textbooks that had been privately produced, but would be entering the textbook business itself—ineptly, most educators felt. The amendment passed when submitted to the people, thus restoring one aspect of state control. In practice, though, the state arranged to use the plates of textbook manufacturers, and the state superintendent and board of education worked closely with county and city superintendents in making selections.[65]

After the decentralization of authority brought about in part by the new constitution, state school leaders spoke less as commanding reformers and more as one among equals. The state education journal became more bland, the words of the superintendent qualified and cautious. In an editorial on whether local school trustees could allow schoolhouses to be used for religious purposes, the superintendent hedged in a way that might have appalled his more decisive predecessors. People disagreed about this matter, and since no one had asked to have the matter settled, "its discussion as an abstract matter of right would be neither popular nor profitable."[66]

The Limits of Expansion and the End of an Era

We have described state authority during the early years of statehood in Michigan and in the development of California's system of public schooling during the nineteenth century. In Michigan reformers like Pierce and Crary wrote into the first constitution a bold blueprint for a state system of schooling, only to see their efforts eroded by economic dislocation during the Panic of 1837. An ensuing public suspicion of strong state government stemmed from disenchantment with aggressive internal improvements that plunged the state into debt. Faced with financial crisis and a rebellion against state control of local districts, the legislature legalized tuition payments and decreed that the superintendent should distribute the common school funds to local schools whether they complied with state regulations or not. In the constitutional convention of 1850 Michigan leaders retained their earlier faith in common schooling as a bulwark of republican values, but they sought to limit state authority and to cut back state expenditures. While not rejecting the goal of a free school system supported by state taxation, they refused to mandate it in the constitution, choosing instead to pass the task to future legislatures.

In California, by contrast, the early years of defining state responsibility in education represented a "protozoic" stage of development in which the government moved unsteadily and obscurely toward defining a centralized system. The first constitution of 1849 was little more than an invitation to legislate, buoyed by the confidence that federal land grants would amply support a public school system. When that hope of bounty proved a delusion, state leaders were slow to finance and regulate the common schools promised in the constitution. Then followed a transition time of governmental legitimacy and universalistic policies during the Civil War and Reconstruction, when the state, guided by reformers like Swett, redefined the legal rules governing the system and moved toward greater centralization and state bureaucratization. Finally, in a return to localism and retrenchment, the impetus toward greater state authority of schools subsided during the latter part of the nineteenth century. The constitution of 1879 crystallized and symbolized this last phase. It was the product of an era of social dislocation and widespread disaffection with government. The proportional growth of enrollments stalled, county and local school authorities became the key actors in educational governance, and state leadership became more bland, its vision limited to matters clerical and pedagogic.

In both Michigan and California the expansion of state authority and centralization did not follow a smooth evolutionary upward curve. Rather, it ebbed and flowed with the vicissitudes of state politics that responded, in turn, to trends in the broader political economy. In both states education continued to expand locally, and in the urban centers it began to take on more complex and differentiated forms with the growth of high schools and other institutions beyond the common school. Within the educational profession a broader agenda for reform was developing in the late nineteenth century, but in few state capitals did lay leaders share the aspirations of educators for a vastly expanded and expertly designed system. It would require a new initiative in the state's political arena, nothing less than a reconception of the relationship between politics and education, to set in motion another surge of expansion aimed at unifying and universalizing the schools.[67]

The 1890s brought another economic crisis in the nation's business cycle, the consolidation of vast corporations, another major realignment of the political system, and a burst of proposals for remaking government. Out of this period of shifting party labels and loyalties a new rhetoric of social reform emerged, giving rise to the Progressive Era, both in education and in governmental reform.[68]

In the next generation the pattern of educational expansion changed dramatically, again stimulated by state legislation and constitutional amendment. Some states enacted reformed city charters that restructured educational governance. The state again became an arena for designing broad social policies and a centralized authority for changing social institutions. Similar reform movements and realignments in state politics occurred across the nation. And again the issue of compulsory school attendance came to the fore, this time connected with an interlocking series of institutional sanctions that cut across schooling, child labor, juvenile justice, truancy officers, and the sorting of pupils into differentiated institutions and curricula. This growth propelled the common school into another world, strikingly different from that which had confronted Pierce and Semple when they had sought to frame systems of education in Michigan in 1835 and in California in 1849.[69]

CHAPTER 4

Law and the Bureaucratization of Public Schools: Twentieth Century

In 1893 an astute observer of American public education commented that "many schools have taken on intensely local conditions that are overlooked by those who expect to mold all public education after a uniform pattern. Even absolute monarchy can not compel uniformity in village or other community administration, much less can uniformity be forced in a great wide country in which diverse groups of people settle for themselves how they will conduct their affairs, and among whom no prosecutor will rise for a popular departure from law which does not attract the attention of outsiders." Despite the gradual growth of state laws governing the schools, he wrote,[1]

> Local option shows itself to be sometimes even stronger than statute law in the administration of school affairs. Communities grow into methods of administration which continue after laws establishing them are repealed or which statute law has not confirmed. This is not confined to illiterate justices of the peace whose interpretations of law in the back settlements point the stories of comic writers, but men in our best communities, carrying high diplomas and charged with the administration of law, . . . do not adapt themselves to changes in law till they are rudely disturbed by some litigation that subjects their methods to a judicial comparison with laws in whose name they conducted public affairs.

Such a condition of school law deeply concerned school reformers at the turn of the twentieth century. They knew that local lay leaders often governed schools in a haphazard way with little regard either for state law or for the professional autonomy and expertise of the educators they hired. These self-confident reformers, whom we call the administrative progressives, believed that they knew what was wrong with the public schools, what changes were needed, and how they could make their blueprints of a new education a reality. Unlike

108

nineteenth century activists, who were often satisfied with essentially symbolic statutes like California's compulsory attendance law of 1874, the administrative progressives were determined to devise effective implementation. A transformation of school law was an essential part of their strategy for reform of public schools.

The administrative progressives were the first generation of professionally trained career educators, many of them graduates of the new programs in education at universities like Teachers College, Columbia, Chicago, and Stanford. The most prominent shapers of policy and activists among them were professors (often of educational administration), city and state superintendents, officers in professional associations, and reformers in foundations and in the U.S. Bureau of Education. Like early common school crusaders, they had a dream, but they were more evangelists of a new professionally controlled and differentiated bureaucracy than of a common school system growing from community roots. They wished to free the professional educator as much as possible from the caprices of lay control; they believed that a science of education might one day replace armchair wisdom or political clout in educational decision-making; and they knew that to bring about such expert design of schooling would require fundamental changes in the governance and finance of public education.[2]

They found much to criticize in public education at the turn of the century. Rural schools were too small, starved for funds, miscellaneous and out-of-date in curriculum, and taught by young and often untrained teachers—conditions the reformers attributed to decentralized lay control, meager state and local taxation, and parochial values quite out of tune with the needs of a rapidly industrializing urban society. Only remodeled state law could reach these rural educational wastelands, thought the reformers. The remedies were to consolidate the hundreds of thousands of one-room schools as fast as possible into modern graded schools, to put more power into the hands of professionally trained county superintendents, to standardize the curriculum, to upgrade the requirements for certification of teachers, and to provide more financial support from the state.[3]

The administrative progressives thought the governance of urban schools equally chaotic, though its faults took different forms. To "take the city schools out of politics" the reformers had to embark on political campaigns themselves to persuade state legislatures to change city charters. They usually had the aid of urban elites who agreed with the reformers' vision of a socially efficient school system based on business models. The administrative progressives knew what was wrong with city schools. As in the countryside, lay people had too much power over decision-making. Large central school boards meddled with the everyday details of running the system, and most big cities also had local ward boards that further tangled what should have been a clear allocation of responsibility. In many cities, patronage and graft were rife and made a mockery of meritocracy in the appointment of teachers and other staff. The solution was clear: the governance of city school systems should be "taken out of politics" and much greater autonomy afforded the professional experts. School boards should be small, elected from the city at large rather than by wards, and composed of business and professional men who would know how to delegate authority to the superintendent. This model was, of course, not apolitical; it was simply a way to disguise politics as impartial administration.[4]

Changes in governance could prepare the way for substantive reform of the school system. The old-guard rural trustees and urban ward bosses of education were not only intrusive and sometimes corrupt, thought the administrative progressives; they were also pedagogical mossbacks. The reformers believed that the old undifferentiated common school had become antiquated in an age of specialization and in an era when more and more pupils of widely differing backgrounds were staying longer and longer in school. Educational science showed, they thought, that students of varying capacities and destinies in later life should be educated differently. The educational reformers, powerfully assisted by lay allies, wanted to restructure schools to make vocational training and guidance central functions of the system, to introduce tracking systems for students of different abilities, and to revise the whole curriculum to make it "socially efficient."[5]

Another problem reformers attacked was chronic shortage of funds and the Rube Goldberg patchwork of school finance. Their plans to expand and restructure the school cost money that was often hard to find in impoverished rural areas or in cities struggling to keep up with the rapid expansion of enrollments. To supplement local financing of vocational education, for example, the reformers turned first to state governments and then to the federal government, which began its first large program of categorical aid in the Smith-Hughes Act of 1918. Educators also lobbied both state and federal governments for increased general aid to local districts, sometimes urging them to narrow the range of expenditures between communities with different tax bases.[6]

Finally, reformers turned to state governments to correct what many of them saw as the most important defect of public education: poor training and professional qualifications of teachers and administrators. Like many other occupational groups in the Progressive era, educators wanted to improve the status, pay, and autonomy of their group by raising state-mandated standards. Especially in rural districts, nineteenth-century school boards had basically been free to hire anyone they wanted, subject in most states only to cursory examinations and some sort of guarantee of good character. Only a small proportion of teachers had any special training for their work, and many had not even attended secondary school. Reformers thought the remedy obvious: state certification requirements that would mandate teacher education. And more, they pressed for different credentials for administrators and the many other educational specialists who were appearing in complex educational bureaucracies.[7]

Both public educators and professional groups like doctors and lawyers wanted to use the power of the state to restrict entry into their occupations and to win greater autonomy. For teachers and administrators autonomy meant, in part, greater freedom from direct control by lay people, and this, in turn, resulted from creating the sort of bureaucratic buffers that distanced them from the community. Thus a consolidated school in the countryside, supervised in part by a professional county superintendent, distanced teachers from parents or district trustees who used to visit the one-room school. In city school systems, the corporate model of school governance insulated administrators from ward school committees and an activist and large central school board. As Corinne Gilb has noted, in their strategies for achieving professional autonomy through bureaucratization educators differed from doctors and lawyers, who resisted incorporation into large organizations and wished to preserve an individual fee-for-service relationship with their clients.[8]

Even when engaging in political coalition-building and lobbying, educational reformers typically wanted to appear nonpolitical. This seemed an appropriate stance for professionals concerned with the common good, and it had been used in the past by common school crusaders who had also adopted a political strategy of nonpartisan benevolence. But the administrative progressives added another dimension: the neutral authority of science, the claims of expertise. They argued that their system would be above politics because experts could best decide what most benefitted the children and the society. An NEA expert on state legislation advised school people to retain their purity as they pursued their quintessentially political objectives: "Generally speaking, experience seems to show that it is unwise to enter into any form of alliance, concession, or bargain to secure the passage of school legislation. 'Be sure that you are right, then go ahead' is a good motto for a program of school legislation. When school people begin to bargain, they weaken their fundamental position."[9]

The professional concept of school governance and unselfish lobbying for the public good was of course just another model of political influence—an alternate form of rule that substituted expert administration for more open forms of conflict and preferred high-minded pressure to bargaining. The nonpolitical stance may have been an illusion, even if believed sincerely, but also could have been a clever ploy if used cynically to make opponents appear self-interested.

In certain respects, the early twentieth century was an ideal time for the administrative progressives to have campaigned for the legal restructuring of public education. The Progressive era was a time of transformation in state politics and a period of growth in the size and scope of state government. Daniel T. Rodgers has observed that opportunities opened for new coalitions and pressure groups of many kinds to shape public policy because older party loyalties were eroding. Many Americans during the Progressive era were uneasy about extremes of wealth and poverty, feared that immigrant groups might be unassimilable, worried about the social effects of industrialism, and were especially concerned about the welfare of children and youth. For many of these citizens the administrative progressives were the right people with the right program at the right time. They blended the promise of a socially engineered future with reassuring traditional values of hard work, self-help, honesty, and efficiency. Best of all, they promised that if the rising generation were properly educated, the problems besetting the society might be solved without drastic disruption in the lives of adults.[10]

To accomplish such purposes the reformers needed to find potent allies in politics at the local, state, and federal levels in order to pass the laws and regulations that would provide the framework for reform.

The members of the reform coalition differed from place to place, but the most influential were typically business and professional elites who sensed a congruence of purposes and methods between what they were accomplishing in their own enterprises and the goals and tactics of the administrative progressives in public education. Other groups with resources and access to power and publicity joined the campaign: The U.S. Bureau of Education; foundations like the Russell Sage Foundation, the Commonwealth Fund, the Carnegie Corporation, and the Rockefeller General Education Board; elite local Public Education Associations, as in New York City and Philadelphia; various reformist women's associations; and business groups like the National Civic Federation and the National Association of Manufacturers. In a number of school districts it was not the local educators who took the initiative in school reform but rather lay citizens who were members of national or local associations committed to changing traditional education.[11]

Educational reformers used a variety of strategies to persuade the public of the need for change and legislators of the desirability of new laws. One of the most effective was the school survey, a gathering of facts and figures about the current educational system designed to pinpoint problems and advocate remedies. The surveys were fairly predictable, since the surveyors were a relatively small group of leaders who shared the same ideas about what was wrong with American schools and what to do about their defects. In the five years from 1905 to 1910, there was an epidemic of 28 state educational commissions appointed to investigate the schools. The survey itself was often only the starting point of a campaign to line up influential groups to lobby for new legislation. Advocates of reform used the surveys as report cards on how the state was doing in comparison with others. Russell Sage Foundation's researcher Leonard Ayres created an index of efficiency in 1912 that rank-ordered all 48 states. The Rockefeller-financed General Education Board used data-sheets on state systems as part of its campaign to persuade southern states to improve their schools.[12]

Statistical comparisons and surveys provided the reformers with useful ammunition for their legislative campaigns, but lobbies and coalitions still needed to reach lawmakers in the state capitals. Although business groups, women's reform associations, and experts from universities and foundations worked hard for new school laws, the most persistent and probably the most influential lobbies were the groups with the most at stake, the state educational associations. They did not always speak with one voice. Teachers and administrators sometimes clashed on issues like tenure; rural and urban districts disagreed on occasion on formulas for allocating state aid; elementary and secondary teachers might dispute the virtue of a single salary scale, while equal pay for male and female teachers split the ranks from time to time. But by and large the state educational associations, typically dominated by administrators, worked closely with colleagues in the state departments of education, the education schools of universities, and other members of the professional coalition led by the administrative progressives.[13]

In a relatively short time during the Progressive era of the first two decades of the twentieth century, this coalition of administrative progressives and their allies encouraged states to alter much of the legal framework governing public schools. States granted new charters to a host of cities, typically abolishing the old ward school boards and concentrating power in small central school boards. Legislatures passed laws to encourage rural school consolidation, though the pace of change was slower there than in the cities. Laws promoted the differentiation of schooling especially at the secondary level. A number of states, prodded by the administrative progressives and their business allies, investigated the need for more job training and passed laws to encourage or require local districts to vocationalize the high schools. In 1918, after over a decade of lobbying by the advocates of vocational education by numerous educational, civic, and business groups, Congress passed the Smith-Hughes vocational educational act, which provided fiscal incentives for states to adopt a particular model of training for work. Almost every state soon passed a law to take advantage of the Smith-Hughes subsidy.[14]

Laws also established new patterns of teacher education and procedures governing the hiring and firing of educators. Statutes specified, for example, how teachers were to be certified, what their contracts should contain, the grounds on which they might be dismissed, and sometimes what they should teach. State legislatures also gave special legal standing to new professional specialties in education by recognizing new job categories and requiring certification for positions like principal, superintendent, counselor, teacher of special subjects, and school psychologist.[15]

New school codes, devised in part by educational experts, mandated patterns of administrative organization, new curricular programs such as physical education, funds and their apportionment, school building standards, rules for transporting pupils, compulsory attendance regulations, and health and sanitary requirements. Administrative law mushroomed both at the state level and in local districts. In the attempt to bring all schools up to a state-approved level no detail was too small to evade the attention of the reformers: two professors from Teachers College, Columbia, created score cards for country schools that rated them on their window shades, sanitary drinking cups, and toilets.[16]

The administrative progressives had distinct ideas about what shape the new state laws should take. Ideally, state constitutions should establish the general principles upon which public education was based; statutes governing schools should be pruned and organized into a systematic education code; and state legislatures should standardize schools according to the plans of the professional educators. Local administrators then should be free to establish administrative regulations on matters peculiar to the individual district. These were the principles underlying Ellwood P. Cubberley's ideal school code for the state of Indiana, for example.[17]

In a number of states a symbiosis developed—some called it an "interlocking directorate"—between state departments of education, education professors in colleges and universities, and state educational associations (especially the administrators who dominated policymaking). Often these groups had special links with state legislative education committees. In the flush of enthusiasm for reform in the early twentieth century, states often asked administrative progressives like Cubberley to assist in drafting new codes or statutes. State departments of education depended heavily on the local administrators to carry out the new laws and used professional organizations to publicize the new departures. Educators were more likely to enforce laws they had helped to design and pass. Of course, the state-level "interlocking directorate" of professors, state departments, and leaders in professional associations did not always have their own way in legislation. In states that did not trim school law into modern codes, anachronistic laws were apt to stay on the books. Some laws—for example, mandating new items to include in the curriculum—were passed by interest groups that educators regarded as lay meddlers.[18]

As state laws on education became more elaborate, school law itself was becoming a professional specialty, often required in training programs for school administrators and becoming a specialty for lawyers who worked for school boards. New textbooks on school law consolidated the case law. These textbooks were typically organized according to the bureaucratic categories of most utility to school leaders and attorneys. Basic constitutional questions like racial segregation sometimes were treated as an issue of pupil assignment, while religious teaching was construed as a question of curriculum. Thus did even social philosophy become bureaucratized.[19]

In the more sophisticated districts, knowledge and implementation of the law became increasingly the responsibility of administrators and school board lawyers. The effective superintendent in this ideal scheme of school law would combine all three branches of government: executive, carrying out the law; legislative consultant helping to shape statutes; and judge in matters of administrative law referred to him for adjudication. Of course, in the small country districts the state departments of education still had to rely on lay trustees and rather transitory teachers to know and carry out the law; one incentive for compliance was the withholding of state funds if local districts were not up to standard.[20]

The leaders among the administrative progressives believed that if all went well, there would be little place for any kind of litigation in their ideal concept of educational governance. Court suits represented pathology, the result of poor laws, infighting in the profession, or failed procedures through which lay people could appeal the decisions of school administrators. The reality of public education, however, was often far from the ideal, and litigation over schooling did in fact increase. The attempt to construct large pedagogical conglomerates, patterned in part on business corporations, distanced school decisionmakers from the parents and citizens. Buffers between professionals and the lay public became barriers. In the nineteenth century, when control of schools had been highly decentralized and more particularistic, citizens and parents had many ways to settle disputes over public schools outside the courts. In the twentieth century, educational leaders and their elite allies sought to restrict lay participation in decisionmaking, and this constricted the ways to voice dissent effectively. The attempt to take the schools out of politics and to delegate policy to professionals delegitimized older forms of popular control through ward committees or activist school boards, and this made litigation a more common avenue for disaffected individuals or groups.

Thus some of the older means of settling disputes short of going to court worked less well in the twentieth century than they had in an earlier era. It became less common for state legislatures to pass special legislation adapted to the wishes of local communities, and legislatures themselves became more attuned to the desires of the most powerful interest group concerned with the schools, the educators themselves. Individuals' appeals from decisions of local school boards or officials typically went inside the system, up the hierarchical ladder of authority, so that the persons responsible for policies were put in the position of defending their own staff members. As state departments of education and key administrators at the local level began to assert more control over the educational system, local boards had less discretion. The older strategy of seeking to achieve unity in public education through allegiance to a shared worldview, common Protestant-republican principles to which citizens were supposed to subscribe voluntarily, gave way to the state-enforced forms of normative dominance that we discuss in chapter 6, on the one hand, and to specialized expertise and administrative control of schooling, on the other.[21]

Going to Court

Despite the desire of the new educational leaders to create a modernized educational system that would be above politics and above litigation, new laws and administrative regulations prompted challenges in the courts. Statutes, administrative law, and judge-made law interacted with one another. Legal changes created new types of disputes—for example, over consolidation of school districts or transportation of pupils. The expansion of legal sanctions in American education gave litigants new forms of legal standing—such as due process in the firing of teachers covered by tenure laws. With the decline of older means of settling disputes, the courts also loomed larger as a means of redress of parents' grievances than in the past. The insulation of the schools from popular participation in decision-making, the increased size of districts, the rise in administrative law, and the standardization of school practice by state law meant that lay people had fewer means of influencing by informal local methods what happened in their community schools.[22]

As figure 4.1 demonstrates, the rates of litigation fluctuated more sharply during the twentieth century than they had during the steady rises per decade before 1896 (the actual figures used to construct this graph are presented in table A-3 of the Appendix). The apparent sharp increase from 1897 to 1906 is misleading, for it is in part an artifact of late reporting of school cases. Because of a tight 1896 publication deadline of the *West Century Digest*, some cases from 1895 and 1896 were not reported until the 1897–1906 decennial digest. This inflated that decade's total. Thus there was actually a less steep rise between 1897 and 1906 and a less steep drop from 1907 to 1916 than the graph indicates. Despite this aberration, the long term trend in litigation rates ran clearly upwards, with the sharpest increases occuring from 1917 to 1936, then dropping somewhat until the sharp rises of the 1960s and 1970s.

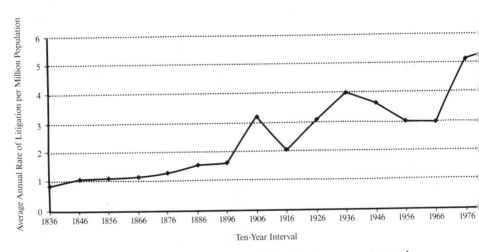

Figure 4.1. **Average annual rate of litigation by ten-year intervals**

As the total amount of litigation rose, some traditional types of cases remained a fairly constant proportion of the total, at least until the 1950s, as illustrated in table A-2 of the Appendix. About a quarter of the cases involved district debt, securities, and taxation, while 14–15 percent dealt with district property, contracts, and liabilities. As school districts grew in size and complexity, borrowed large funds to underwrite building programs, and issued contracts for large sums, they became entangled in the law of contracts and public finance.

Education cases litigated in federal courts illustrate the importance of these bedrock fiscal issues. Of all federal education cases decided between 1850 and 1955, 41.7 percent dealt with bonds, contracts, and taxes. Almost half of the total number of plaintiffs in federal courts were business companies (26.1 percent) and individual taxpayers (22.5 percent), while district school boards were defendants in 57.8 percent of the cases (see tables A-4 and A-5 in the Appendix). Fiscal concerns also continued to load the dockets of state courts during the twentieth century, as they had during the nineteenth.

The increase in the absolute number of fiscal cases involving schools no doubt was disconcerting to educators, but a rise in other kinds of cases after 1900 constituted a more direct challenge to the program of structural and professional change promoted by the administrative progressives. An increase in litigation concerning the many facets of school district consolidation and the teaching staff bothered the educational leaders who sought to centralize and professionalize the system. Many of them thought that educational science was a higher authority than the uncertain outcomes of litigation. They especially deplored the infighting within the educational profession that sometimes led to the courts. Table 4.1 breaks out some relevant subcategories from the West digests that show the changing volume of cases on consolidation and alteration of school districts, school transportation, and legal decisions on the employment, suspension, and compensation of teachers.

TABLE 4.1

Estimated Number of State and Federal Appellate Cases Dealing with the Bureaucratization and Centralization of Public Schools (1810–1981)[a]

	1810– 1896	1897– 1906	1907– 1916	1917– 1926	1927– 1936	1937– 1946	1947– 1956	1957– 1966	1967– 1976	1977– 1981
1. Constitutional & Statutory Provisions for District Creation	18	8	56	116	115	51	103	70	72	9
2. Boundary Changes; Annexation & Detachment of Territory	60	53	57	171	106	74	136	86	57	16

TABLE 4.1 (continued)

	1810–1896	1897–1906	1907–1916	1917–1926	1927–1936	1937–1946	1947–1956	1957–1966	1967–1976	1977–1981
3. Consolidation and Union of School Districts	9	10	13	51	38	25	64	56	39	4
4. Proceedings for District Alteration & Review of Proceedings	106	71	89	178	22	112	272	424	274	49
5. Submission of District Alteration to Popular Vote	25	28	17	71	47	51	123	97	50	9
6. Transportation of Pupils/ Busing	5	2	13	35	81	61	54	61	216	86
7. Teachers: Selection, Employment, & Tenure	16	27	13	27	105	299	225	178	755	647
8. Teachers: Suspension, Removal, & Due Process	84	71	38	60	146	402	*308*	379	*1539*	*1426*
9. Teachers: Compensation	96	31	49	47	62	111	111	78	226	192
10. Compulsory Attendance/ Truancy	7	13	7	23	15	20	25	23	37	27

[a]Italicized figures refer to estimates based upon a 30 percent sample of pages and entries per page.

Consolidation of rural schools and the expansion of the size and scope of school districts was a key goal of educational reformers. Small, isolated schools were barriers to bureaucratization and professionalization in public education, they believed. How was it possible to provide enriched educational opportunity for children and autonomy for teachers in poor and sparsely-settled rural districts where lay trustees outnumbered the teachers and where parsimonious farmers fought improvements that cost more money?[23]

The figures of reported cases on the creation and alteration of districts given in table 4.1 (see categories 1 through 5) show waves of increased litigation that correlate roughly with enabling legislation and mandatory laws on consolidation and reformation of school districts in the 1920–1940 period and in the postwar years. In the mid-1920s, for example, such cases accounted for a large proportion of the cases in Texas, Arkansas, and Oklahoma. The cases themselves reveal a multiplicity of interests and values in conflict: of educators pressing for larger, modern school systems; of legislators passing laws that may have been deliberately ambiguous because of sharp differences of opinion in the state assemblies on the virtues of consolidation; of local board members and citizens who disagreed among themselves about the kind of schools they wanted; and of adjacent districts quarreling about boundaries and who was to pay for what.[24]

Part of the conflict over consolidation arose from the clash of formal state authority and local loyalty and custom. Constitutional doctrine was clear enough: school districts were the creation of the state, which at any time could alter them. The school property of these local communities technically belonged to the state. In the beginning of settlement, towns and school districts in new territories might have seemed arbitrary, the artifact of the surveyor's transit and the land speculator's blueprint for wealth. But once inhabited, communities came to have a symbolic and real life of their own. Local loyalties were strong and rivalries divided adjacent districts. The school was often the center of community life, typically built by the hands of the settlers themselves, taught by their sons and daughters, and affording their children a mental window on the world beyond. To merge this school with neighboring districts could easily splinter a community.[25]

State legislators, coming in large numbers from such rural areas, were caught between the desires of constituents who wished only to be left alone and the claims of educators and their allies that a modernized school system demanded consolidation, standardization, and centralization. The education laws they passed often held in tension these competing demands, encouraging the enlargement of districts and upgrading of schools but leaving room for local self-determination through elaborate procedures for posting notices for meetings, submitting alterations of boundaries to popular vote, and reviewing actions. The result was often laws full of deliberate ambiguities or provisions for due process and public hearings which dissenters could use in reversing decisions through the courts. The cases reported in table 4.1 reveal this increase in litigiousness that may have signalled a questioning of the legitimacy of the program of consolidation forced by state statutes.[26]

Table 4.1 also documents the rise of a new kind of court action related to consolidation: transportation cases (category 6). As widely separated schools were united into larger units, it became necessary to convey pupils from home to school, first by wagon or sled or boat and then (with the rapid improvement of roads and technology) by bus. The transportation cases reveal the bureaucratization of this service. At first the laws passed by the legislatures contained ambiguities about who was entitled to be transported and where the public money was to come from. Many of the early cases came from parents eager to get their child on the wagon or bus—not, as in the last generation, to get their child *off* (there was a great increase in transportation cases, many of them "anti-busing," in the 1967–76 period). Litigation also shaped bus routes, the development of procedures for awarding contracts, and new rules of safety and liability.[27]

Another domain of public education that became rapidly bureaucratized during the twentieth century was the employment and dismissal of teachers and other professional employees. In the nineteenth century, the typical teacher was young, relatively untrained, and hired by local trustees in what amounted to an open market. Under such circumstances, teachers had few rights litigatable in court; typically, disaffected teachers simply left. Even if they had a written contract—most probably did not—their chances for redress of grievances were slight. But in the twentieth century statutes increasingly defined the status of teachers and created procedures for due process in hiring and firing. Teachers themselves often pressed for state laws creating clearer contract terms and tenure (usually limited to the larger districts in the more liberal states). By the mid-1920s, for example, 23 states specified what should be included in contracts; 44 indicated causes for dismissal; 21 provided appeals processes within the educational system; and 11 legislated some form of tenure. These legal developments in education mirrored those in other sectors of public and unionized employment.[28]

Sometimes the administrative progressives were ambivalent about or even hostile to these new rights of due process won by teachers through their unions and professional groups. Ellwood P. Cubberley, for example, deplored teachers who went to court—as creating "newspaper notoriety" for superintendents and boards. They were especially hostile to militants like Margaret Haley of the Chicago Teachers Federation and adversarial leaders of the American Federation of Teachers. Teachers did in fact take increasingly to litigation, as shown in table 4.1, beginning in the Great Depression and rising sharply in the years since 1967, partly because teacher organizations increasingly supported the claims of individual teachers in court. In California, to take one example, 42 percent of 811 education decisions of appellate courts from 1858 to 1979 involved personnel issues like dismissal, tenure, salary, and similar matters, the great bulk of them coming after 1930.[29]

Although local school districts were often able to block consolidation of schools through court challenges, and teachers won new rights of due process in hirings and firings, individual parents and citizens did not fare so well in challenging the new bureaucratization and centralization of authority in education. In the first half of the twentieth century, judges largely upheld school officials when parents questioned school curriculum, disciplinary regulations, or assignment of pupils. Until quite recent times, liability laws also gave the benefit of the doubt to school employees as representatives of the state. One analyst of parental rights observed that the new statutes, administrative regulations, and court decisions produced a situation in which, by and large, the parents "may not decide what school they wish their child to attend; whether or not the distance to school is so unreasonable or the way sufficiently dangerous to require transportation; at what age their child should begin school; what subjects he will study once he is in school and from what texts; how long he should continue his education; under what circumstances they may withdraw their child from school."[30]

The child was indeed legally becoming as much the creature of the state as of the parents. Litigation was not a powerful means of stemming the tide of bureaucratization, but statutory law became a powerful tool in the hands of those who wished to employ the power of the state over parents. One legal expert asserted that "the public school exists as a State institution simply because the very existence of civil society demands it. Education formulated by the State is not so much a right granted pupils as a duty imposed upon them for the general good."[31]

Cases arising from compulsory school laws illustrate the relative power of parents and the state. The appellate decisions on compulsory attendance and truancy listed in table 4.1 only partially reflect a central feature of the bureaucratization of public schools in the twentieth century: the creation of machinery for enforcing school attendance, in which the courts played an ancillary but important role. By the end of the nineteenth century almost all states outside the South had passed compulsory attendance laws, but enforcement was spotty, save in a few states and a number of cities. The passage of more effective attendance and child labor laws after 1900, however, created criminal sanctions for delinquent parents and pupils and a large array of attendance officers to sweep children into school and parents into court if they proved to be refractory.[32]

One study of court enforcement of compulsory attendance in the 1920s found that five judges in New York City in six sessions heard 3,383 attendance cases. In these court appearances 55 percent of the defendents pleaded guilty, 16 percent not guilty, and 29 percent made no plea. Of the 2,348 who were sentenced, 68 percent received a penalty of fine or jail, 30 percent a suspended sentence, and the rest other punishments.[33]

Few compulsory attendance cases reached appellate courts. New York probably had an unusually aggressive attendance department, yet from 1871 to 1925 only six cases were appealed and reported in that state. John F. Bender found only 46 such cases nationwide in those years. There seem to be several reasons why so few defendants appealed. One is the low socio-economic background of the defendants; they probably lacked the funds to appeal their cases. Another is the relatively light fines assessed by judges who recognized that there were often mitigating circumstances. Although they might have been sympathetic to individual parents or children, judges were at the same time eager to uphold the constitutionality of the statutes and to support the enforcement of attendance. The state, according to the theory quoted above, had a compelling interest in securing the education of every child. As early as 1901, in *State v. Bailey*, Indiana held that compelling attendance was a legitimate exercise of the state's police power, although judges in many jurisdictions did sometimes display ambivalence toward putting parents in jail. By 1950 a court declared in *Knox v. O'Brien* that there was no need to cite authority for "the right of a sovereign state to adopt legislation to direct the paths of its children to seek education for enlightenment and literacy." It continued:[34]

> A democracy would fail to meet the challenge if it were not to approve the right of the state to adopt legislation having for its ends standards of education which may forever destroy illiteracy, and to clothe its youthful citizens with academic attainments wherewith to enjoy the high cultural and secular heights thus far reached. To preserve this American way of life and its full enjoyment, this nation has only recently emerged from a global conflict.

It was in the Progressive era that educational reformers began to equate *education* with compulsory *schooling*. This was an ideological corollary of their larger campaign to enlarge the scope of state action in education, to recharter and reform urban school governance, to consolidate and standardize rural schools, to lengthen the school term, to increase state and local taxes, to refashion the required curriculum, to expand the bureaucratic complexity and scope of school systems, and to create new rules for certifying, hiring, and firing school workers.

In all of this expansion of public authority state legislation played an important part. The state government became a fulcrum whereby reformers levered major institutional change. More than ever before, the state became an arena for designing broad social policies and centralized authority in changing social institutions. Similar reform movements and realignments swept in time from state to state, beginning first in the more urban and industrially developed sectors but eventually reaching most communities. For the most part the courts upheld the new policies and institutional structures in education even though they sometimes struck down other state initiatives, such as child labor legislation.[35]

The state and its legal system were hardly at the equal beck and call of every group. Statutory law was a powerful tool of those professional educators and their elite allies who sought to transform the educational system into bureaucracies buffered from lay influence. Litigation remained a recourse for disaffected individuals and groups who had legal standing and the funds to have their day in court—usually on some financial issue. Litigants were mostly members of favored groups. The most common federal cases, as we have said, were those involving the bond market, and here typically the plaintiffs were corporations (which initiated over one-quarter of all federal suits involving public schools until *Brown v. Board of Education*). Until 1954 there were almost as many education cases in federal courts involving money markets as there were cases involving race and questions of constitutional rights (see table A-4 Appendix).[36]

While litigation revealed conflict in society and in the schools, few cases successfully challenged the assumptions underlying the bureaucratic reforms of the administrative progressives. And for those groups that suffered the most severe forms of discrimination—in particular the poor and racial and religious minorities—the legal system moved only weakly toward redistributive justice and the protection of minorities against majoritarian laws that violated their rights. Those legal concerns for outsiders would arrive in force only with *Brown* and its aftermath.

PART II

Majority Rule and Minority Rights in School Law

SOCRATES: Well, how would you gentlemen compose your fundamental principles, if a majority, exercising its fundamental right to rule, ordained that only Buddhism should be taught in the public schools?

[WILLIAM JENNINGS] BRYAN: I'd move to a Christian country.

[THOMAS] JEFFERSON: I'd exercise the sacred right of revolution. What would you do, Socrates?

SOCRATES: I'd reexamine my fundamental principles.

WALTER LIPPMANN,
American Inquisitors

The Many Faces Of Power

As Lippmann's conversation between Socrates, Bryan, and Jefferson suggests, the relation between majority rule and minority rights—like the connection between law and social justice—is fraught with complications. In Part I we have foreshadowed some of these ambiguities in the belief that linked public schools with republican ideology. There we examined how citizens used state constitutions, statutes, and the courts to build, refine, and contest common schools in a nation of republics. We stressed that open political conflict over means typically occurred within a commonly voiced commitment to these ambiguous but potent republican purposes of public education.

These conflicts and agreements took place, however, only among people empowered to decide questions of education law in constitutional conventions or legislatures or school boards and among a relatively small group of people who had the resources and desire to enter the courts. In the nineteenth century within most political forums a majority of the people were denied participation because they were not full citizens, women and blacks being the most obvious examples. "Majority rule" in law, then, meant the decisions of enfranchised white males. Even among this body of citizens many were unable to place their concerns on the agenda of political parties or governmental bodies, thereby making them public issues subject to legal resolution. The real outsiders—the poor and powerless— were often not able to take part in the arenas of legal dispute over school policy.[1]

With only a slight shift of focus, the agreements of the policy-makers in education, underlying even the issues of finance and governance they so vigorously disputed, might be regarded as a form of hegemony that buttressed their position in society. They could contend over particulars with passion partly because the contest did not challenge the political and economic order that gave them influence; they could afford to lose with some degree of composure because next time they might win. There were deep dividing lines in American society—of economic class and gender, for example—that rarely became translated into matters of education law; they were simply ignored as issues.[2]

The relationships between law-making majorities and relatively powerless minorities were varied. Majorities could use their legal power to oppress minorities, as Southern white citizens did when they disenfranchized blacks and cheated them of school funds, as Californians did when they barred Asians from public schools, or as the federal government did when it sought to destroy tribal cultures of Native Americans by resocializing their children in reservation schools. But majorities could also protect the rights of minorities through law, providing them the equal protection of the laws. At times—during Reconstruction in the South, for example—reformist factions among political majorities could even use law to reorder the social system to enfranchise and educate minorities like the freed blacks.[3]

Law-making majorities were hardly monolithic and unchanging, and under certain circumstances minorities—even groups without the vote—were able to exert a strong influence over the legal frameworks governing education. Such was the case, for example, when disenfranchised females in the Women's Christian Temperance Union were able to persuade legislators in every state to mandate instruction on the evils of alcohol. Some politically potent minorities could win concessions from the majority because they were able to vote and could swing elections. In some communities, for example, immigrants won the right to use their own language in public schools, while Catholics sometimes secured public funds for their parochial schools.[4]

Some minority groups wished to gain full entry into the political system, to win access to public schools and to participate as citizens. Such was the goal of many blacks under Reconstruction who used a reformulated republican ideology of schooling as part of their justification for inclusion in the polity and the common school. Other minority groups—the Amish are a prominent example—wanted to be left alone to pursue their separate life. In between were a number of ethnocultural groups that wanted to participate in the mainstream of American political and economic life but resisted the attempts of Americanizers to promote a homogeneous culture and rejected the demands of evangelical Protestants that schools use Bible reading as the basis of a "nonsectarian" moral training.[5]

One might suspect that the courts, not legislatures, would have been the chief protectors of minority rights against infringements by majority rule. Over recent decades the U.S. Supreme Court has greatly enlarged the scope of civil rights, civil liberties, religious and intellectual freedom, and due process in education. In the landmark second flag salute case of **West Virginia Board of Education v. Barnette** in 1943 the court declared that "if there is any fixed star in our constitutional constellation, it is that no official, high or petty, can prescribe what shall be orthodox in politics, nationalism, religion, or other matters of opinion."[6]

It was an eloquent statement, and did reflect some protections the Supreme Court had afforded citizens through its interpretations of the First Amendment after World War I, but it surely did not describe the course of intellectual freedom in public education. In public schools legislatures and officials often prescribed values "in politics, nationalism, religion," and other domains.

In fact, the courts have rarely used this fixed constitutional "star" to shield minority rights violated by legislatures and school boards. Until the middle of the twentieth century there have been very few appellate cases in education under religious instruction—the West Digests list a mere 87 from 1810 to 1981—and until the Bible and prayer decisions of the 1960s these cases reached quite diverse conclusions. Throughout most of American history, local majorities seemed to have had their way with religious elements in the curriculum. These local majorities were typically Protestant, and the "compromise" they most favored—teaching the King James Bible without comment—was hardly fair to Catholics, Jews, or non-believers. Likewise, despite the large number of state statutes requiring "Americanization," outlawing the use of foreign languages in public elementary schools, and prescribing the contents of textbooks in social studies, we have found very few appellate court cases on compulsory patriotic instruction or questions of linguistic or ethnic diversity. As we shall suggest, even the landmark case of **Meyer v. Nebraska**, dealing with the abolition of instruction in German, reserved, like *Pierce v. Society of Sisters*, much leeway for majorities to use the public schools to prescribe political orthodoxy. Thus until the middle of the twentieth century the courts have not interfered much with the right of the majority to "prescribe what shall be orthodox in politics, nationalism, religion, or other matters of opinion." Local and state contests over such questions, or over racial policies, were typically perceived less as constitutional issues to be adjudicated in the courts than as questions of who had the most political power.[7]

Political contests over school law, then, reveal much about the changing relationships between majority rule and minority rights in public education. Part II of this book explores some of the forms these conflicts took. In, chapter 5 we examine the attempt of the freed blacks and their allies in Congress and in the South to use the brief constitutional moment of Reconstruction to build racially inclusive systems of common schools as part of the larger battle to enfranchise blacks. In chapter 6 we analyze how lobbies that regarded themselves as moral majorities successfully legislated their own views of temperance, patriotic instruction, and religious orthodoxy into curricular mandates—that is, how they gave their norms the force of law. Chapter 7 is a case study of an Oregon compulsory public school attendance law in which we scrutinize the political background of legislation that led to a landmark Supreme court decision, the case of *Pierce v. Society of Sisters* in 1925, which sought to delimit the power of the majority of a state legislature to use education to combat the supposed perils of pluralism.

CHAPTER 5

The Constitutional Moment: Reconstruction and Black Education in the South, 1867–1954

F. L. Cardozo, a black teacher and politician, was aware that his people had reached a turning point in their history after the Civil War, a time of promise and precarious power for the former slaves. The delegates meeting in the Reconstruction convention during the winter of 1868 were framing a new constitution for South Carolina. "I do desire we shall use the opportunities we now have to our best advantage, as we may never have a more propitious time," said Cardozo in arguing for a compulsory school attendance provision. "We know that when the old aristocracy and ruling power of this State get into power, as they undoubtedly will, . . . They will never pass such a law as this. Why? Because their power is built on and sustained by ignorance. They will take precious good care that the colored people shall never be enlightened."[1]

"Seize the present moment," George Sumner told his fellow United States Senators a year before the delegates met in Charleston. "You have prescribed universal suffrage. Prescribe now universal education." The reason was clear, he told them:[2]

> In a republic Education is indispensable. A republic without education is like the creature of imagination, a human being without a soul, living and moving blindly, with no sense of the present or the future. It is a monster. Such have been the rebel States. They have been for years nothing more than political monsters. But such they must be no longer.

To ensure that a new order be created from the old in the South, Congress must insist that before admission to the Union, former Confederate states guarantee the establishment of "public schools which shall be open to all without distinction of race or color, to the

This chapter was co-authored by David Tyack and Robert Lowe.

end that where suffrage is universal, education may be universal also, and the new governments find support in the intelligence of the people." Sumner in Washington and the black delegates in South Carolina were seeking a racial and educational revolution.[3]

Public education was a central concern of those Radical lawmakers who sought to bring about a republican political order that would include blacks as full citizens. Eric Foner argues that republican ideas were central to the "attempt to forge from diverse elements in the black and American experiences a coherent political response to the unprecedented situation of emancipation. . . . Perhaps black leaders can best be understood as those most capable of appropriating the available political language of American society and forging from it an expression of the aspirations of the freedmen." New constitutions, like statutory law, were instruments used by Reconstruction Radicals to reshape Southern society by creating universal republican citizenship and by breaking the hold of the planters over the political economy. Reconstruction offered a brief constitutional moment between two periods of white supremacy under slavery and a tightening caste system.[4]

In the prewar years there had been stark exceptions to the egalitarian values that informed American republican ideology. The most notable was white supremacy and its institutional embodiment, slavery. Before the Civil War, foes of slavery argued in Congress that a slave state could not be a "republican form of government" and that a "republican slaveholder" was a contradiction in terms. Southerners disagreed, and in the educational clauses of their constitutions sometimes intoned the conventional rhetoric linking the diffusion of knowledge to the preservation of republican institutions. In few Southern states, however, did governments build even rudimentary foundations for public schools for whites before 1861. All excluded blacks from public schools and many made it a crime to teach them to read.[5]

After the Civil War, when Radical Republicans cast about for a constitutional basis for reconstructing and readmitting the Confederate states during the late 1860s, some of them turned to Article IV of the U.S. Constitution with its provision that Congress must guarantee a republican form of government throughout the nation. Charles Sumner called this provision a "sleeping giant." Under the Military Reconstruction Acts passed in 1867 Congress empowered the generals of the armies of occupation to call for new constitutional conventions in which blacks were to participate along with whites in elections, serving as delegates, and ratifying the new documents. Although there was a dilemma in using military rule to ensure self-government, there was little chance to restructure the Southern political system without protection by Congress and the Army.[6]

W. E. B. Du Bois demonstrated that "the first great mass movement for public education at the expense of the state, in the South, came from Negroes." After the war, blacks engaged in a collective movement to educate themselves, seeking help where they could find it—from the Freedman's Bureau, from Northern philanthropic agencies, and other white groups—but at first relying mostly on their own efforts. In Radical Reconstruction conventions blacks pressed for modern common schools modeled on the best Northern state systems. The educational provisions of those Radical Reconstruction constitutions and the debates on education in the conventions reveal how passionately the freedmen and their white allies believed in the traditional ideology that linked schooling and republican citizenship. A comparison of the prewar educational provisions in Southern constitutions with those of the Radical Reconstruction period demonstrates that blacks and their white allies in Congress and in the Reconstruction conventions were the architects and advocates of free and universal state schools in the South.[7]

Their triumph was short-lived. After Reconstruction when white supremacists regained political control, they gave only a trickle of funds to black schools and then, in the 1890s, began to deny the vote to them because they were illiterate (by the racially biassed standards set by the white registrars). In a petition to the constitutional convention of 1895 that disfranchised them, a group of blacks in Louisiana pointed out the cruel inconsistency of this practice: "To punish a man for his ignorance by withholding the right to the ballot, without which the distinction between self-government and a despotism disappears, when that ignorance is due to the neglect of the State, would be a most unnatural crime." An "unnatural crime" it was to require literacy for suffrage after stifling education, but that is precisely what happened not only in Louisiana but in other Southern states. During the years following 1877 in the black system of that state, no more than 30 percent of school-age children were enrolled, salaries of teachers declined, and school terms shrank, while the white schools gained greater resources. State constitutions and statutes, for a time a source of hope and an instrument for reconstructing the social order, became once again a means of subordinating blacks.[8]

The experience of blacks in the South constitutes an anomaly in the way state legal authority was typically used to promote common schools. By 1860 most Northern state constitutions and statutes on public education established a structure of finance and governance designed to induce local communities to build schools and to encourage parents to enroll their children for public instruction. Northern states were moving toward similar educational policies that distinguished public education from charitable education, that sought to stress common civic and moral values (while avoiding, in theory, sectarian and partisan teaching), and that judged the success of the system by its universality—that is to say, by its appeal to all groups and its ability to enroll ever-increasing numbers of children.[9]

Blacks in the South—and in some Northern states as well—found that such forms of majority rule and such uses of state authority did not include them. Convinced of the need for schooling, they required no stimulus from the state to found schools. Immediately after emancipation they banded together to provide education from their meager private resources. What initial help they did receive came largely from the North and from private philanthropic and religious groups, not from state or local governments in the South. For a brief constitutional moment, when they enjoyed the support of Radical Republicans in Congress, blacks sought to use the authority of the state to create universal and free schools open to all. The political power to put this vision into practice was fleeting. With the restoration of white supremacy, blacks in the South were forced to attend schools universally segregated and increasingly starved of funds in comparison with the white schools. Whites who hoped to restore the old political order after Reconstruction did not dismantle the common school systems that blacks and their allies had created, but they used those educational systems to reinforce the caste system. When majority rule in the South came to exclude blacks as citizens, it relegated the black underclass to separate and grossly unequal schooling.[10]

Not until a hundred years after emancipation would *de jure* segregation be effectively challenged in the majority of Southern communities. Education for Southern blacks was not an entitlement due to each individual and a guarantee of equal opportunity and republican citizenship. Education was something blacks provided for themselves, received as a charity, or wrung from a reluctant state. With the exception of that brief period of hope in the late 1860s and early 1870s, black public education in the South contradicted the principles that linked schooling to the republican form of government.[11]

Beginnings: Self-Help and Aid from the North

In Savannah, children went to school in the Bryant Slave Mart, where windows were still barred and where they could see, as museum pieces, slave whips and handcuffs. The black leaders of the city formed the Savannah Educational Association shortly after the Union occupation. With funds collected from the ex-slaves they hired teachers to instruct their children in whatever quarters they could find. In North Carolina black teachers and children congregated in churches across the countryside for weekday classes and sabbath schools. In a Virginia community black parents gave the teacher five eggs and a chicken for tuition. A young man told his teacher, after she had shown him how to form a word from letters, "I shall have to stand up and shiver first before I write it."[12]

At the close of the Civil War Southern blacks joined together in a massive and multifaceted social movement to upraise themselves. They were creating their own separate churches, attempting to transform labor relations, participating in politics, and building schools. Emancipation made it possible for ex-slaves to act collectively on values they shared and to preserve their culture. The desire to gain an education was one of the most powerful "communal values" in black communities, as James D. Anderson has demonstrated. Diverse motives fueled this educational movement. One was economic: blacks knew that whites used their knowledge to cheat freedmen unable to read contracts or to compute accounts. Another was religious: ex-slaves wanted to read the Good Book, all of it and not just the safe portions their mistresses or masters had recited to them. And blacks, as they made clear in Reconstruction conventions, recognized the bond between citizenship and literacy, knowledge and power. To express this political aspiration, blacks used American republican ideas about citizenship in new ways to upraise a freed people. For them equal political rights and unbound labor were not traditional values undergirding everyday experience but a hard-won achievement. The learning that whites had kept to themselves was one cause of their hegemony, and blacks were determined to win the educational opportunities that undergirded participation.[13]

Blacks themselves were the prime movers of the educational crusade in the South, but poverty and illiteracy obstructed the work. They needed allies with money and the ability to teach. In the period of Presidential Reconstruction, from 1865 to 1867, before the concerted attempt to create state systems of schooling during radical Reconstruction, help from the North came from philanthropic groups, the Union army, and the Freedman's Bureau. If one took as a legal and institutional norm the kind of public education that had evolved in the North—free, controlled and supported by state and local governments—this combination of forces was odd indeed: the federal government as represented by the military and the Bureau, voluntary groups (many of them religious), and blacks who had organized themselves spontaneously in local communities. Soon both Radical Republicans in Congress and blacks and white allies in Southern state conventions would insist that states institute the Northern model of state-controlled and publicly financed non-sectarian education.[14]

The early coalition of blacks, philanthropists, and federal and military officials was not so incongruous as it might seem, given the values of the individuals involved and the conditions they faced in the conquered Southern states. Whether they worked in the military, the Bureau, or private benevolent groups, many of the white women and men shared evangelical religious convictions (many of the men were ministers); they believed in the power of education to upraise blacks from the degradation of slavery and to make them productive workers and citizens; and they believed that the "army of civilization," the teachers, were carrying on the war by reconstructing the South on Northern principles. The "pious general" who headed the Freedmen's Bureau, O. O. Howard, gave "genial, Christian talks to the colored children" in Sabbath schools and appointed ministers and army officers of his religious persuasion to carry on the millennial task. The diverse agencies also agreed to a general functional division of labor. The Bureau coordinated the administration of schools through its state superintendents and helped with materials for schoolhouses and other logistical support, while the voluntary associations concentrated on providing teachers and funds.[15]

The creation of schooling for blacks in Louisiana during the war under the military rule of General Nathaniel Banks—a Massachusetts man—illustrates the dynamics among the different groups and the diverse motives that impelled them. Avid for education as a means of liberation and social change, blacks and their abolitionist advocates in the North pressured Banks to create schools. William F. Messner argues that Banks and his staff had their own reasons for providing schooling for blacks:[16]

> Both on the plantation and within the army, the military considered education not only a source of black enlightenment, but also a potent tool for black control. Government officials believed, in fact, that control was the cornerstone of black enlightenment. Education would be a civilizing influence upon the freedmen, preparing them for... their place as military and plantation laborers.

In 1863 the army began schooling black soldiers, aided by books and supplies donated by Northern philanthropic associations. Banks then extended the educational campaign to the families of laborers on plantations and blacks in New Orleans. Again the voluntary associations assisted in the work, sending teachers and funds. Banks sought to make white planters and citizens of New Orleans supplement the donations of the blacks, the benevolent associations, and the army, but he encountered strong resistance.[17]

Although Southern blacks generally welcomed the funds and teachers, conflicts sometimes broke out between black people and Northern whites. In Savannah, Georgia, the black Educational Association and officers of white philanthropic groups argued over who was to lead the educational crusade. White educators sometimes doubted the capacity of black teachers to instruct their communities, and some acted as if the goal of schooling should be to "civilize" blacks according to a Northern evangelical and capitalist model of social control of a working class. For their part, blacks responded negatively to condescending whites, chafed at the way some white teachers observed Southern conventions of race etiquette outside the classroom, and sometimes disagreed with the sectarian leanings of missionary teachers. Although the majority of the missionary teachers were courageous and competent and sought to provide a liberating literacy, undercurrents of mistrust and misunderstanding marred the relationships of Northern whites and Southern blacks in a number of communities.[18]

If relations between Northern whites and blacks were sometimes stormy, Southern whites were generally hostile to the idea of giving blacks an education commensurate with republican citizenship. In a few states—North Carolina, for example—some whites were willing to teach the ex-slaves, often as a means of holding blacks as workers on their plantations in a time of labor shortage. To force employers to teach them to read and compute, blacks sometimes included educational provisions in their labor contracts. But Southern whites were generally hostile to schools for blacks when these were conducted by blacks or Northern whites. In many communities they burned schoolhouses, ostracized or beat teachers, and sought to intimidate the families who went to school.[19]

Since Southern whites were able in this way to thwart the educational gains of the freed people, blacks and their allies concluded that a firmer foundation must be laid for a just society. Self-help, philanthropy, and occasional subsidies from the Freedman's Bureau were too impermanent and fragile a base for a lasting system of universal schooling. Radical Republicans in the Congress and in the Southern states were demanding by 1867 a basic reconstruction of the rebel order. With that restructuring would come the first comprehensive constitutional provisions for universal and free education enacted by Southern states.

Legalizing Universal Education—An Opportunity Seized

In the late 1860s Congress became for the first time a major battleground for equal education. Radical Republicans fought on several fronts, urged on by petitions and delegations from blacks and former abolitionists and eager, in Sumner's words, to "seize the present moment" to overturn the old order. Underlying their various proposals was a desire to use the federal government more aggressively. Radicals were among the leading spokesmen for a federal department of education, which was signed into law on the same day that Congress passed its first Reconstruction Act. They sought to amend that act to require, as a precondition for readmission to representation in Congress, that the Confederate states "establish public schools which shall be open to all without distinction of race or color, to the end that where suffrage is universal, education may be universal also, and the new governments find support in the intelligence of the people." They attempted to establish a modern and racially mixed public school system in the District of Columbia. Republicans proposed plans to give massive federal aid to states to eradicate illiteracy, most of which would have gone to the South. Persistently, Sumner and his allies tried to enact a civil rights bill that would outlaw school segregation.[20]

The notion of using federal influence to encourage states to provide public education was not new, but substantial support for the use of federal authority to enforce educational standards on states was unprecedented. The Department of Education, founded in 1867, meant many different things to different people. To radicals like Sumner and Ignatius Donnelly it promised to be an opening wedge for action to equalize schooling. Donnelly conceived of the agency as one "whose duty it shall be to enforce education, without regard to race or color, upon the population of all such States as shall fall below a standard to be established by Congress." There was little doubt about which states he had in mind, since he believed that the war itself was "traceable, in a great degree, to the absence of common schools and general education among the people of the lately rebellious states."[21]

As after other wars, Americans thought education or reeducation of the vanquished an appropriate aftermath to victory, and in the South the Union army could buttress the Radical educational regimes. In the Senate debate on the bill to form a department of education Sumner said that "through the agency and under the influence of the national Government education is to be promoted in the rebel States." The department, later demoted to bureau, in fact fulfilled no such aspirations. Republicans repeatedly but unsuccessfully tried another strategy to equalize schools in the South: granting federal aid for schools based on the proportion of the people who were illiterate, which would have had the effect of redistributing public funds from the wealthier states to the more impoverished. Despite the failure of these plans to use the bureau and federal funds to improve schooling in the South, Radicals in Congress did play an important role in assisting blacks to achieve their educational goals.[22]

On Saturday, March 16, 1867, Sumner and his Senate allies sought to amend the Reconstruction Act to require all Confederate states to create free public schools open to all as a precondition for statehood. Sumner believed that Article 4, Section 4, of the United States Constitution, which declared that "the United States shall guarantee to every State in this Union a Republican Form of Government," authorized Congress to insist on such provisions for education in the constitutions of states readmitted to representation. If Congress had the power to demand universal (manhood) suffrage, he argued, it had the duty as well to ordain universal education. Senator Morton concurred: "Republican government may go on for awhile with half the voters unable to read or write, but it cannot long continue. Intelligence is the very foundation of republican government." Others contested the constitutional justification of the precondition or the wisdom of forcing such a requirement "by the bayonet." When the vote was called on Sumner's amendment it lost by a tie of 20 to 20.[23]

Despite the defeat of this far-reaching measure, the Radicals had demonstrated their strength of commitment to equal opportunity in state systems of public education. The message was not lost on the delegates to state constitutional conventions in the South. Sumner had hedged somewhat in answer to a direct question about whether his amendment would require "that each and every school shall be open to children of both races." That was his desire, he said, "but the proposition is necessarily general in its character; it does not go into details." The important matter was to let Southerners know that they must provide free schools or Congress would reject their constitutions.[24]

Sumner and his radical allies continued to press in Congress for biracial schools. In Virginia the delegates had inserted vague language concerning mixed schools into the constitution they wrote in 1867–68, but the conservative governor elected in 1869 made it clear that he opposed desegregation. Blacks feared that one day separate schools would lead to educational inequalities, and they were right. When Congress was deciding whether to readmit Virginia to representation, Virginia radicals asked their friends in Washington to insert a clause into the bill declaring that both races would participate equally in the school fund and in school privileges. Radicals wanted educational equality to be recognized as a basic civil right beyond the power of the state to deny. After a considerable legislative skirmish, in which the constitutionality of such a provision binding states to action in the future came under attack, Congress inserted the following stipulation in its act admitting the state to representation: "that the constitution of Virginia shall never be so amended or changed as to deprive any citizen or class of citizens of the United States of the school-rights and privileges secured by the constitution of said State."

Shortly thereafter they inserted similar provisions into the bills readmitting Texas and Mississippi.[25]

Even the Radicals in Congress, however, took no action when these states flouted the mandate of equality (in 1870 Virginia passed a school law requiring segregation, for example). And when Congress enacted its Civil Rights Act of 1875, it deleted the clause banning segregation in public schools for which Sumner had labored. In Washington, D.C., segregation persisted and blacks had to struggle for even a semblance of equality in separate schools, despite the efforts of abolitionist allies like Thaddeus Stevens. Alfred E. Kelly points out that it was a small band of idealists who pushed for racial equality in Congress, and only when their mission "happened to coincide with the momentary tactical or strategic interests of the Republican party" did they succeed in passing mixed school provisions.[26]

Radical whites and blacks in Congress were able to exert their greatest pressure for educational equality on the ten Confederate states covered by the Reconstruction Act of March 2, 1867 (the eleventh, Tennessee, had already been admitted to representation in Congress in 1866). In those states the army supervised elections for delegates to the conventions, thus facilitating the participation of the freedmen in the political process. Delegates also realized that Congress would look closely at the educational and other provisions included in the constitutions. Congressional Radicals, like their counterparts in the Southern states, regarded education as a basic civil right for all individuals and believed universal schooling to be a collective necessity in a republican form of government. In Mobile, Alabama, the Republican newspaper said that the party was unanimous that the new constitution should guarantee "that every child in the state must and shall have an opportunity to acquire an education."[27]

The contrast between provisions for public education in the antebellum and Reconstruction constitutions of these ten Confederate states is striking, though lack of specific educational provisions in prewar constitutions did not necessarily signify that states were failing to develop systems of public education. The older states in the North and a few of the older slave states chiefly used statutory law rather than organic law to elaborate their public schools. Conversely, specific provisions in constitutions did not assure that states were putting what was on paper into practice. The Reconstruction constitutions often were utopian, indicating the future that blacks and white Radicals aspired to create more than the current realities they faced. For example, several Reconstruction constitutions authorized compulsory school attendance legislation at a time when they lacked the schoolhouses and teachers to put it into effect. But aspirations deeply held were important clues to the Radicals' plans for reconstructing Southern society. Moreover, much of their constitutional legacy remained, for even when white Southerners regained control of state governments, they kept the central features of educational governance and finance created by these constitutions. Indeed, poor whites profited from the educational revolution wrought by Reconstruction, for their education had been neglected in most communities before the Civil War.[28]

The prewar constitutions of the ten states paid little attention to public education. South Carolina's constitutions made no mention of education. Alabama, Arkansas, and Florida had brief general clauses about encouraging the means of education and about using the proceeds of federal land grants to support schools. A clause in the Georgia constitution of 1777 about schools was omitted in later revisions, though provision was made in 1798 for promoting "seminaries of learning." Mississippi and North Carolina included general sentiments about the value of learning in their constitutions but no specifications about state schools. Virginia used a "capitation tax" for the use of white primary schools. Louisiana and Texas went somewhat further than the others, providing for superintendents, a school fund, and state school systems, but hedging the language somewhat; in Louisiana, for example, the Constitution of 1852 said that the legislature might abolish the superintendent's office, while in Texas the legislature was to establish a school system "as early as practicable." The clause was repeated in 1866, suggesting minimal progress in Texas.[29]

The haphazard and halting provisions for education in the prewar constitutions were transformed into elaborate bureaucratic blueprints for free schools in the Reconstruction constitutions. Table 5.1 indicates the major educational provisions in the revised constitutions of the ten ex-Confederate states. A count of provisions tells only part of the story. The language shifted from vague clauses to decisive *shall* declarations and highly specific requirements. Six constitutions stated that local districts would forfeit state aid if they did not keep schools open for a minimum number of months; several prescribed sources and minimum levels of taxation; almost all specified precise systems of governance. In its first clause on education Florida stated the assumption that underlay the Radicals' political philosophy of education: "It is the paramount duty of the State to make ample provision for the education of all the children residing within its borders, without distinction or preference." Convention delegates, a number of them educators from the North or men who had been active in the Freedmen's Bureau schools, borrowed freely from educational provisions of Northern states. In South Carolina, where three of the five members of the Committee on Education were black, and Cardozo was the chair, delegates modelled educational clauses partly on the system of education in Massachusetts. In Alabama, delegates emulated the constitution of Iowa. The only state to write a perfunctory education provision was Georgia, whose convention was dominated by Southern whites. In 1869 Congress once again put Georgia under military rule after the legislature excluded black members.[30]

TABLE 5.1
**Educational Provisions in the Reconstruction Constitutions (1868–70)
of Ten Former Confederate States**[a]

	Percent of States
Requirement of state free school system	100
Provision for state superintendent	100
Provision for state board of education	60
Provision for county superintendents	40
Provision for common school fund	90
Provision for county or local taxation	50
Provision for state taxation	100
Minimum school term prescribed for state aid	60
Clauses concerning compulsory attendance	50
Clauses concerning federal land grants	80
Clauses forbidding aid to sectarian schools	40

SOURCE: Franklin B. Hough, *Constitutional Provisions in regard to Education in the Several American States of the American Union*, U.S. Bureau of Education, *Circular No. 7, 1875* (Washington, D.C.: GPO, 1875).

[a]Alabama, Arkansas, Florida, Georgia, Louisiana, Mississippi, North Carolina, South Carolina, Texas, Virginia.

In these Reconstruction conventions delegates largely agreed on the need to establish free and universal public schools. Controversy centered on the issue of whether to establish separate black and white schools. Two states—Louisiana and South Carolina—constitutionally banned legal segregation. Louisiana declared that "all children shall be admitted to the public schools... in common without distinction of race, color, or previous condition"; South Carolina had a clause that said that public schools "shall be free and open to all the children and youths of the State, without regard to race or color." South Carolina's was the only convention where blacks were in the majority (59 percent of the delegates), while in Louisiana, according to Richard L. Hume's estimates, slightly less than a majority were black (but the convention voted for integration 63 to 12). In the conventions as a whole, however, almost half the delegates were Southern whites and only a quarter were black. Social equality was anathema to all but a small percentage of Southern whites, and thus desegregating schools was an extreme measure to adopt. Four of the conventions followed a common pattern of disputes over segregation. First a Southern white proposed racially separate schools, which delegates voted down (in one a black delegate unsuccessfully suggested integrated schools). Then the delegates passed educational provisions that failed to require separate schools.[31]

Given the hostility of whites to integration and the racial composition of the conventions, silence on race constituted one form of victory for the blacks and their allies. Silence did not imply black acquiescence in segregation. Even in the Reconstruction conventions in 1868, black delegates often faced blatant prejudice. In the Arkansas convention, after hearing an unreconstructed white declaim against "this precipitate enfranchisement of an inferior, ignorant, and dissimilar people," a black member rose to speak:[32]

> I have longed to see the line of separation withdrawn. And every time these gentlemen come to this hall, they represent the negro as a goat—a goat! They have forgotten that we have tied their shoes, that we have clothed them, that we have driven them in their carriages, we have reared them, in their castles, we have furnished them with all the means they now possess in the world, and we have furnished them money to employ the overseers to drive us in the field, where they have driven us all the day and half the night, and then again before the morning light. And now, when we are free, they say that we have no right! no right!

Prior to the war, all Southern educational provisions were silent on race, since black access to public schools was unthinkable in a polity based on slavery. After the war, when blacks were winning a place in classrooms, blocking legally mandated segregation was a step toward equality. In North Carolina a black delegate, speaking against a motion to create separate schools, argued that legally segregated schools for blacks would soon become inferior to those for whites, and hence that legal separatism was retrogressive. But he did not favor mixed schools because of their untoward effects on blacks:[33]

> I do not believe that it is good for our children to eat and drink daily the sentiment that they are naturally inferior to the whites, which they do in three-fourths of all the schools where they have white teachers. . . . I shall always do all what I can to have colored teachers for colored schools. This will necessitate separate schools as a matter of course, wherever it is possible, not by written law, but by mutual consent and the law of interest. For this reason I am opposed to putting it in the organic law. Make this distinction in your organic law and in many places you will have good white schools at the expense of the whole people, while the colored people will have none or but little worse than none.

In Louisiana and South Carolina delegates differed in their views on the likely effects of banning distinctions based on race. Some delegates in South Carolina voiced the aspiration that if white children attended school with black students, over time fierce white prejudice would diminish. A militant integrationist declared that "we are laying the foundation of a new structure here, and the time has come when we shall have to meet things squarely, and we must meet them now or never. The day is coming when we must decide whether the two races shall live together or not." Others stressed that the point was to guarantee open access to schools but that separatism would be likely to continue. One said that progress might eventually dissolve racial hatreds but that he "did not believe the colored children will want to go to the white schools, or vice versa." To a Confederate veteran who protested that delegates were forcing racial integration Cardozo replied[34]

> We have carefully provided in our report that every one shall be allowed to attend a free school. We have not said there shall be no separate schools. On the contrary, there may be separate schools, and I have no doubt there will be such in most of the districts. In Charleston, I am sure that such will be the case. The colored pupils in my school would

> not like to go to a white school. Without flattery, I think I may say I
> have not been in as good a public school in Charleston as my own.

Most probably believed, as did Cardozo, that schools would remain
racially distinct, at least into the near future.

The constitutional bans on segregation in Louisiana and South
Carolina had only meager impact. In Lousiana desegregation took
hold only in New Orleans, and there it crumbled when the compromise of 1877 denied blacks federal protection. In South Carolina the
first state superintendent of education was a Massachusetts educator,
Justus K. Jillson, who had been a member of the convention and who
believed in mixed schools. But when he tried a first step—desegregating
the state School for the Deaf and Blind, where many children could
not even tell the color of their peers—it failed when the faculty
resigned in protest.[35]

Despite their inability to prevent separate schools, blacks made
gains in the short period of time between the constitutional moment
of Congressional Reconstruction and the reestablishment of Southern
white political supremacy. In five states of the deep South where they
constituted an important part of the electorate, blacks were elected as
state superintendents. Many blacks served as county superintendents
and members of school boards. Enormous problems confronted educators in the South: poverty, dispersion of population, a high ratio of
children to adults, the moral and fiscal cost of maintaining separate
schools, and corruption in the appropriation and diversion of school
funds. This last problem was hardly new in the Reconstruction period,
for before the Civil War Southern, like Northern, states had already
squandered and stolen hundreds of thousands of dollars derived from
the sale of federal school lands.[36]

Despite these obstacles, educators and legislators and state officials
gradually established public schools on the legal foundations laid
down by the new constitutions. The story of problems and achievements varied state by state. Some were laggard and contentious, some
corrupt, some prompt and earnest in putting ambitious constitutional provisions into effect in education. But overall, as Du Bois maintained, the Reconstruction conventions and legislatures were responsible
for founding universal public schooling in the South. Largely as a
result of the public schools thus created, black illiteracy dropped
from 79.9 percent in 1870 to 44.5 percent in 1900. Enrollment of
black children in public schools jumped from 91,000 in 1866 to

150,000 in 1870 to 572,000 in 1877. In states where blacks and their allies had seized the constitutional moment, the Reconstruction years were a period of hope and substantial educational progress for the freed people. This achievement helped to prepare blacks to survive the repression to come, as Du Bois wrote: "Had it not been for the Negro school and college, the Negro would, to all intents and purposes, have been driven back to slavery. His economic foothold in land and capital was too slight in ten years of turmoil to effect any defense or stability." But by founding schools and by organizing the black church, the freed people "had acquired enough leadership and knowledge to thwart the worst designs of the new slave drivers."[37]

Law as an Instrument of Inequality

Educational revolutions can breed counterrevolutions. After the Southern whites regained control of state governments, white supremacy became a dominating principle of law and party unity among Democrats. "The loyalty and discipline that prevailed in the white man's party were inspired by the revolution that established it in power," writes C. Vann Woodward. "After the two objects of that revolution were achieved—the crushing of Negro power and the ousting of foreign control—party discipline was still dependent upon keeping vividly alive the memory of these menaces." The chair of the South Carolina Constitutional Convention of 1895 showed that the memory of Reconstruction was alive at that date. The constitution of 1868, he told the delegates, "was made by aliens [that is, natives of other American states], negroes and natives without character, all the enemies of South Carolina, and was designed to degrade our State, insult our people and overturn our civilization."[38]

The constitutions the Redeemers—white Democrats—wrote after Reconstruction legally required racial segregation in schools. They also generally altered the governance and finance of public education in ways that would assure that it would remain in white hands. There was, however, no wholesale demolition of the structures that the Reconstruction governments had created and no strong movement to abolish the education of blacks. In several states funding of black schools remained for several years nearly equal to that in white schools, in part because of promises Redeemers had made to blacks to win their support and in part because of legal safeguards still in state constitutions. So long as blacks could vote—for a time it looked as if the Fifteenth Amendment assured enfranchisement of blacks—and retained their deep commitment to schooling, it was politically dangerous to tamper too much with the educational system. In addition, there were Southern white political leaders who believed that it was best to educate the freed people—if their schooling was under the control of Southern whites—since an illiterate populace might constitute a danger to the restored white social order.[39]

The Southern white governments were committed to retrenchment in a regional economy already afflicted by poverty. Under the Redeemers, in a decade the school term dropped by an average of 20 percent, and by 1880 the average expenditure per enrolled pupil (black and white combined) was only 59.5 percent that of 1871. As time went by, the grip of white political leaders became more secure and the threat of black backlash receded. Eager to bypass provisions for equal apportionment of the meager school funds to white and black schools, whites experimented with different methods of cheating the black communities. One was to increase the number of pupils enrolled in black schools while paying black and white teachers about the same salaries. Another was to pay teachers according to the certificates they held and then to assign lower certificates to blacks. A strategy used in the District of Columbia, Kentucky, Maryland, and Delaware shortly after the Civil War, and then emulated in local communities in several states, was to divide the school fund according to the poll tax or real estate taxes paid by the two races, thereby creating a racially distinct tax base.[40]

With the effective disfranchisement of blacks in a number of states in the 1890s and early 1900s—by using such devices as literacy and grandfather clauses in constitutions—the campaign to short-change blacks had an open field. One common technique in the deep South was to assign state funds to white county officials to allocate as they chose. The result in heavily black counties was to permit officers to pour the money into white schools and to give tiny sums to the black ones. A report issued in 1916 on funding of black schools in the South showed that in counties where 75 percent or more of the students were black, the whites received $22.22 per capita compared with $1.78 for blacks. Such a device also cheated poor whites outside the black belt, for powerful planters from the black counties kept school taxes low. Class as well as racial conflict shaped the politics of Southern school finance. Populists placed better education high on their agenda for reform. But whites of different classes were agreed, for the most part, that laws to improve the schools should keep blacks in their place.[41]

As Louis R. Harlan has documented, the campaign to improve public schools at the turn of the twentieth century in the South was aimed at whites and sharply increased the disparities between the schools the two races attended. In addition to the regional discrepancies that divided North and South in public education, he writes, "an institutional fault line separated the Negro school from the white school in the same community." As in the days immediately following emancipation, blacks found that Southern whites were content to give them less than half a loaf and that blacks were expected to fund schools from their own pockets or from Northern charity. As late as World War I, secondary education for blacks in the South was almost entirely private. When Southern legislatures sought to modernize education—providing such new services as busing or guidance or technical training—the improvements went first to white schools, thereby increasing the fiscal gap between white and black schools.[42]

Such were the results of the use of law to recreate inequality. Delegates to the Reconstruction conventions had predicted that these disasters might befall blacks. In South Carolina blacks had argued against both the poll tax and the literacy requirement for suffrage on the ground that such devices might later be used by whites to disfranchise them. In North Carolina and in other states, Radicals had blocked provisions for legally separate schools, preferring silence on race since they believed that legally distinct schools would soon become unequal. Subsequent events confirmed their predictions. In 1935 Charles H. Thompson wrote that in the Southern states, where most blacks lived,[43]

> Negroes have little or no voice in the administration of school funds, either directly or indirectly; neither do they have the opportunity to hold any offices which have any direct relation to policy-making; nor are they allowed to participate to any appreciable extent in the selection or election of school officials. . . . The entire educational system is controlled and run *by* the white people and mainly *for* the white people.

Under such circumstances blacks had few alternatives if they wanted to change the system, Thompson said. Migration might help a fraction of blacks but was not a mass solution. Revolution was "suicidal." Seeking the ballot was necessary but entailed a long and difficult campaign. Trying to persuade local whites to be just was a favorite tactic of moderates, but what had such appeals brought? Despite the popularity of "race-relations" approaches, educational discrimination had increased, not decreased, Thompson claimed. The best available remedy, he said, was court action.[44]

Despite the racially repressive character of the Southern legal system, blacks did turn to the courts to win the rights that the Reconstruction constitutions had sought to guarantee. Several cases dealt with the question of who was black. This was seemingly a metaphysical issue when a person was so light-skinned as to be ambiguously white or black or neither, as were Chinese Americans. But to be assigned to the lower caste was to be denied meaningful citizenship. In a case in Mobile, Alabama, children who looked white and lived in a white neighborhood sought admission to the white school. The court sustained the school board's exclusion, saying that it was "incumbent upon the plaintiffs to prove the race they claim." At times, legislators, lawyers, and judges learnedly quibbled about what fraction of "blood" made a person black. The crazy-quilt world of some of the cases only makes sense if one remembers that caste—itself a social construction—had immense economic, social, and political consequences for those on top and those on bottom.[45]

In other cases blacks joined in collective efforts to challenge segregated schools, to attack separate taxation for the support of black and white schools, and to compel equal educational advantages. They won all cases protesting separate taxation. They lost about two-thirds of cases in which they argued that black schools were unequal. In cases protesting the constitutionality of segregation in states where separate schools were established in law, they lost every case to 1935. In 1927 the U.S. Supreme Court even refused to consider the question of constitutionality of segregation, declaring it well settled in precedents.[46]

The issue was, of course, not settled. "If, in retrospect, the outcome of the postemancipation struggle appears all but inevitable," writes Foner, "it is equally certain that Reconstruction transformed the lives of Southern blacks. . . . It raised blacks' expectations and aspirations, redefined their status in relation to the larger society, and allowed space for the construction of institutions that enabled them to survive the repression that followed." The racist counterrevolution had proved durable, but the Reconstruction principle that educational equality was an individual entitlement and a civic necessity also persisted. Questions of educational justice that the law of caste had sought to close would be reopened again in a new constitutional moment in 1954, this time in the Supreme Court in the *Brown* decision.[47]

CHAPTER 6

Moral Majorities and the School Curriculum: Making Virtue Mandatory, 1880–1930

For over a century, state government has been in the classroom, mandating the values that informed the curriculum. From the last quarter of the nineteenth century onwards, and especially during the two decades surrounding World War I, groups claiming to be moral majorities prevailed on state legislators to enact into law their own conceptions of what should be taught as moral certainty. Advocates of temperance, Bible reading, and patriotic instruction sought to insert their values by law into the curriculum and to prescribe for all children in the state the moral indoctrination that once had been the province of local school boards and educators.

In 1891 a group of educational leaders made explicit the attitudes underlying this shift from persuasion and local option to compulsion by the state. They agreed that all pupils must learn English and American moral and political principles. One put the reasons bluntly: "when the people established this government they assumed a certain standard of intelligence and morality; and that an intelligent and moral people will conform to the requirements of good citizenship." Such an assumption no longer was justified, he declared. "People have come here who are not entitled to freedom in the same sense as those who established this government." It was necessary to force the newcomers to attain the level of the original Americans lest the society "lower this idea of intelligence and morality to the standard" of foreigners. When custom failed to reproduce virtue and wisdom, law must enter to legalize virtue through the curriculum.[1]

Americans have always attempted to prescribe values through education. The founders of public education were strong-minded reformers who wanted their convictions to prevail in classrooms. Exemplars of

Victorian morality, school leaders of the middle of the nineteenth century typically assumed that other citizens would share their views on reading the Bible without comment, teaching about the evils of alcohol and tobacco, inculcating nonpartisan citizenship, and Americanizing immigrants. It was not necessary or desirable to legislate on such matters but simply to remind other right-minded citizens of self-evident moral and civic truths. During the middle of the nineteenth century, when the common school was still an uncertain innovation dependent on the good will of citizens in local communities, school promoters mostly believed that divisive value questions were best settled by local public authorities or left to voluntary moral suasion. Rarely did such matters become subjects for state legislation or authoritative determination by the courts before 1870.[2]

As the United States became more urban, industrialized, and heterogeneous in its population and values in the late nineteenth century, politically powerful WASP groups concluded that they must find new ways to enforce traditional social controls once exercised informally in smaller and more homogeneous communities. They became worried about declining consensus on religious and political values, dismayed by drunkenness and urban ills, concerned about the assimilation and loyalty of new immigrant groups, and frightened by violent strikes and class conflict. Organized into effective pressure groups, they urged states to pass statutes that gave their convictions the force of law.

Although the movement to mandate virtue by law was already well under way by the late nineteenth century, World War I provided an especially favorable political climate for this drive toward homogenization through public education. Many normatively prescriptive laws were passed during the second and third decades of the twentieth century. The experience of mobilizing the population for World War I stimulated this campaign to inculcate fundamental values by law. During the war, officials used the schools to promote Americanism and to eradicate divergent thinking. After the war, uneasy conservatives continued to promote orthodoxy through public education. Were Darwinism and skepticism undermining traditional patterns of faith? Then forbid the teaching of evolution and require the teaching of the Bible. Was the United States a nation of hyphenates? Then outlaw the teaching of foreign languages in elementary schools. Were Bolsheviks plotting to corrupt the minds of the young? Then weed out teachers who could not prove their patriotism. Was a cynical spirit abroad in the land? Then pass laws requiring textbook writers and teachers to be reverential toward the Founding Fathers. If society seemed centrifugal, schools must be clamped into narrow circles of orthodoxy.[3]

The groups that sought to enforce their values on others by state law were composed of people who believed that the United States was not only God's country but also *their* nation. They were mostly native-born Anglo-Saxon citizens of pietist Protestant persuasion and respectable station. They were confident that their values were the only ones reasonable people could share and believed that they represented the belief system of the majority of the people. By the end of the nineteenth century, they were no longer willing to rely on voluntary action or unselfconscious consensus to secure the principles they cherished. Instead, they believed that state laws must mandate their values in the school curriculum.

In this chapter we discuss three crusades: for temperance instruction, for compulsory Bible reading and the banning of Darwin, and for patriotic rituals and Americanization. The activists in these pressure groups differed in membership and goals from one another but shared a common assumption that orthodox schooling could correct social and civic ills. The Women's Christian Temperance Union (WCTU), for example, concentrated on the evils of alcohol; evangelical Protestants attacked the modernism that they believed was undermining the fundamental religious truths that should inform the worldview of their children; the advocates of patriotic instruction worried about the Americanization of immigrants and about radicalism. The activists in all of these groups agreed that the young were unformed and vulnerable to the poison of incorrect belief. They had enormous faith in the power of proper education to correct social ills. Because the public school system reached nearly all children, it seemed a more effective way to shape the future than attempts to change adults, already socialized and often recalcitrant.

Since these pressure groups were typically organized in federated institutions, they enjoyed special advantages in devising and enforcing curricular legislation. At the national level, they could establish unified policies; in state capitals they could lobby for laws; in their local chapters, posts, and churches they could keep an eye on the implementation of the statutes. These activists were confident and mobilized members of social movements out to reshape a wayward society to their own specifications. Their motivations were a complex but compatible mixture of fear and hope, a worldview expressed in the best seller of evangelical reform, *Our Country* by Josiah Strong, who called on the moral aristocracy of the nation to preserve the "certain standard of intelligence and morality" that once could be assumed but that was threatened in the new order emerging at the end of the nineteenth century. These groups, speaking as American moral majorities, achieved major successes in translating their program of social regeneration into curricular law.[4]

"Scientific Temperance Instruction"

The temperance movement exemplified this shift in educational strategy from persuasion to compulsion. No longer satisfied with enticing students to virtue through pious homilies in the McGuffey Readers and Webster Spellers, temperance advocates turned in the 1880s to state and federal laws that mandated a prescribed version of "scientific temperance instruction" in public schools. Prohibition of alcohol was an issue that shook state politics during the nineteenth century. Even politicians in favor of temperance were not sure that they wanted to alienate voters by proscribing drink. Children, however, were another matter; they did not vote, and they might safely be taught to shun what many parents cared little to abandon. By the turn of the twentieth century every state and territory had laws mandating the teaching of the evils of alcohol. Many of these laws were more specific and binding than legislation on any other branch of the curriculum. Twenty-two million schoolchildren were exposed to this instruction. Fifteen states required special observance of temperance day, sometimes called Frances E. Willard day. In his study of legislative control of the course of study, Jesse K. Flanders remarked in 1925 that teaching about temperance "is our nearest approach to a national subject of instruction; it might be called our one minimum essential." Laws mandating scientific temperance instruction aroused relatively little controversy in legislatures or in the courts.[5]

The tireless and astute political activity of the WCTU produced these laws on temperance instruction. Leaders like WCTU President Frances Willard and Mary Hunt—a chemistry professor who became the chief advocate of scientific temperance instruction—found that voluntary efforts to persuade educators and school boards to teach about the dangers of alcohol had not produced results. Tough laws were the answer, the WCTU concluded in 1882. From then until the end of the century the members devised strategies that would be copied later by other pressure groups: mass petitions, letter-writing, endorsements from leading citizens, lobbying efforts in Congress and state capitols, approval from experts for their program, and effective implementing legislation. The largely middle-class, native-born, well-educated, and Protestant leadership of the WCTU had many advantages in carrying out this campaign. Geographically dispersed, they could work in each state capitol and in local communities. United by a common moral conviction, they could share successful strategies through their national organization. They had access to influential people and time to devote to the cause. Many of the leaders were teachers who could claim expertise about schooling, and mothers could maintain that they were remaining in woman's sphere of caring for children even while politicking.[6]

The WCTU campaign swept the nation. In 1883 three states came into line with compulsory laws; the next year New York passed a law after 39,000 signatures on petitions arrived at the legislature in one day. In North Carolina, where women presented a petition containing 17,000 names, the legislature voted for temperance instruction unanimously. In Washington, D.C., Mary Hunt masterminded the lobbying effort that produced a stringent law for the District and all the territories, maneuvering around a hostile chairman of a House committee who wanted to bottle up the bill. By 1895 Hunt was able to produce a "temperance education map of the United States and territories" that showed only three states as hold-outs: Arkansas, Georgia, and Virginia. Table 6.1 shows the number of states that incorporated various provisions.[7]

Laws on the books were one thing, enforcement another in an era when state departments of education were minuscule. The WCTU had two major advantages in policing enforcement. One was that the educational profession as a whole was sympathetic to temperance. The National Education Association, for example, was well nigh evangelical on the subject, even into the 1930s when most Americans had given up on prohibition, and U. S. Commissioners of Education like William T. Harris and Philander P. Claxton were converts. Teach-

TABLE 6.1

Number and Percent of States with Legal Provisions
for Scientific Temperance Instruction, 1895

	Number of states	Percent of states
Scientific temperance a mandatory study	45	100
A penalty clause attached to non-compliance	22	49
Temperance instruction required for all pupils in all schools	15	33
Textbooks on temperance required for all pupils able to read	10	22
Temperance to be taught as thoroughly as other required subjects	19	42
Relevant textbooks must devote one-quarter of space to temperance	7	16
Only teachers who pass test on temperance can be certified	27	60

SOURCE: U.S. Commissioner of Education, *Report for 1894–95*, 1896.

ers stood to lose little from prohibition anyway, since communities typically expected them to be teetotalers.[8]

Another advantage of the WCTU was that its members—about 150,000 in 1892—were scattered in communities across the nation and could monitor compliance with the laws on temperance instruction. When, in an unusual gesture of defiance, teachers in New York state protested a highly prescriptive temperance law, the WCTU mobilized influential local members to make sure that teachers were obeying the statute. The WCTU legislation contained strong enforcement clauses. The federal act covering Washington, D.C., and the territories, for example, and those of several states said that any school official or teacher who failed to comply would be removed from office. In other states, no money could be distributed to schools until officials had affirmed by affidavit that temperance instruction had been provided as required by law. It was no secret who had lobbied for Alabama's baroque law of 1919, which mandated that the state normal schools should pay WCTU temperance workers to lecture to future teachers on the effects of alcohol, that the state WCTU should prepare the program for the celebration of temperance day in the

schools, and that the state should bear the expense of printing materials such as placards showing "the evils of intemperance."[9]

Enacting laws and making sure they were enforced were only part
of the crusade. WCTU leaders in scientific temperance instruction
also wanted to dictate the content of the textbooks. Some of the
physiology texts were "not safe in that they did not preach total
abstinence" and most did not allot the desired proportion of pages—
at least one-fourth—to the WCTU's alcohol science. In 1886, after
persuading Congress to require the use of a WCTU-approved text in
Washington, D.C., and the territories, Hunt wrote a petition to publishers with a checklist for selecting texbooks that would comply with
the temperance instruction laws. Books should stress, she said, that a
little drink creates an uncontrollable craving for more, illustrate the
"appalling effects of drinking habits upon the citizenship of the nation,"
and omit reference to the fact that doctors used alcohol for medicinal
purposes. Temperance should not be relegated to an appendix; it
should "be the chief and not the subordinate topic" in physiology
texts, she wrote. WCTU members, following Hunt's lead, barraged
publishers with petitions signed by school board officials and educators. Aware of the market being created by the new laws and eager to
avoid offending the temperance lobby, seven major publishers promptly
submitted their physiology texts to Hunt for review, while many others
later decided it was best to have her endorsement. In 1891 she presented the WCTU convention with a list of 25 approved books.[10]

In *The Temperance Educational Quarterly,* the advocates of prohibition described how temperance was to be taught in the public schools.
Some articles gave scripts for teachers and pupils to use on Frances E.
Willard day. Others printed pledges for children to sign in meetings
modeled on revivalist principles. Others again told horror stories
about drunkards and offered quotations from writers on the evils of
liquor. The magazine featured prize essays by pupils on alcohol,
smoking, and other evils and furnished detailed lesson plans. This
pedagogy, like the textbooks approved by the WCTU, was one of
moral absolutism, a lurid world of virtue and vice. It appealed to the
teacher "to become a social worker, a community reformer, fighting
for the rights of children. She insists that each child has a right to be
well born, sanely reared, and surrounded as it grows up by construc-
tive, elevating influences instead of destructive and degrading forces."
Children were given Thirty Scientific Facts like these to recite:[11]

Alcohol ruins the character.

Alcohol prevents men from obtaining good positions.

Nearly all business houses refuse to employ smokers because they can not be trusted. They are careless, dull and irresponsible.

The members of the WCTU were attacking a genuine medical and social problem, alcoholism. Their methods and message, however, disturbed many people, among them scientists appalled at the simplistic and moralistic physiology that the WCTU managed to install by law as orthodoxy in the classroom. They attacked the veto power that the Union had achieved over textbooks. In 1903 a committee of scholars issued a scathing study of instruction on alcohol which asserted that "under the name of 'scientific temperance instruction' there has been grafted upon the public school system . . . an educational scheme which is neither scientific, nor temperate, nor instructive." Another study of what children actually remembered from their physiology classes reported one pupil's response: alcohol "will gradually eat away the flesh. If anyone drinks it, it will pickle the inside of the body." The gross inaccuracies and the scare tactics of the temperance crusade could only backfire when children grew up and learned the real facts, critics said, and the child who witnessed moderate drinking at home would have reason to doubt the teacher or to fret about parents' damnation. Norton Mezvinsky argues that such opposition to the WCTU's program did not harm the organization or its work but rather stimulated it to find new allies and adherents. When Hunt wrote a reply to the scientific critics, it was published as a U.S. Senate document, and more than 100,000 copies were distributed.[12]

The WCTU was perhaps the most influential lay lobby ever to shape what was taught in public schools. Though it was a voluntary association, it acquired quasi-public power as a censor of textbooks, trainer of teachers, and arbiter of morality. As Ruth Bordin has shown, the WCTU gave tens of thousands of women an opportunity to learn the uses of political power long before they had the vote. Part of its goal was to educate a generation of children who would vote for prohibition when adults—which did happen, though the role of scientific temperance instruction in passing the 18th amendment is difficult to measure. In moving from persuasion to legal compulsion the WCTU was a pioneer in the codification of social values within the school curriculum, using strategies later employed by other groups that wished to give their religious and political values the force of law.[13]

Religion in the Public School: Majority Rule?

In the nineteenth century, religion had often been at the center of ethnocultural disputes, especially in cities. Most of these disputes took place in local communities without recourse to the courts or to legislatures. Sometimes they led to pitched battles in the streets between Protestants and Catholics or to endless battles of words, as between Horace Mann and his orthodox opponents. But it was not until the twentieth century that there was a widespread movement of Protestants to lobby state governments to legislate their fundamental values—in particular, Bible reading and the banning of teaching about evolution—into the school curriculum.[14]

When the common school took root in the middle of the nineteenth century, evangelical Protestant churches were a robust force in American life. Almost everywhere, Protestant ministers and lay people were in the forefront of the public school crusade and took a proprietary interest in the institution they had helped to build. They assumed a congruence of purpose between the common school and the Protestant churches. They had trouble conceiving of moral education not grounded in religion. The argument ran thus: To survive, the republic must be composed of moral citizens. Morality is rooted in religion. Religion is based upon the Bible. The public school is the chief instrument for forming moral citizens. Therefore, pupils must read the Bible in school. To say that the schools were "nonsectarian" was not to imply that they were without religion. Rather, it meant that the Protestant churches agreed to suspend their denominational quarrels within the public schoolhouse.[15]

Until well into the twentieth century, arguments over Bible reading in public schools were normally perceived more as a question of local option and who had political power than as a constitutional issue. In 1844 a Presbyterian leader, Robert Baird, wrote about religious instruction in common schools, "I can see no other course but that of leaving the question to the people themselves; the majority deciding, and leaving the minority the alternative of supporting a school of their own." He believed the prospects for evangelical Protestants were favorable, for in most communities "a pious and judicious teacher, if he will only confine himself to the great doctrines and precepts of the Gospel, in which all who hold the fundamental truths of the Bible are agreed, can easily give as much religious instruction as he chooses."[16]

When Catholics and other plaintiffs protested the reading of the King James Bible in court, they generally lost. Otto Hamilton has analyzed 25 cases in 19 states involving constitutional issues concerning religion and the Bible from 1854 to 1924. In three-fourths of the cases the courts upheld the right of school boards and officials to limit individual rights. Three-fifths of these complainants were Catholic. Cases upholding Bible reading outnumbered those declaring it sectarian and unconstitutional by roughly five to one. Because eloquent state supreme court decisions argued both sides of the Bible issue, judges found it easy to cite precedent either way.[17]

The earliest landmark decision on Bible reading was a Maine case, *Donahue v. Richards* in 1854. The school board of Ellsworth had expelled a fifteen-year-old girl, Bridget Donahue, for refusing to read from the King James version since the priest had told her and her father that it was sinful to use the Protestant Bible. Her lawyers contended that this requirement preferred Protestants over Catholics and hence constituted "a religious test." This led to an unconscionable kind of majority rule justified as "the greatest good of the greatest number":[18]

> as protestants regard instruction in protestant christianity as the most essential branch of education, therefore if the majority of the school be protestants, the committee may enforce such a system of instruction upon all; and Mahomedans, catholics, or Mormons may follow their example if they get the power. 'The greatest good of the greatest number.' This tyrannical doctrine of pure democracy, we generally hear only from the lips of demagogues.

The court found for the school board, arguing that the Bible was not used for sectarian instruction but as a reading book calculated to instill the virtues demanded by the state constitution.

So deep were the differences of religious outlook between Protestants and Catholics in the mid-nineteenth century that they often seemed incapable of understanding one another. Enraged by compulsory reading of the King James Bible and by textbooks that derogated Catholicism and often the lands from which Catholic immigrants had come, Catholics in many communities came to believe that they must build their own school system. It was only just, they said, that they receive public money to do so. Protestants, on the other hand, were equally angry. Only agents of the anti-christ—like Catholics— could be opposed to *the* Bible; surely no public funds should go to them.[19]

Most public school people shared the outlook of the Protestant ministers and politicians who believed that Bible reading was essential to effective moral and civic education. The NEA was dominated by a Protestant outlook and its members largely shared Horace Mann's "nonsectarian" solution of reading the Bible without comment. Let the majority rule quietly and keep the Bible in the classroom, and out of "politics"—this was the message of many NEA speeches. And in most communities teachers and pupils probably did read the Bible without much conflict. In the 1880s a school superintendent estimated that about 80 percent of American schools permitted the practice, while later surveys set the proportion at about three-quarters of the districts.[20]

During the nineteenth century only Massachusetts had passed a law mandating the reading of the Bible in public schools (in 1826). In the twentieth century many advocates of Bible reading were less willing to leave such an important matter to the decisions of local school boards or school people. As with temperance, they came to believe that local initiative and persuasion by voluntary groups were not enough; state prescription of Bible reading was necessary. So great were the dangers that beset the republic—crime, radicalism, class violence, intemperance, Darwinism and agnosticism, and loose morals—that only moral training through required Bible reading could reach those most in need of correction. Here was a crusade to reestablish the fundamentals, led in part by religious fundamentalists.

Between 1913 and 1930 eleven states and the District of Columbia passed laws requiring the reading of the Bible in public schools. Five states banned the teaching of evolution, and many more hamstrung the teaching of biology. Willard B. Gatewood, Jr., observes that the two legislative campaigns were probably connected and that required Bible reading may have been easier for fundamentalists to achieve than the more controversial banning of Darwinism. Table 6.2 lists the states that prescribed Bible reading.[21]

Besides the states that required Bible reading in all classrooms, seven states passed laws permitting the reading of the Bible but leaving it up to local option. In addition, North Dakota passed a law

TABLE 6.2

States Requiring Bible Reading, by Year

Massachusetts	1826	Maine	1923
Pennsylvania	1913	Kentucky	1924
Delaware	1915	Florida	1925
Tennessee	1915	Idaho	1925
New Jersey	1916	District of Columbia	1926
Alabama	1919	Arkansas	1930
Georgia	1921		

SOURCES: Keesecker, *Legal Status;* Johnson and Yost, *Separation*, 33–34; Gatewood, *Controversy*, 169—see note 21, chapter 6 of the present work.

requiring all public schools to place "the Ten Commandments of the Christian religion in a conspicuous place" in each classroom, and Mississippi required in every grade a course in morality that included the Ten Commandments. The wording of both the compulsory and optional laws on Bible reading showed similarities from state to state, suggesting that similar groups were sponsoring the bills. The compulsory Bible laws typically required teachers to read aloud a certain number of verses every day and imposed stern penalties for failure to comply, such as revoking the teacher's certificate or stopping state fiscal support. Urged on by their ministers, local church members stood ready to ensure that the law was enforced. In every state where the laws compelling Bible reading were challenged they were upheld by state supreme courts until the 1950s. The preamble of Maine's law suggested the conservative and retrospective motivation behind the bills: religious instruction was necessary, it announced, "to ensure greater security in the faith of our fathers, to inculcate into the lives of the rising generation the spiritual values necessary to the well being of our and future civilizations." The Idaho law side-stepped questions about which Bible to use—a vexed source of argument among Protestants, Catholics, and Jews—by prescribing "the standard American version."[22]

Part of what bothered religious conservatives in the decade after World War I was precisely the questioning they saw all around them of "the standard American version" of religious truths that once had been taught as received wisdom. It was time, many of them thought, to go on the offensive, to attack heresy and to prescribe old beliefs. One of the most pugnacious campaigns was the assault on the teaching of evolution in public schools. Between 1921 and 1929 the foes of evolution introduced 37 bills in 20 state legislatures to ban the teaching of Darwinism. Only five states—Arkansas, Florida, Mississippi, Oklahoma, and Tennessee—passed such laws, but in many other states the battle was furious and the effect on the teaching of biology chilling. In some states—for example, California, Louisiana, North Carolina, and Texas—the administrative branch of government restricted teaching about evolution. The anti-evolution lobby intimidated textbook publishers. Several of the largest publishers agreed to omit mention of evolution, and the treatment of that topic declined in biology texts from 1925 through the next two decades.[23]

Fundamentalist groups orchestrated the campaign to pass these laws and other restrictions on teaching of evolution. In 1922 the World's Christian Fundamentals Association passed a resolution at its meeting in Los Angeles: "As taxpayers we have a perfect right to demand of public schools that they cease from giving to our children pure speculation in the name of science, and we have an equal right to demand the removal of any teacher who attempts to undermine...the Christian faith of pupils." This statement expressed two themes that ran throughout the anti-evolution campaign. The first was that the majority had the right to dictate the doctrines taught to students in public schools, since the people paid the bills. The second was that children were pure but vulnerable, ready targets for a conspiracy of modernists who planned to poison their minds with faith-destroying beliefs. Governor Miriam Ferguson of Texas spoke for many of the anti-evolutionists when she declared: "I am a Christian mother, and I am not going to let that kind of rot into Texas textbooks." Like temperance advocates who fought the poison of alcohol with absolute certainty in their cause, the fundamentalists believed that they struggled not just for their own children but for the health of society. An Oklahoma legislator, arguing for a rider to a free textbook bill that would ban the teaching of evolution, angrily shouted "I promised my people at home [Sallisaw] that if I had a chance to down this hellish Darwin here that I would do it."[24]

New fundamentalist organizations sprouted to carry on the campaign, bearing names like the Bible Crusaders of America, the Supreme Kingdom, the Defenders of the Christian Faith, and the Flying Fundamentalists. The motto of the Crusaders was "Back to Christ, the Bible, and the Constitution." Many of the members of these groups were devout people who believed that they were doing the Lord's work; some of the leaders were opportunists eager to cash in on the money that wealthy fundamentalists contributed to the cause; and a number of the organizers were allied with racist groups like the Ku Klux Klan. Lobbyists employed by the fundamentalist action groups went from state to state to plead with or bully legislators to support their cause. In Mississippi a leader of the Bible Crusaders, T. T. Martin, who had written a pamphlet called *Hell in the High Schools*, lectured the legislators:[25]

> Go back to your homes and face your constituents and tell them that you bartered the faith of your children for gold; go back to the fathers and mothers of Mississippi and tell them that because you could not face the ridicule and scorn and abuse of Bolshevists and Anarchists and Atheists and Agnostics and their co-workers, you turned your children over to a teaching that God's word is a tissue of lies and that the Savior who said it was God's word was only the illegitimate son of a Jewish fallen woman.

William Jennings Bryan was the leader of the fundamentalist crusade, the author of its most influential speeches, and the defender of the faith against Clarence Darrow in the Scopes trial in Dayton, Tennessee, in which a local biology teacher was found guilty of teaching evolution to his pupils against state law. True to his convictions, and convinced that he represented a majority of Americans in wishing the faith of the fathers restored to the schools, Bryan did not worry about whether he appeared atavistic to sophisticated intellectuals. He liked to point out that only two percent of Americans had completed college, while the other 98 percent still had their souls. The massive publicity given to Darrow's demolition of Bryan's arguments in the monkey trial, however, gave the modernists their most potent weapon against the fundamentalists: ridicule. In legislature after legislature, the foes of the anti-evolutionists used derision or warned that their state might become a laughingstock in the national press. In Delaware, the evolution bill was referred to the committee on fish, game, and oysters; in Missouri an opponent suggested that the penalty for breaking a proposed law should be to spend a month in the St. Louis zoo; elsewhere, facetious legislators suggested that teachers should tell students that the world was flat, as it said in the Bible.[26]

The conflict between religion and science was more serious than the ballyhoo that attended it. Like the advocates of temperance, who believed in their own version of "science," fundamentalists in religion and politics held firmly to convictions which they took to be grounded in established truth, but these were at odds with the views held by modernists. At one level, the battle was one of distorted simplicities, bigoted hayseeds versus godless sophisticates. At the deeper level that Walter Lippmann probed in *American Inquisitors,* the dispute between fundamentalism and modernism was a conflict of basic ways of understanding the universe and of shaping the future through educating the rising generation. Public educators were caught in the middle, many of them attuned to more cosmopolitan kinds of thinking but subject, as civil servants, to the will of the majority as expressed in legislation. In the nineteenth century and in homogeneously Protestant communities in the twentieth century, many teachers never sensed that there was a conflict between the fundamentals of religion and the pursuit of knowledge. What an evangelical community wanted for its children was what teachers knew and cherished themselves. But with the extension of modernist outlooks and the increasing pluralism of the society, the fundamentalist majorities in Bible belt states turned to law to preserve what once had been consensual wisdom.[27]

Some modernists of the 1920s regarded such majority rule in religion as the last gasp of a regressive and dying cause. By the 1980s it became apparent that the imminent death of fundamentalism was a delusion. No segment of American private education grew more rapidly in the late 1970s than the Christian day school, an institution designed to inculcate the certainties that fundamentalists had once hoped to embed in public schools. Many fundamentalists turned away from the public school system, which they regarded as secular or worse, instead holding that education was a *parental* duty and not properly a state function. This represented a retreat from their attempt to enforce their fundamentalist views on all children. But other religious lobbies and politicians in Washington and the states attempted at the same time to reverse the Supreme Court's bans on prayer and Bible reading, thereby restoring religion to the public school by constitutional amendment. Majority rule on religion in public education was an issue that refused to go away.[28]

"The Americanization of America"

Like religious fundamentalism, political fundamentalism in education reached its apogee in the decade following the outbreak of World War I, when politically mobilized pressure groups demanded state laws to enforce what the American Legion called "the Americanization of America." If its proposals for mandatory civic instruction were adopted, the Legion promised at its first convention in 1919, "the next generation will see this country rid of the undesirable element now present in its citizenship, foreign colonies a thing of the past, the spirit of true Americanism prevailing throughout the length and breadth of our country, and our ideals of government secure." The Sentinels of America, even more optimistic about the malleability of youth, declared that with the right kind of training—theirs— "in less than five years we can build up a body of real Simon-pure citizens." Utopian faith in schooling to right wrongs was not new, nor belief that education was essential to the survival of the republic. Heresy-hunting was not novel, either. What was unprecedented was the success of political fundamentalists in enacting their own political norms into binding state law.[29]

Protestant-republican ideology had infused the common school of the nineteenth century, inspired its leaders, and spoken with clear voice in the textbooks of the time. At the end of the century, challenges to this political consensus and to the dominant position of the prosperous WASP segment of the American people caused alarm. Nativists associated immigrants with violence, radicalism, poverty, ignorance, and disloyalty. Leaders began to worry whether so disparate a population could constitute one people, speak one language, honor one flag. World War I heightened these anxieties. Fears of a domestic fifth-column fueled the crusade for 100-percent Americanism during the war, while the Russian Revolution and the Red Scare that followed it in the United States created a frenzied conservative backlash. As in religion, a gulf separated the modernists from the fundamentalists in political thought. Disillusionment with the war made many intellectuals skeptical about the polity, while many conservatives were eager to return to a supposed era of political certitude. As skeptical historians found faults with the heroes of the past, pressure groups persuaded legislatures to pass laws like that of Oregon banning any textbook "that speaks slightingly of the founders of

the republic, or of the men who preserved the union, or which belit-
tles or undervalues their work" (a statute that was not overruled by
the courts until 1984). War had taught the uses of propaganda. It was
time, thought many, to shape the impressionable minds of the next
generation to American specifications.[30]

Laws prescribing patriotic instruction took many forms. States
mandated courses in U.S. history, civil government, the U.S. Constitution, citizenship, patriotism, and similar subjects. Flag displays, salutes,
and patriotic ceremonies on special days became popular. More and
more states required that all instruction be given in English, reversing
earlier law or custom that had allowed ethnic groups to teach public
school pupils in their parents' languages (particularly German). A
campaign by the National Security League to ban the teaching of
German, both through law and through persuasion, achieved remark-
able success; the percentage of high school students studying German
dropped from 24 percent in 1915 to less than one percent in 1922.
Legislatures required teachers to pass tests on the Constitution or U.S.
history, forced them to sign loyalty oaths, and banned non-citizens
from teaching. They dictated the content of textbooks in history and
civics. One-third of the states passed laws to hasten the Americanization of immigrants.[31]

In 1885 there had been relatively few such statutes. Then only 11
states mandated American history (or similar civic instruction) by
law, and only nine required that instruction be conducted in English.
The campaign to mandate patriotism by law gained momentum in
the 1890s and accelerated after World War I. Table 6.3 indicates this
rapid growth during the years from 1903 to 1923, when the total
number of state prescriptions on patriotic instruction more than
doubled, from 147 to 304.[32]

Many pressure groups sought to influence such legislation. Veterans' groups like the Grand Army of the Republic and the American
Legion had large memberships and considerable political clout. As
federated organizations—in this respect they were similar to the WCTU
and fundamentalist churches—they could shape a unified national
policy, lobby legislatures, and ensure compliance at the local level
through posts in communities throughout the nation. Many different
groups, drawing on different social classes and ideologies, joined in
the crusade for patriotism. The American Bar Association played a
central part in legislative campaigns to require the teaching of the

TABLE 6.3
Number of States Prescribing Patriotic Instruction or Rituals
(Percent of all states in parentheses)

	1903	1913	1923
History of the U.S.	30 (67)	32 (67)	43 (90)
Constitution of the U.S.	9 (20)	9 (19)	21 (44)
History of the State	13 (29)	20 (42)	29 (60)
Citizenship	1 (2)	1 (2)	39 (81)
Patriotism	0 (0)	1 (2)	12 (25)
Flag Displays	17 (38)	29 (60)	39 (81)
Flag Exercises	3 (7)	4 (8)	10 (21)
All Instruction in English	14 (31)	17 (35)	35 (73)

SOURCE: Flanders, *Legislative Control*, 62—see note 32, chapter 6 of the present work.

U.S. Constitution and American history. Patriotic lobbies like the Daughters of the American Revolution, the National Security League, the Constitution Anniversary Association, and the Better America Federation—conservative and elite in their orientation—worked to secure orthodox political instruction. Politicians like Mayor William Thompson of Chicago and John Hylan of New York courted votes by attacking the allegedly pro-British and unpatriotic cast of history textbooks.[33]

Union veterans banded together in the Grand Army of the Republic (GAR) were the first potent pressure group to call for correct patriotic instruction. Their campaign began in the mid-1880s, when state and local groups inquired into the American history textbooks their children were reading and found them wishy-washy, so diluted in order to appeal to the Southern market that pupils could not determine "which [side] was right and which was wrong" in the Civil War. Not surprisingly, Confederate veterans had a different view from that of the GAR. Southerners who erected statues to soldiers who fought in "the war for Southern independence" had a contrasting version of history from the Northerners who celebrated the "war of the great rebellion." Southerners also wanted their own orthodoxy taught through legal prescription. In Florida the legislature passed an act to secure "a Correct History of the United States, Including a True and Correct History of the Confederacy."[34]

In the 1890s the national encampment of the Grand Army broadened its concerns. It attacked radicalism and sought restriction of immigration as well. Members of the GAR and its women's auxiliary worked zealously at the state and local levels for patriotic instruction and rituals, the display of flags in every school, flag salutes, patriotic essay contests, special days for patriotic observances, and the singing of the Star Spangled Banner (the GAR started the custom of standing while singing the national anthem). They were the most influential advocates of the pledge of allegiance or flag salute recommended by George T. Balch in his book *Methods of Teaching Patriotism in the Public Schools* (1890).[35]

The crusade for patriotism rapidly bore fruit. By 1895 seven legislatures required schools to display American flags, and the commander could report that the stars and stripes floated over 17,988 of the 26,588 schools within the GAR departments. Legislatures passed laws specifying in minute detail the size of flags and height of flagpoles. In 1898, on the day after the Spanish-American War was declared, the New York legislature required the flag salute as a daily ceremony in all schools. The next year the Grand Army officially adopted Balch's pledge—the one still in use, minus the phrase "under God," added in the 1950s—and urged that it be mandated in schools, together with a simpler version for primary students: "I give my hand, my head, my heart to my country. One country, one people, one flag." Within a few years four other states followed New York's example, and in a GAR stronghold, Indiana, the law required children to sing all the verses of the Star Spangled Banner "upon all patriotic occasions." In Michigan, pupils had to pass an examination on "the first verse of the Star Spangled Banner and the words of America" in order to graduate from eighth grade. Between 1900 and 1917, 32 states required the study of American history, and many mandated instruction in the federal and state constitutions. New Hampshire compelled all eighth-graders to read both the state and U.S. Constitutions aloud, ritualizing the sacred documents. Severe penalties were often attached to failure to comply with these laws. In Oklahoma, teachers neglecting properly to conduct flag ceremonies were subject to discharge, fines, even jail sentences.[36]

Organized in 1919, the American Legion was another veterans' group that sought to promote patriotism through public education. It urged legionnaires to lobby in state capitols for laws that would mandate instruction only in English and that would require students to study U.S. history and the constitution before they could graduate from high school. Like the GAR, it placed great stress on the ceremonies of patriotism. Worried about the deficient Americanism of some teachers, the Legion pressured legislators to pass loyalty oaths and kept watch in local communities for signs of radicalism or pacifism in the schools. It commissioned its own text, *The Story of the American People*, a book that preached on "every page a vivid love of America"; a dissident historian, finding it vacuous, called it "The Marvelous Story of Us." With a mass membership in over 10,000 local posts, the Legion seemed omnipresent.[37]

Another group that sought compulsory Americanization was the American Bar Association (ABA). It cooperated with the American Legion and other patriotic groups to secure laws requiring the study of the constitution. In 1921, the president of the ABA warned his colleagues that communists and anarchists were propagandizing against American institutions. The most insidious were teachers who injected "questions into the unformed minds of the coming generation." The "half-baked, so-called educator in the schools" dared to ask "whether in fact things are right as they exist." A committee appointed by the ABA in 1922 reported on what the Association should do to ensure proper citizenship: the ABA should call upon "every true American" to "stem the tide of radical, and often treasonable, attacks upon our Constitution, our laws, our courts, our law-making bodies, our executives and our flag, to arouse to action our dormant citizenry, to abolish ignorance, and crush falsehood, and to bring truth into the hearts of our citizenship." The committee said that "the schools of America should no more consider graduating a student who lacks faith in our government than a school of theology should consider graduating a minister who lacks faith in God." It did not add "lacks faith in lawyers," though popular distrust of the profession rankled the members of the bar.[38]

The committee recommended the establishment of a standing committee and bureau to oversee the "education, training, and development of a better citizenship." Its program was to enact laws requiring "the study of and devotion to American institutions and ideals" in every school, public and private, in every state; to appoint "a committee in every community, whose duty it shall be to see that the Constitution of the United States is taught in every school" and to report to the bureau "the courses in each state, the textbooks used, and the qualifications of teachers for teaching American citizenship"; and to promote patriotism and counteract un-American ideas. In 1923 and 1924 the committee reminded the bar of the continuing need for vigilance because of "socialistic doctrines" taught in the schools and said that some school people were dragging their feet. It concluded that progress was being made, for seven new states had passed satisfactory laws by 1924. The continuing problem was to instill the right attitude of "bed-rock Americanism" in teachers. The committee furnished cartoons and articles to the press, sponsored "Constitution Week," and wrote a "citizenship creed."[39]

In the politically virulent years of World War I and the Red Scare, numerous other conservative political organizations sought to enforce orthodoxy through the schools, sometimes lobbying state legislatures in concert to secure passage of prescriptive laws. The National Security League sought to Americanize America through banning the study of German, the abolition of German literary and musical clubs, and laws compelling teaching in patriotism. The League formed a Committee on Constitution Instruction and a Civic Department and had 281 local branches. It carried its campaign to all presidents of state boards of education and every county and district superintendent in the nation. The League prepared bills for state legislatures that required courses on the Constitution and claimed success when 36 states enacted such laws, many of them verbatim copies of its legislation. It also lobbied to require teachers to pass tests on the constitution in order to gain certificates; by 1925, 33 states had required these examinations. The League estimated that by law over 200,000 teachers were teaching the constitution to more than four million pupils. A major problem, said the Committee on Constitution Instruction, was that there were no texts that correctly transmitted "the basic principles of our government to the minds of children." It advocated "short stories" on the Constitution "readily understood by the average child" and taught by teachers who "reverenced" the constitution. The League distributed almost one million copies of its "Catechism of the Constitution" to schools and offered training to teachers seeking to pass the state tests on government that were required for certification. Its civic secretary, Etta Leighton, wrote a teachers' manual called *Our Constitution in My Town and My Life.*[40]

In 1923 the Constitution Anniversary Association joined the fundamentalist political movement to stem "our drifting in recent years away from representative government toward direct action; from individual property rights to socialism; from individual responsibility for individual conflict toward class consciousness, class agitation, and class legislation." Its director was Harry F. Atwood, who believed that the United States had shifted far from its republican foundation to democracy; "what drunkenness is to the individual," he wrote, "democracy is to government." Atwood joined forces with conservatives in the Better America Foundation to sponsor a National Oratorical Contest on the Constitution.[41]

Without state-by-state case studies it is impossible to disentangle the contributions of each of these organizations—the Legion, the American Bar Association, the National Security League, and the rest—made to the passage of laws requiring patriotic teaching. The 100 percent Americanism of the war years and the Red Scare created a public mood that predisposed legislators to heed the right-wing lobbies. The new laws on patriotic instruction and the concurrent loyalty oaths required of teachers endangered educators who dissented from political orthodoxy. A New York legal journal editorialized thus in 1922 about the Lusk Act of that state, which had been denounced as an "un-american inquisition":[42]

> the unformed and undiscriminating minds of children should not be subjected to any form of propaganda. Parents are required by law to send their children to school, and have a right to expect that they will be taught nothing there except the established fundamentals. Matters of opinion have no place in the public schools and should not be allowed to get in by indirection.

As in the case of religion, these political fundamentalists feared the impact of views divergent from their own on the "unformed" minds of children and could not see that their convictions were quite as much "matters of opinion" as the political values they attacked.

Although some educators protested such 100 percent Americanism, some taught a more liberal interpretation of constitutional rights than conservatives desired, and many suffered as victims of heresy-hunting, school people generally agreed with the pressure groups that promoted patriotism, seeing it as part of the reform movement to make schools "socially efficient." Some protested against lay people telling professionals what and how to teach, and others complained about the overloading of the curriculum with required topics and rituals. But the majority of educators probably shared the values of the patriots although they were nervous about the extremes of zealotry. The NEA worked closely with the American Legion and the National Security League in promoting National Education Week, in which a nativist version of patriotism was a prominent theme. Professor Carlton Hayes, an expert on nationalism, observed that the leaders of public education "lead a kind of double life; they must be superteachers... getting an example of the highest idealism for their teachers; they must be also more or less servile representatives of the state, holding their teachers in check, guarding their pupils against radicalism and novelty, and generally maintaining such standards in their schools as reflect most faithfully the collective spirit of the taxpayers."[43]

Once the public schools had become well established, they were a ready target for lobbies that claimed to represent moral majorities and that wished to write laws to inculcate their version of truth and virtue in the rising generation. Educators typically shared the values of temperance, non-sectarian religion, and patriotism thus embedded in law. Once placed on the books, such legislation was rarely challenged successfully in the courts, although sometimes it was reversed in electoral politics. Judges have mostly upheld the plenary powers of the legislature to establish whatever curriculum it deemed necessary to mandate civic virtue.[44]

Since it was easier to instruct the captive—and presumably malleable—audience of the young rather than to alter the beliefs or behavior of adult voters, WASP citizens found it expedient to shift reform to the next generation, to find educational solutions to intractable problems. Thus the alcoholism of adults, the supposed dangers posed by unassimilated foreigners, or the decline of faith and the threat of new ideas like evolution could be overcome by the proper socialization of the next generation. The legislative campaigns of WASP reformers to conquer evil by indoctrinating good offer a screen on which they projected their hopes and fears concerning the social order.

The groups claiming to be moral majorities were not simply trying to persuade others to adopt their values when they mandated them into school law. They were in effect declaring dissenters to their values to be un-American if not illegal. The law thus conferred special dignity on certain civic and religious and moral convictions and denied equality of dignity to others in a society that was pluralistic in culture and belief. We pursue these issues further in chapter 7 in examining an episode in the politics of education and in constitutional interpretation of school law that tested the limits of coercion.

CHAPTER 7

Compulsory Public Schooling and the Perils of Pluralism: The Case of Oregon, 1922

The King Kleagle, Pacific domain, of the Knights of the Ku Klux Klan warmed to his theme. We are facing now, he said in 1922, "the ultimate perpetuation or destruction of free institutions, based on the perpetuation or destruction of the public schools." To defend the common school "is the settled policy of the Ku Klux Klan and with its white-robed sentinels keeping eternal watch, it shall for all time, with its blazing torches as signal fires, stand guard on the outer walls of the Temple of Liberty, cry out the warning when danger appears and take its place in the front rank of defenders of the public schools." The King Kleagle and his hooded colleagues had just helped persuade the citizens of Oregon to pass an initiative requiring all children between eight and 16 to attend public schools and essentially outlawing private elementary schools. Now they were awaiting a court test of the law by their opponents.[1]

Grotesque though it may be to imagine the KKK as defender of the common school and liberty, the Oregon experiment with compulsion was not a lonely aberration but a cresting of social attitudes and political currents that had flowed and ebbed in the past. Thus like a cartoon that caricatures but reveals salient forces, the Oregon events present in bold outline a widespread American fear of diversity and an impulse to coerce uniformity through public schooling. The political furor this measure aroused and the landmark decision of the U.S. Supreme Court in *Pierce v. Society of Sisters* in 1925 together illuminate majority rule and minority rights in education in a pluralistic society.

The themes the KKK stressed in their campaign for compulsory *public* schooling had sounded many times before in American history. Anti-Catholic, anti-immigrant, anti-elite, anti-radical, and anti-intellectual attitudes were hardly new. But in the early 1920s in Oregon the KKK and their allies in the school fight found that many citizens were responsive to their peculiar mixture of fear, paranoia, nostalgia, and hope. This hope was in some ways the most traditional and yet puzzling part of the story. The Klan taught the inherent superiority of WASPs and the inferiority of aliens, blacks, Catholics, and Jews, and yet it somehow persuaded itself that to force all children to attend public schools together would avert the ruin of the republic. Conflicting assumptions about heredity and environment sat side by side in mute antagonism in their writings on the school question. In urging that the common school could produce social solidarity by mixing all ethnic groups, all social classes, the KKK echoed the claims of Horace Mann.[2]

But the time was 1922, not 1840, and compulsion, not persuasion, had become the watchword. The educational leaders of the mid-nineteenth century had hoped to make the public school so attractive that citizens would desire no other; they had tried to find a common core of Christianity and patriotism acceptable to all. After the Civil War a number of state legislatures went beyond exhortation by passing laws compelling parents to send their children to some school, public or private. In the nineteenth century these laws were generally not strictly enforced, save in a few cities. They represented a stamping of the foot, an accusation against delinquent parents, a symbolic show of state authority. But in the early twentieth century compulsory attendance laws had become far more than symbolic gestures. Part of the genius of the progressive era in education was organizational—learning how to sweep up truants and process them in the bureaucracies of schools and courts. By 1920 *compulsory attendance* meant just that in many states: children had to go to school or their parents had to prove why not. The provisions of the Oregon initiative were Draconian: if a parent did not send children to public schools between the ages of eight and 16, they were subject to fines for each day of delinquency and to jail terms of not less than two days.[3]

Before the Oregon law there always were limits on the state's power to compel. Whether for religious or other reasons, parents could send their children to the schools of their choice. Now all that might change, wrote the editor of the Portland *Telegram:* "We, the majority, have decided what is necessary. . . . The public schools please us. Why not make them please the other fellow? Why not march him up to the school of our choice and say to him in effect: 'There, take that, it's good for you.' " The next step, wrote another Oregonian, was clear: "some self-appointed patriots calling themselves 100 percent will come along with a petition requesting that all babes be removed from the home from the mother's breast lest the babes hear some unpatriotic lullaby song, fed on Eagle Brand milk, and placed in a state institution." A defender of the initiative bought a half-page advertisement in the *Silverton Appeal* to declare that "young children in private schools have no defense against any private ideas antagonistic to our free institutions. We cannot afford to run this risk any longer, and we positively know that traitors are now at this deadly task." "Private schools" meant "private ideas"; "private ideas," by definition, were dangerous.[4]

Why should an anti-immigrant, anti-Catholic, anti-Bolshevist, anti-elite, anti-private school campaign have appeared in Oregon? At first glance it was an unlikely place to press for a public monopoly of elementary schooling. In 1920 the state had only 13 percent foreign-born inhabitants (one-half of them naturalized), only 0.3 percent blacks, only about 8 percent Catholics. Schooling was already practically universal for children seven to 13 (95 percent were enrolled). Only 1.5 percent of people ten and older were illiterate. The major city, Portland, had few slums and few of the problems of the crowded polyglot eastern metropolis; outsiders congratulated Portland for its "Teutonic," orderly, Americanized school-children. Only 7 percent of elementary pupils attended private schools and the ratio was dropping fast. Public and private schools had peaceably coexisted since the first settlements (indeed, the minister considered to be the father of Oregon common schools also founded private schools). It was fanciful to assert that Oregon exemplified the perils of pluralism or that the private schools, steadily declining in the proportion of students they served, constituted a threat to public education.[5]

Why, then, Oregon? Perhaps it was because Oregon did approximate the ideal WASP society that partisans like the Klansmen chose it as a test case for compulsory public education: there were so many of US and so few of THEM. A similar plan had failed in Michigan, but if the Oregon campaign proved successful, a dozen other states were next in line.[6]

The Politics of Paranoia

The beginnings of the 1922 law for compulsory public education lie shrouded in the obscurity of secretive organizations. The men who put the measure on the ballot claimed as inspiration a resolution of the Scottish Rite Masons, Southern Jurisdiction of the United States, May, 1920:

> *Resolved*, That we recognize and proclaim our belief in the free and compulsory education of the children of our nation in public primary schools supported by public taxation, upon which all children shall attend and be instructed in the English language only without regard to race or creed as the only sure foundation for the perpetuation and preservation of our free institutions.

The Scottish Rite Masons were mounting a national campaign against an alleged effort of Catholics to sap the strength of the common school and against the specter of "Bolshevist" instruction in private schools. They claimed that the antidote would be to teach children in public schools "along standardized lines, which will enable them to acquire a uniform outlook on all national and patriotic questions." But in Oregon the Masons split on the issue of outlawing private schools, and there is much evidence that the KKK was using the Scottish Rite as a front.[7]

Because of the secret membership and "invisible government" of the Klan, probably no one will ever know how fully it infiltrated the Oregon Scottish Rite Masons or other groups allied in support of the school initiative, such as the Federated Patriotic Societies. The Salem *Journal*, one of the few newspapers to attack the KKK openly, said in an editorial called "Masonry the Goat" that the state monopoly of education "was introduced into the campaign for the purposes of stimulating membership in the Ku Klux Klan in its appeal to religious prejudice and racial hatred." That was doubtless one intent of the Klan leadership. In any case, the school initiative became the most heated and bitter issue in the election. The bill has "set the brush on fire and . . . rent asunder communities," said the La Grange *Observer*. The fact that it passed by a comfortable majority (115,506 to 103,685) suggests that the KKK appeals tapped deep public concerns.[8]

The Klan in Oregon had many faces and more masks. Many of the leaders and salesmen saw chances to make a profit from anxiety and hatred. The KKK became a semi-open political party that ran its own candidates (men they endorsed won the governorship, the mayoralty of Portland, and a potential deciding vote in the legislature). In some communities it became an underground and hooded police troop enforcing prohibition, marital fidelity, and fundamental morality. It also harassed minorities who insisted on their rights. But most of the Klansmen were not the rural, violent night riders of the popular stereotype. Over half the Oregon members lived in Portland. If they fit the larger pattern of urban Klansmen described by Kenneth Jackson, a large percent were probably blue-collar fundamentalists, arrested in their careers at a menial level amid the contemporary cult of success, troubled by assaults on the familiar certainties, looking for dignity and significance. Jackson has observed that "fear of change, not vindictiveness or cruelty, was the basic motivation of the urban Klansman" of this type. They thought they represented not extremist values but the mainstream of traditional Americanism. In elaborate rituals and offices Klansmen found an excitement and a companionship often missing in their drab lives. The Klan's absolute versions of Christianity and patriotism soothed troubled minds (the names of the days in the Ku Klux Kalendar were "Desperate, Dreadful, Desolate, Doleful, Dismal, Deadly, Dark"). Its assurances of the superiority of the native-born, white Protestant gave Klansmen status they were denied elsewhere.[9]

The Klan adapted the traditional ideology of public education to its own purposes. Along with pure womanhood, white supremacy, the Constitution, uncorrupted religion, and the common people, Klansmen were sworn to uphold public education: "I believe that our Free Public School is the cornerstone of good government," they recited, "and that those who are seeking to destroy it are enemies of our Republic and are unworthy of citizenship." Only bluebloods or people who placed church above state could oppose compulsory public schooling; in either case, they were traitors to American institutions.[10]

In the Oregon Klansmen's writings on using the public school to solve the problems facing the United States, there were contradictions that could be resolved only by an illogical jump of faith in the powers of education to redeem inferior people. Lem Dever, a Klan publicist, wrote that the KKK was determined to "keep our country from becoming a vast Mongrelia." He thought that the Army intelligence tests had proved the stupidity of southeastern European immigrants and that urban masses had "no more pedigree than the street dogs and cats" and were "the product of innumerable crossings with the mongrel horde." Such assumptions about genetic inferiority of certain "races" went far beyond the Klan's traditional assumption of white superiority over blacks. How the schools were to deal with "inferior" genes was simply ignored. But Dever made it clear that the public schools were to replace immigrant cultures with 100 percent Americanism and wanted to Protestantize the Catholics by requiring "their priests to marry and live normal lives" and by forcing Catholics to "abolish the parochial grade school and join with other Americans in building up the Public School."[11]

The Klan's propaganda piece in favor of compulsory public education—called *The Old Cedar School*—was a curious mixture of nostalgia, paranoia, anti-clericalism, Populist egalitarianism, anti-intellectualism, and bitter fantasy. In his introduction the King Kleagle wrote that the conflict was "a battle of the mass of humanity against sects, classes, combinations and rings; against entrenched privilege and secret machinations of the favored few to control the less favored many." The author of the pamphlet, George Estes, cast the narrative in the form of a conversation between an old Oregon pioneer and his alienated and perverse children who chose to send their children to private schools. In the dialect of the common man the father told of building a school on a ridge east of Portland "so us children could learn to read an' write an' cypher a little so't we couldn't git beat out o' everything when we growed up an' maybe when it come time to votin' we'd know enuff to vote agin fool laws an' graftin' men." But his children grew up to be snobs and sectarians. And in the end Estes' pioneer transformed his family's apostasy from Americanism into a public apocalypse, as a cabal put the torch to the public school:[12]

> Our Old Cedar School House, next in my heart to Mother's grave, was tumblin' to the ground, in flames, the crushed an' shriveled form of old Silas Parker, its teacher for mor'n fifty years, lay dead with his snow-white head hangin' out of the open front door... and the burnin' flag on the tall spire, THE LAST TORCH OF LIBERTY, FADIN' FROM THE WORLD.

In their public pronouncements the Klan specialized in this sort of common man melodrama. Probably more powerful, though often underground, was the fanning of anti-Catholic hatred. A citizen of Glendale put the matter candidly: the bill "is not a question of Catholic's [sic] having the right to follow the teachings of their Dago pope, but the right of Protestants to educate their children by the best school system in the world." The majority has the right to rule, he said, for after all, if the papists had a majority they would destroy our institutions. "Catechized monstrosities" were emerging from parochial schools intending "to destroy all of our public schools," wrote a man in Silverton. The Klan trotted out renegade nuns to retail stories of Catholic smut and conspiracy. The lies of the Klan cut deeply into the lives and feelings of many Catholics. One mother said that her daughter could not find work because of virulent prejudice: she almost had a job until questioned what religion she professed. To her astonishment she was refused the place because of the name Catholic."[13]

Counterattack

A sense of outrage united an otherwise miscellaneous collection of opponents of the school initiative. Religious leaders—Catholic, Protestant, and Jewish—deeply resented the implication that "sectarianism" was unpatriotic. Businessmen feared increased taxes for schools and a lower rate of investment and population growth because of such "freak legislation." Minority groups like blacks, Jews, and the foreign-born detected totalitarian notes in the arguments of the bill's supporters. Private school proprietors fought for their very existence. And liberals attacked the tyranny of the majority in a law that threatened religious liberty, freedom of thought, parental rights, and constitutional rights.

In the campaign against the bill in press, pulpit, and forum, opponents charged that promoters had secured the initiative by fraud and publicized it by deceit. The measure bore the misleading title "Compulsory Education" (misleading because Oregon already had an effective compulsory school attendance law). The Portland *Spectator* said that advocates had won signatures by telling citizens that the purpose of the law was "to give every child an education." Many signers of the petition said later that they did not realize that the act would ban private schools.[14]

Several groups coordinated the attack on the measure: the Portland Committee of Citizens and Taxpayers (largely businessmen); the Lutheran Schools Committee, which had prior experience with a similar bill in Michigan in 1920; the Non-Sectarian and Protestant Schools Committee (the central clearinghouse for speakers and newspaper publicity), and the Catholic Civil Rights Association of Oregon. In the highly emotional campaign, subtleties about constitutional law and religious liberty were less potent than arguments that the bill would raise taxes and invade parental rights. Opponents as well as supporters wrapped themselves in the American flag. The bill was clearly Prussian or communist in intent, said the critics, and a cartoon in the *Telegram* showed Lenin and a hooded Ku Kluxer upholding a placard bearing the message "State Monopoly of Schools Is an Absolute Success in Russia."[15]

Ethnic minorities recognized that the majority could become tyrannical if public schools became compulsory and groups like the Klan could shape the curriculum. The Jewish community opposed the bill; even Jesse Winburn, a Jewish backer of the Klan candidate for governor, Walter Pierce, inserted advertisements in newspapers across the state condemning the law. The Portland black newspaper attacked "the diseased mental state caused by ignorant bigotry" and urged all blacks to "stand against it, knowing the methods of the public school system in the South." First- and second-generation immigrants, especially German Lutherans, bristled at the bill not only because they had parochial schools to defend but also because they knew that their way of life was threatened. One writer flatly denied the basic premise that only public schools could Americanize children. Indeed, he wrote, a sympathetic teacher in a private school could be more successful in bridging the foreign and the American culture for the child:[16]

> there are as many nationalities represented in the private schools as in the public schools . . . the discipline and intercourse of the pupils are just as democratic . . . there is absolutely no difference in the tone and teaching of the private and the public schools in matters affecting American ideas and ideals. . . . In some respects . . . the private schools prove to be better Americanizers . . . if the teacher be of the same religion as the foreign-born parents or pupils, and can speak the native language of both pupils and parents, it establishes a tie of sympathy between them that contributes immensely to the Americanization of the pupils.

To Lutherans, Seventh-Day Adventists, and Catholics, the basic issue was freedom to educate their children in accord with their own religious convictions. "This measure virtually involves a union of Church and state," said a spokesman for the Adventists. "The government that turns its citizens into subjects and makes them mere cogs in a wheel, without any rights of their own, is a government that is transforming itself into a tyranny." Liberal Presbyterian, Unitarian, and Congregational ministers agreed that the bill violated the First Amendment; "if the Protestant majority sets aside the rights of the Catholic minority, shall we call it patriotism?" one asked. Catholics tried to keep a low profile in the public debate since they were the prime targets of the opposition.[17]

While differing in motives, the opponents generally agreed about the purposes and limits of public education. They had no quarrel with the principle of free public schools or the need to create one people from many. They objected, rather, to a state monopoly that would destroy their private schools, impose a deadening uniformity on ethnic and religious groups, give Oregon a reputation for extremism, and punish any departure from the views of the majority.

Where Did Oregon Public School People Stand?

Public educators were justifiably proud of the institution they served and vocal in defending it against unjustified charges. But they quite missed the set of constitutional questions raised about the bill and distorted the issue of compulsion; the question, as others constantly said, was not whether there should be compulsory school attendance. That already existed. The question was whether children could only attend *public* schools. Hypersensitive, school people seemed to assume that a vote against the bill was a vote against public education. They obscured rather than illuminated the legal, moral, religious, and even pedagogical issues involved in the battle.[18]

When educational leaders across the nation were asked to comment on the compulsory public school bill, they almost always attacked it. The president of Columbia called the initiative " 'A Bill to Make Impossible the American System of Education in Oregon,' " while the Yale president saw it as a form of thought control. Others declared it unconstitutional, said it violated toleration and good faith, and destroyed the useful emulation of private and public systems.[19]

Newspapers gave wide publicity to such opinions of outside educators, but in the Oregon teachers' semi-official magazine, *Oregon Teacher's Monthly*, the editor departed from the usual safe apolitical approach to urge teachers to "study" the bill and then proceeded only to argue for the measure. She interpreted arguments against the bill as "a direct or implied arraignment of the public schools." Look at "the Boss Crokers, who grew up without schools, and the Morgans who were splendidly but selfishly educated," she said; were not the most "hated, feared, caricatured" villains the class-conscious men who missed "the humanizing influences of the public schools?" In the next issue of the *Monthly* an anonymous teacher wrote an article defending the school bill, claiming that statistics in New York proved that parochial schools produced three to four times more criminals than the public schools. A high school principal ran as the unsuccessful Klan candidate for state superintendent of public instruction. A convention of 133 teachers in Columbia County voted to support the bill.[20]

The one-sided and distorted reactions of such educators to the school bill made plausible the view of some critics that compulsory public education would reinforce existing autocratic tendencies in the public schools. A mother wrote that the measure "will only serve to give certain officials more power, which power they have already abused. The parents have precious little to say about their children now. There are teachers, principals, and officials of all kind . . . so high and mighty that you feel like a serf at times." Another complained that state monopoloy would simply increase rigidity, require political orthodoxy, and stultify the curriculum. The level of debate in the campaign over the bill—what *The Survey* called "a childish outburst of anti-Jewish, and anti-Catholic, and anti-foreign bigotry" —raised a fundamental question about the quality of the education of the citizens of the state, wrote John Mecklin. Despite all the talk of "Americanism," the schools in Oregon were "after all a very mechanical affair. . . . These prospective citizens have not been schooled to the critical analysis of their intellectual heritage. So long as one is clever enough to clothe his propaganda in the familiar dress of . . . stereotypes he finds ready and uncritical acceptance.[21]

The Controversy Enters the Courts

Once the vote was over, on November 7, 1922, the post-mortems on the victory of the bill began, as did the immediate appeal to the courts. The vote was a political upset. The Portland *Oregonian* had reported before the election that betting odds were ten to seven for its defeat. But in the post-election analysis the newspaper claimed that the school bill had passed largely because of anti-Catholicism and the "invisible government" created by the Klan and the other secret societies, the school question being "the most upsetting factor in the history of Oregon since the agitation over slavery." "It was impossible for us to overcome the ruthless activities of the Masons, the minor lodges, the Ku Klux Klan, the Federated Patriotic Societies, the Royal Riders of the Red Robe, etc., etc.," wrote a member of the Lutheran Schools Committee.[22]

Immediately, representatives of church and private schools met to discuss how to test the law in the courts. "Since we have been defeated by a narrow margin, we feel that Oregon will have an ideal case to test out the constitutionality of such laws in the Supreme Court of the United States and thus through its defeat put itself in a position where it can be of service to our people in other states," wrote a Lutheran. "We are so confident of this that we look upon the defeat as a God-sent blessing in disguise." The National Catholic Welfare League and the Knights of Columbus raised funds for the legal battle, believing that the "educational welfare of the Catholics generally may hinge upon" the result of the decision. The American Civil Liberties Union offered to help.[23]

The Society of the Sisters of the Holy Names of Jesus and Mary and the Hill Military Academy both filed bills of complaint against Governor Pierce and his agents. The legal briefs on both sides dealt partly with procedural and technical legal matters. Lawyers argued about whether the suit was premature since the law would not take effect until 1926; what were the legal precedents for the state depriving businesses of their property rights; and when did state interference with patronage of a business become arbitrary. Both the initial injunction by the lower federal court against enforcing the statute and the U.S. Supreme Court decision in *Pierce* addressed such questions and found that the private schools had been deprived of their "property without due process of law" and with no compelling necessity that justified the use of the state's police power.[24]

But some of the arguments of the parties and the decisions went beyond the technical legal points to explore broader questions of public policy in education, and in so doing they revealed current thinking on the outer limits of majority rule and the scope of protection of minority rights. A lawyer for Governor Pierce argued that requiring parents to send their children to public schools was not an abridgement of their privileges and immunities and that the preservation of the state justified the action:[25]

> the great danger overshadowing all others which confront the American people is the danger of class hatred...don't know any better way to fortify the next generation against that insidious poison than to require that the poor and the rich, the people of all classes and distinction, and of all different religious beliefs, shall meet in the common schools, which are the great American melting pot, there to become ...the typical American of the future.

His colleagues added that the initiative had been passed by the will of the people, and that the government was "one in which majorities rule."

The attorneys for the schools denied such charges in their defense of the role of private education in American life and of the constitutional rights of parents. They did not contest the power of the state to compel school attendance or to set standards for schools. But no one had demonstrated that private schools were inefficient. The right to conduct and patronize private schools had long been recognized as natural and inherent, subject to violation by the police power of the state only in cases of compelling necessity. But the state had shown no such need, and on the contrary, its law would undertake "to have a monopoly of education, to put it in a straitjacket, by the fixing of unalterable standards and thereby to bring their people and their citizens to one common level...." The real danger to democracy came not from the children but from the secret societies like the KKK that sought "to defeat law and order." The claim that the public school mixed the rich and the poor was fraudulent. Children go to school where they live, and the rich typically do not live next to the poor. Pieties about democracy sounded hollow when they came from the very people who, in passing the school bill, created "more class hatred" than ever existed in the state and then used majority rule to compel parents to submit to their orthodoxies.[26]

After hearing such arguments, the three-man federal court found in favor of the plaintiffs on March 31, 1924. It declared that it could understand "the desire of the legislature to foster a homogeneous people with American ideals." But the court concluded that compelling parents to send their children only to public schools was a means of achieving homogeneity that exceeded "the limitations upon the power of the state" and conflicted with the plaintiff's property rights.[27]

As the *Pierce* case went on its way to the Supreme Court, the *Catholic Sentinel* was cautiously optimistic: "the plain implication of the decision is that freedom of education means freedom of education," it said, and "not a pale simulacrum of liberty as conceived by the Ku Klux Klan." The Klan thought otherwise. It continued with its battle to outlaw private education in the neighboring state of Washington and declared the decision a violation of human rights in the name of property rights. To them it was a self-evident American principle that "the first duty of a democracy is self-preservation of itself through enforced education of individuals." If the Supreme Court did not see the point, then it was time to change the Constitution.[28]

In the briefs to the Supreme Court the lawyers for Pierce elaborated their earlier arguments, claiming that private schools produced more than their share of paupers, vagabonds, delinquents, and subversives. "If the Oregon School Law is held to be unconstitutional," they argued, "it is not only a possibility but almost a certainty that within a few years the great centers of population in our country will be dotted with elementary schools which instead of being red on the outside will be red on the inside." Only "a compulsory system of public school education will encourage the patriotism of its citizens, and train its younger citizens to become more willing and more efficient defenders of the United States in times of danger."[29]

The lawyers for the plaintiffs took the offensive. The Oregon law had passed from democratic to totalitarian methods. "The young minds of the nation should not be cast in any such straight-jacket. . . . the excess of power which results to the state from such a device clearly serves to maintain and preserve despotism and checks the normal evolution of liberty," replied the brief for the Sisters. It mattered not whether tyranny was exerted by a majority or a minority; it was tyranny nonetheless. Like other forms of pluralism, religious diversity would disappear in education, to be replaced by "religion prescribed by the state and dictated from time to time by a majority of the 'voters of Oregon.' " In a supporting brief, Louis Marshall stated that more was at stake than the survival of a few private schools:[30]

> Fundamentally . . . the questions in these cases are: May liberty to teach and to learn be restricted? Shall such liberty be dependent upon the will of the majority? Shall the majority be permitted to dictate to parents and to children where and by whom instruction shall be given?

If such power can be asserted, then it will lead inevitably to stifling of thought.

When the Supreme Court rendered its verdict, it upheld the contention of the lower court that the private schools had been deprived of their property without due process of law and without a clear demonstration that an "emergency" existed that justified such an exercise of state power. It went on to assert that private schools were "engaged in an undertaking not inherently harmful, but long regarded as useful and meritorious." It further addressed the rights of parents in an eloquent passage often quoted for its defense of libertarian principles:[31]

> The fundamental theory of liberty upon which all governments in this Union repose excludes any general power of the state to standardize its children by forcing them to accept instruction from public teachers only. The child is not the mere creature of the state; those who nurture him and direct his destiny have the right, coupled with the high duty, to recognize and prepare him for additional obligations.

The Supreme Court thus protected the right of private schools to exist and the rights of parents to "direct the destiny" of their children. By upholding private choice in education the *Pierce* decision helped to define the outer limits of coercion.

But the court still left intact large portions of the police power of the state and the right of the majority to prescribe orthodoxy:[32]

> No question is raised concerning the power of the State reasonably to regulate all schools, to inspect, supervise, and examine them, their teachers and pupils; to require that all children of proper age attend some school, that teachers shall be of good moral character and patriotic disposition, that certain studies plainly essential to good citizenship must be taught, and that nothing be taught which is manifestly inimical to the public welfare.

Oregon laws requiring that instruction be only in English and censoring the content of history books remained valid, still falling well within what the lower court had referred to as an understandable American desire to "foster a homogeneous people."

The Supreme Court cited as precedent its earlier case *Meyer v. Nebraska,* which has sometimes been regarded as a charter of freedom in education. Like *Pierce, Meyer* also left large scope for the imposition of majority beliefs, however. Further to explore this question of majority rule and minority rights—raised so sharply in the

Oregon statute and the *Pierce* decision—we examine briefly how the Supreme Court dealt with statutes of other states outlawing the teaching of foreign languages and requiring flag salutes.

The *Meyer* case resulted from a Nebraska law forbidding the teaching of elementary pupils in any language other than English. The plaintiff was punished for teaching a ten-year-old boy to read German. The attorneys for the state of Nebraska used the familiar arguments of patriotism: that English should be "the language of the heart" of all Americans; that under the police power, the state could compel every parent "so to educate his children that the sunshine of American ideals will permeate the life of the future generation"; and that this right of the state "corresponds to the right of self-reservation of the individual." Lawyers defended Meyer by asserting that the statute denied him equal protection of the law when it denied him the exercise of a legitimate calling. The United States Supreme Court based its decision in *Meyer* primarily on that narrow ground—that it interfered with Meyer's job. The court recognized as valid "the desire of the legislature to foster a homogeneous people with American ideals" and did not contest its "power to prescribe a curriculum" or to demand that instruction be in English. Thus the court left large discretion to Americanize America.[33]

The first Supreme Court flag salute case, *Minersville v. Gobitis* (1940), coming fifteen years after *Pierce,* also indicated how firmly embedded was the assumption that the need for national unity transcended individual rights or diversity of beliefs. Jehovah's Witnesses objected to the flag salute on religious grounds, believing the flag to be a "graven image." In *Gobitis* the Supreme Court upheld several state court decisions that regarded refusal to salute the flag as punishable insubordination. The court admitted that the salute violated the religious convictions of parents and children, but it claimed that "the wisdom of training children by those compulsions which necessarily pervade so much of the educational process is not for our independent judgment . . . the courtroom is not the arena for debating issues of educational policy." *Gobitis* thus reflected decades of judicial nonintervention in compulsory civic socialization and other forms of curricular prescription.[34]

Only three years later, the decision in *West Virginia Board of Education v. Barnette* (1943) reversed *Gobitis* on the constitutionality of the compulsory flag salute. We have already quoted a key part of that ringing affirmation of First Amendment and minority rights: "if there is any fixed star in our constitutional constellation, it is that no official, high or petty, can prescribe what shall be orthodox in politics, nationalism, religion, or other matters of opinion or force citizens to confess by word or act their faith therein. If there are any circumstances which permit an exception, they do not now occur to us." The fixed stars of the majority of the citizens of Oregon in 1922 were different, and the questions of minority rights and majority rule have continued to vex public education in a nation in which many have still seen peril in pluralism.[35]

Barnette marked a departure from earlier cases that had defended the majority's right to use schools to "foster a homogeneous people." It also foreshadowed the later activist role of the U.S. Supreme Court in support of minority and individual rights. In the years following *Brown v. Board of Education* (1954) the Court, contrary to *Gobitis*, did indeed become an "arena for debating issues of educational policy." In our Epilogue we reflect on how the new uses of the law in its many forms compare with the past uses we have been exploring.

Epilogue

Nineteen-eighty-four marked the thirtieth anniversary of the landmark racial desegregation case *Brown v. Board of Education*, a major turning point in the use of law to shape public education. During those thirty years reformers used litigation, legislation, and administrative law to reconstruct public education. They sought to desegregate schools; to ban prayer and the ceremonial reading of the Bible; to combat sex bias; to enhance due process and freedom of expression for students and teachers; to improve schooling for the children of the poor and those with limited knowledge of English; to secure an adequate education for the handicapped; to equalize school finance; and even to defend male students who wanted to wear their hair long.[1]

Groups that had long felt powerless to influence the schools in their communities turned to the legal system for redress of wrongs. As Donald L. Horowitz observed, the desegregation decisions "created a magnetic field around the courts, attracting litigation in areas where judicial intervention had earlier seemed implausible." Changes in constitutional doctrine, a broadening of judicial jurisdiction, and the new activism of public interest lawyers and responsive judges made the courts an active forum for reform in education. Also in the 1960s and 1970s the Congress and federal agencies created statutes and administrative regulations that in tandem with judge-made law enhanced the rights of protest groups and advanced new remedies in response to their claims.[2]

Today there are many Americans—both among the general public and among educators and legal scholars—to whom the pre-*Brown* era represents a golden age of the proper use of law in education. To them the growth of reformist legislation, governmental regulation, and activist courts represents pathology. There has been too much intrusion of government into the classroom, they say, too many judges exceeding their proper zone of discretion and competence, too many citizens rushing to court to litigate matters best settled elsewhere, and too much factionalism and special interest in education legislation. Some people are nostalgic for the days when educators and school boards were left alone to run their schools.[3]

If one went back to the early 1950s, one would find less litigiousness than today, less prescriptive legislation concerning rights and programs, fewer and less complex federal and state regulations, and more deference by government officials and judges to educational leaders. One would also find legal segregation of the races, legal compulsory religious exercises in a multitude of school districts, legal sex-based discrimination, gross inequities in the funding of schools between districts and between rich and poor neighborhoods within districts, systematic favoring of middle-class and prosperous students in many districts, and pervasive lack of due process and violations of freedom of expression for both students and teachers. Education lawyers represented mostly the prosperous clients who could pay for their services. Judges largely took the role of neutral umpires adjudicating the disputes that the parties brought to the courts, using the traditional doctrines of common and public law to decide cases. Few basic issues of constitutional rights entered education law. It was a comfortable world for those who wanted to preserve the status quo, but it left untouched some of the most pressing questions of social justice in public education.[4]

In this brief epilogue we do not intend to examine in detail the doctrinal changes in education law since *Brown*, fascinating and important though they are. Rather, we wish to suggest how the new uses of law in education appear in broad outline from the perspective of the history we have explored thus far. Seen from this viewpoint, the character of educational legislation, regulation, and litigation since *Brown* has undergone a transformation. We recognize that much education law has continued to occupy itself with familiar topics like contracts, bonds, taxes, personnel decisions, and state policies on traditional matters like teacher credentials or standardization of curriculum. But here we focus on how law has become a major tool in the quest for social justice in education.[5]

There never was a lawless golden age of comity or depoliticized justice before education became "legalized." Groups have always used education law to carry out various political purposes, though not all types of conflicts have found legal expression (access to the political process and the courts has been restricted for many social groups). One gains greater leverage in understanding how law has operated to shape schools by looking at how various groups have used different kinds of law—constitutions, statutes, administrative regulations, and court cases, often in interaction with one another—to accomplish manifold purposes. We have suggested in this book that in public education

1. *Law has provided a forum for expressing, contesting, and legitimating broad social agreements.* It has been one means of defining the boundaries of common cultural beliefs. The political leaders who wrote and revised educational provisions of state constitutions, for example, were confident that they were expressing popular convictions about the link between common schools and republican government (however partial in fact was the consensus and incomplete the inclusiveness of the polity).

2. *Law has shaped the institutional structures of education.* State constitutions and statutes have built legal frameworks for the expansion of common schools, legislatures have mediated and courts have arbitrated conflicts in the governance and finance of education, and educational leaders operating as a powerful interest group have used legislation to standardize schools according to a professional model. Institution-building and law have operated in interactive fashion; changes in practice have also stimulated litigation and new constitutional and statutory provisions.

3. *Law has offered groups a political opportunity to assert or contest normative dominance.* Organizations claiming to be moral majorities have lobbied legislatures to impose their values on society through curricular legislation. On occasion, dissenters have challenged these laws in court. Law has also helped to shape what is compulsory in public education and what is not.

4. *Law has regulated the relations between majorities and minorities in public education.* In issues of religion and race, statutes and court cases typically have reaffirmed the power of dominant groups over outsiders. On rare occasions, law offered oppressed minorities avenues for redress of wrongs, as when blacks and their white allies sought to use law to remake a racist society during Reconstruction.

What is new in the post-*Brown* era is not the activity of pressure groups in shaping educational legislation and litigation but rather the greatly increased volume of education law, the new types of issues raised and constitutional doctrines employed to decide cases, the scope of education jurisprudence, and the activism of outsiders formerly excluded from political and legal action. In the past, reformers often sought to bring about educational change by rewriting state constitutions, to create in effect a new social compact concerning public schools. Activist lawyers and judges in the post-*Brown* era sought instead to reconstruct the constitutional doctrine by which existing constitutions—both federal and state—were interpreted. Courts have shown a new willingness to redress the claims of minorities, while reformers have passed statutes that gave them new remedies at law. The past thirty years has been a period of unprecedented turmoil in education law and in the schools. Activists have sought to use the legal system to right old wrongs, sometimes appealing to the egalitarian consensual values that Gunnar Myrdal called the American creed and sometimes developing new value claims.[6]

As the Appendix shows, there has been a marked rise in educational litigation in the 1960s and 1970s, the total number of cases nearly doubling from 1957–66 to 1967–76 and the rate per million population rising from 2.93 to 5.09. This increase marks education as part of what Lawrence Friedman calls a "selective explosion" of litigation. We estimate that federal education cases jumped sharply from 112 in the decade 1947–56 to 729 in 1957–66 to 3,486 in 1967–76, rising from 0.07 per million population to 1.9.[7]

There have also been shifts in the character of cases. The traditionally dominant categories of funding and governance have declined as a proportion of the total cases in the last three decades. The ratio of cases dealing with teachers jumped from 17 percent in 1957–66 to 29 percent in 1967–76 to 45 percent in 1977–81, reflecting in part the rise of teacher militancy and collective bargaining, legal questions raised by layoffs during school retrenchment, and the increased funding of the legal arms of teachers organizations (see table A-2 in the Appendix). Segregation cases mushroomed from a previous high of 151 in 1957–67 to 1,457 in the decade 1967–76, when litigation based on constitutional cases and civil rights legislation flourished. Pupil discipline cases jumped from 46 in 1957–66 to 601 in 1967–76. Cases involving student rights jumped from 0.8 of appellate decisions in 1959–68 to 3.6 in 1969–78 as students challenged the discretion of school administrators and made federal cases of such matters as dress codes, hair length, and rights of free expression (75 percent of these cases were decided in federal courts). The education of the handicapped and the question of sports eligibility also became important legal issues in the past decade. In California, five-eighths of all individual rights cases in education ever decided by the state Supreme Court appeared after 1960.[8]

While old issues such as religion, language policy, and school finance commanded attention in novel ways, relatively new issues emerged such as sex equity, rights of privacy and expression for students, due process in suspension of pupils, and scrutiny of the classification and treatment of handicapped children. Many of these cases were class action suits and thus went well beyond the individual litigants in their impact. These issues of civil rights, individual liberties, and entitlements increasingly entered the courts because of rapid changes in constitutional doctrine in education law. Legal scholars reinterpreted traditional jurisprudence. Lawyers and judges construed the First Amendment in new ways in cases involving religion and free expression in the schools, and they invoked the equal protection and due process clauses of the Fourteenth Amendment to address questions previously thought to be outside the ambit of education law.[9]

It would be simplistic to see the upsurge in education litigation and the changes in legal doctrine as just the products of activist lawyers and judges working in a political or social vacuum. An important impetus to reform in education law came from social movements determined to correct social wrongs. Members of protest organizations often found local elites unresponsive to their demands, not surprisingly since such elites had often been the agents and beneficiaries of injustice in the first place. The dissenters turned to outside agencies for redress: the federal courts, the federal Congress or administration, and liberal allies in the churches, the foundations, and national voluntary groups. The *Brown* decision itself was the product of decades of hard work, personal sacrifice, and carefully honed strategy on the part of the NAACP and countless blacks in local communities. It foreshadowed a rise in education cases in states—especially in the South—where the courts had formerly buttressed inequality.[10]

In the 1960s and early 1970s one social movement after another—women, Hispanics, the handicapped, Native Americans—mobilized political support for educational reform, inspired by the successes of blacks in the civil rights movement. For a time it seemed that better schooling was the door to progress and that law offered the key to the

door. Reformers went to court armed with new constitutional doctrines and found many judges alert to civil and individual rights and
to governmental neglect or abuse. Courts offered reformers an end
run around unresponsive state legislatures or school boards, for example
in securing more equitable funding of schooling within districts or
between districts where the tax bases were grossly uneven.[11]

Reformers also fought for federal (and in some cases state) statutes
and regulations on civil rights, bilingual education, special education, multicultural curriculum, funding for poor children, and sex
equity. Such statutes and administrative law, representing a new aware-
ness of issues of social justice on the part of elected officials, worked
in tandem with educational litigation. New doctrines of educational
equality gave rationales for new legislation, while legislation gave
protest groups new standing in court. Public interest lawyers, funded
in part by the federal government and by foundations, used class
action suits to represent groups that had formerly been outsiders in
education law.[12]

In the past, courts often put the brake on social reforms enacted by
legislatures, as in the case of child labor laws during the Progressive
period. Conservatives turned to the courts to strike down legislation
they did not like. In recent years, however, in response to protest
groups, courts have often led the other branches of government in
calling attention to social wrongs and devising remedies for them.
Commentators have differed sharply in their evaluation of judicial
reform of public education. Some have seen activist lawyers and
responsive judges as heroes of social justice, seeking to correct problems long ignored by legislatures and school boards and educators.
Others have regarded the rush of education cases as evidence of the
pathology of a litigious society and have condemned an "imperial
judiciary" for exceeding its proper scope in trying to usurp the role of
political bodies in educational policy.[13]

Some observers favorable to the desired outcomes of judicial
intervention—who agree, for example, on the need for desegregation
or for equitable school finance or for meeting the linguistic needs of
immigrant children—argue that the nature of the legal system and
the indeterminate character of education do pose problems in achieving reform through litigation. It is one matter for judges to prohibit a
practice on constitutional grounds. Forbidding action on the part of
government has a long constitutional history, although implementing

court orders may be difficult, as in the case of the Bible and prayer decisions. But critics of judicial activism claim that it is more complicated—and arguably not within the expertise or time available to most judges—to devise remedies to wrongs that involve the courts in actually restructuring how schools run. As Horowitz notes, adjudication deals with particular rights and duties in focused cases; it is piecemeal, depending as it does on the timing and character of the cases brought to the court; and it requires a decision even where the social facts are much in dispute. But many questions of educational policy require weighing competing needs—how much to increase school funding for the handicapped versus targeting dollars to the poor, for example—that is hard to do within the bounds of a court case but that is normal in the give-and-take of legislative law-making. Other governmental bodies—administrative branches and legislatures —often have far larger resources to investigate, weigh alternatives, and follow through on compliance. But lest one conclude that legislatures, school boards, or administrative agencies are preferable to judges in educational reform, it is important to recall that judges became involved in correcting inequities because protest groups found other branches of government unresponsive to their needs. Even if courts have some limitations in settling questions of educational policy, they have been essential in correcting educational injustice, especially in insisting on finding remedies for classes of litigants.[14]

Courts have not worked in isolation from other law-shaping bodies. David Kirp has argued that "the primary effect of judicial involvement in defining equal educational opportunity may well lie not in court-defined resolution of these questions, but more nebulously in the judicial impetus for an essentially political solution, with courts affording new legitimacy to particular equity-based concerns." In practice court decisions and legislation have often operated interactively to secure changes in educational policies and practices. Many aggrieved groups, such as the handicapped, women, and language minorities, have won more pervasive reform though favorable statutes and regulations than through litigation. And in recent years, especially in the more conservative judicial climate since the Supreme Court rejected a constitutional "right to education" in the school finance case *Rodriguez*, judges have often preferred to base decisions on statutory law rather than on constitutional doctrine.[15]

In the initial phases of both litigation and legislation reformers and their allies mostly shared a traditional faith in the power of education to right social wrongs. They insisted that outsiders be included in the educational system on equal terms. They questioned not the common school but exclusion of some people from its full benefits. Many early protest leaders shared an integrationist dream of equal access to public schools as one of the mainstream institutions of American civic, economic, and social life. Blacks demanded entry into white schools, feminists sought access for girls into separate boys' schools and segregated programs in vocational education and sports, advocates sought to serve the handicapped in the "least restrictive environment" of regular classrooms, and reformers wanted sufficient added resources to enable the children of the poor to participate equitably in the academic mainstream. Universalistic legal principles of equal protection fit such demands well, and some of the language of court cases and statutory rationales echoed claims that might well have been heard in state constitutional conventions of the nineteenth century. In this sense, social movements collaborated with legal allies to assure through litigation, statutes, and favorable administrative regulations that the old republican case for universal schooling would include them as well.[16]

But some leaders of social movements began to question these universalistic, liberal values of integration into a majoritarian mainstream. They came to advocate various forms of separatism and pluralism. They did not dispute the *right* of individuals in their group to participate on equal terms in the public educational system; to do so would have been to deny their status as full citizens. But they questioned the *realism* or *wisdom* of the assimilationist dream of amalgamation of all people as individuals in a "great community" that shared similar notions of the common good. Enforced segregation was abhorrent, but voluntary separatism was different. It enabled the group to consolidate and perpetuate its values and to gain new power. The desire for separatism also reflected distrust of those who had held power and suspicion about the "consensus" they might foster. Thus some blacks called for community control and curricula to create black pride; some Hispanics sought to maintain their language and culture through special classes; and some feminists argued that females might require some degree of separatism to enhance and develop a new consciousness and common purpose. There were ample precedents in public education for this type of pluralistic response, for blacks had for a century debated the virtues of separate schools run by blacks, in the nineteenth century immigrant groups had bargained successfully to retain their languages in public schools, and women had long argued the claims of single-sex schools.[17]

Such group consciousness and group demands, however, posed tricky legal questions largely unanswered by both the old and the new education jurisprudence. It was a clear principle to assert that no *individual* should be denied educational opportunities because of race, religion, national origin, or sex—this fit both universalistic legal doctrine and liberal republican doctrine. This view of equality maintained that all individuals, whatever their "minority" status, had a right to join the "majority," that is, had all the rights of American citizens. But could *groups* command from the state special entitlements, legal standing, or rights denied to non-members, and if so, which groups? Because of the separation of church and state, religious groups like the Amish could make certain claims not so readily accorded to others. Because of the history of oppression of blacks, their rights deserved special constitutional protection. But the legal implications of other group memberships—of gender, ethnicity, and economic class, for example—were less clear. Just when one set of issues concerning the rights of individuals seemed settled in legal doctrine if not in practice, the new politics of pluralism introduced new complexities in education law: what principles should govern relations between the state and social groups?[18]

Changes in education law not only altered the rights and entitlements of different groups, thereby producing changes in power between them, but also gave some previously potent groups the perception that they had become, for the first time, outsiders. The Oregonians who had voted for the compulsory public education bill in 1922 would have understood their outrage. Many evangelical Protestants, long accustomed to seeing the common school as in some sense their creation and a bastion of their values, regarded the Bible and prayer decisions of the Supreme Court as a betrayal of that tradition. Predictably from the long history of "nonsectarian" religious teaching in the schools, conservative groups angrily protested the Bible and prayer decisions of the Supreme Court, while sympathetic politicians vowed to pass a constitutional amendment permitting prayer in public schools.[19]

Conservative protest movements arose to combat other legal changes as well. In the aftermath of *Brown*, Southerners organized massive

resistance to desegregation, and when the campaign against segregation spread to the North, bitter opposition developed there as well. A
powerful backlash hit bilingual instruction programs. Groups of self-
appointed censors attacked books and courses that treated questions
of race, sex, patriotism, or religion in unfamiliar and, to them, abhorrent ways. Tax-cutting lobbies undermined attempts to equalize school
finance. Conservatives in Congress countered the feminist campaign
against sex bias by proposing a Family Protection Act that would
have reinforced traditional gender roles. Certain segments of a once
confident WASP majority now found themselves on the defensive, and
many decided to leave the public schools for private institutions like
the fast-growing Christian day schools, where they could continue the
religious practices they had once imposed by law on public education.[20]

For their part, school officials have had mixed reactions to the new
legal activism. They have been bothered by the decline in judicial
deference toward the traditional authority of school administrators
to deal with students—for example in discipline or suspension cases
or cases involving reins on free expression. Yet despite accusations
that students were becoming precocious lawyers, there was no cloud-
burst of litigation on such issues. In 1979–80, for example, there were
only 16 appellate cases involving due process in suspension of students, only a few more than on athletic eligibility. But school officials
felt that they were acting in the "shadow of the law" and were losing
autonomy. They have also protested the flood of paperwork associated
with mandated programs and the increase of regulations affecting
their everyday work. Accustomed to dealing with local elites in the
1950s, school superintendents found themselves confronted in the
1960s by angry minorities and other alienated groups who took to the
courts to gain equality.[21]

New court decisions, civil rights legislation, and federal and state
regulations seemed to complicate school administrators' lives at the
very time that they were being asked to do their regular work of
instruction more efficiently. The legalization of schooling from above
by centralized authority seemed to introduce *disorder*, not order, into
the everyday work of local school people, an irony John Meyer has
noted. A common response of educators to new legal mandates has
been, deliberately or not, to remain ignorant of their demands, as
surveys of the legal knowledge of school people have demonstrated.

Selective attention has been another common strategy. The force of institutional inertia has been powerful.[22]

Despite resistance to new forms of legalization of education, educators have been historically committed to certain visions of equality. In the nineteenth century school people conceived of equality as free and open access to public schools; in some places, of course, groups like blacks or Asians were excluded. Reformers during the Progressive era added a new and complicated dimension—equality of opportunity. They believed in compulsory attendance in a school system that was differentiated according to the abilities of students and the needs of society. In theory, what equality of opportunity meant in such a system was the chance to develop one's talents to the utmost. The administrative progressives believed that there were great differences between individuals—and between groups—and that educational experts were best qualified to determine what opportunities were most appropriate for students. In practice, their negative beliefs about the abilities of low-status groups often constricted the operational meaning of educational opportunity, while their ethnocentrism gave short shrift to the dignity of non-WASP groups.[23]

Many of the court decisions and legislative reforms of the last generation can be understood as an attempt to broaden these traditional concepts of equality of access and equality of opportunity by making them real for excluded groups. By and large, educators shared this liberalization of the goal of equal schooling; to have done otherwise would have seemed to deny their own best ethical traditions as a profession.[24]

The history of law in the last generation has thus been one of transformation but with some elements of ideological and institutional continuity. Protest groups have demanded attention to their claims. Older notions of WASP supremacy been challenged by a new pluralism of values in which equality of dignity has been a goal of excluded groups. The insulated management of school systems by professional experts—the ideal of a one best system championed by reformers early in the twentieth century—has lately been eroded both by lay groups wanting to participate in decision-making and by the regulations promulgated by federal and state governments. Amid the justified clamor for social justice by some groups and opposition to their demands by others, older conceptions of public education as a common good have been obscured. The strains on the public schools have been formidable as people have struggled with the creative tension between common purpose and respect for diversity, majority rule and minority rights. Seen in historical perspective, the conflicts of the last thirty years show how law has been employed to remedy injustices condoned or even created by the use of law in the past.

APPENDIX

NOTES

INDEX

APPENDIX

Introduction

This appendix seeks to familiarize the reader with how we estimated the volume, character, and long-term changes in educational litigation in federal and state appellate courts since the early nineteenth century. We discuss the sources and procedures used to count education-related court cases in different historical periods, evidence which is formally incorporated in the tables in chapter 2 and 4. This appendix also reports a number of new tables which present a more continuous picture of changes in educational litigation over the past 170 years.

The use of court caseload statistics and litigation rates to analyze the business and demands placed upon the courts is a significant recent development in the fields of political and legal history. Early work examining court caseloads over time concentrated on the federal court system, primarily because data on case filings and decisions were more readily available. For instance, there is an extensive literature which looks at the factors associated with changing caseloads in the Supreme Court, the U.S. Courts of Appeals and Federal district courts.[1] Studies of the federal court system, however, paint only a partial picture of litigiousness in American society. The vast majority of litigation occurs in state trial and appellate courts, estimated recently to be the initial address of over 95 percent of all court cases filed in the United States.[2]

Research on the patterns of litigation in state courts employs a variety of sources and methods to estimate the number of cases filed, decided, or delayed. One important primary source is the actual records of the court. Studies of lower level courts —such as those reported by McIntosh, Friedman and Percival, and Young and Company—have assembled data by using existing tabulations of court cases made by court officials, by actually counting case filings or decisions from court records, or by employing some sampling procedure to estimate overall litigation. These studies provide a detailed report of the business of selected local courts over an extended historical period.[3]

In order to compare caseloads and litigation rates across states, researchers have turned to secondary data sources. For example, a comprehensive study by Kagan, Cartwright, Friedman, and Wheeler of 16 state supreme courts sampled published opinions in Shepard's Citations to estimate the number and type of legal disputes between 1870 and 1970. Marvell reported annual, though not always complete, statistics for the number of cases decided in 27 state appellate courts by examining annual reports of judicial councils, state court administrators, and law review articles, some beginning as early as 1860.[4]

The level and specificity of statistics concerning case filings or decisions obviously limits the questions one can address. Particulars concerning the litigants, the disputes at issue, and the length and course of the trial demand quite detailed data bases. Comparative and longitudinal analysis of trends in caseload statistics across states or for the nation as a whole—as well as the factors affecting those changes— requires a more general data base. In this initial foray into the world of educational litigation, we gathered statistics of the latter type, statistics which allow us to gauge long-term historical changes in the development of school law both for the country as a whole and for different regions.

The most comprehensive source from which one can compile longitudinal data on educational cases is the series of historical digests issued by the West Publishing Company, references that legal researchers have used for almost a century. These digests record and classify cases litigated in all appellate courts, both state and federal, beginning in the early nineteenth century and continuing until the present day. In 1887 the West Publishing Company began issuing the yearly American Digest System which gave brief synopses of all reported appellate cases. In the ensuing years its staff of lawyers-editors prepared the monumental *Century Digest*, published in 1897, which West described as "a complete and definitive digest of all American case-law from the establishment of government down to 1896" and which classified over a half million appellate cases in an elaborate classification scheme spanning fifty volumes. For the next and each subsequent ten-year interval, West published successive decennial editions based on slightly modified versions of the original classification scheme.[5]

In this research we focus on cases classified under the topic of "Schools and School Districts." This rubric includes all cases concerning elementary and high schools and excludes cases dealing with universities and colleges. Under the school law heading nine major legal categories and 78 subcategories are listed (see table A-1). The issues covered in these categories range from the establishment of school lands, school funds, and school districts to busing, the discharge of teachers, and the classification of pupils. A particular virtue of the West digests is the relative consistency over time in the taxonomy of cases. Although there were some changes within the categories the digesters used—the subdivisions became more elaborate in later years, for example—the basic classification of the cases remained the same. This permits relatively precise comparisons within most major and many minor categories over a long historical period.

As we mentioned in the text, however, one must be cautious in using the digests to estimate the volume and character of educational litigation. One problem is the selectivity of reported appellate decisions. It is difficult to generalize about the character or number of lower court cases from reported appellate court decisions. Because of different legal structures, the ability and propensity of citizens, school officials, and teachers to appeal losing cases are likely to vary substantially by state. In some areas of school law—compulsory education, for example—lower court litigation seldom resulted in appeals, whereas in other areas such as racial discrimination, appeals were more frequently initiated.[6]

Another problem inheres in the legal categories themselves. For social historians interested in the social context of educational litigation, the taxonomy used in the West digests sometimes obscures more than it reveals. Vital issues like religion and race may be placed under unlikely umbrellas. From the first decennial (1897–1906) through the seventh decennial (1957–66) the topic of "Separate schools for colored pupils," for example, was placed under the rubric "Establishment, School Lands and Funds, and Regulation in General." In retrospect, it is clear that legal categories are neither time-free nor ethically neutral. Such classifications do illuminate, how-

TABLE A-1

List of the Major Legal Categories and Subcategories under the Topic of 'Schools and School Districts' in the First Decennial of the American Digest System

1. Private Schools and Academies

Cases Concerning Public Schools:

2. Establishment, School Lands and Funds, and Regulation in General
   A. Power to establish and maintain in general
   B. Constitutional and statutory provisions
   C. School system, and establishment or discontinuance of schools
   D. Application of school system to cities and incorporated towns and villages
   E. Separate schools for colored pupils
   F. State and county educational institutions
   G. Application to school purposes of school lands and proceeds thereof
   H. School funds
   I. Regulation and supervision of schools and educational institutions in general

3. Creation and Alteration of School Districts
   A. Nature and status as corporations
   B. Constitutional and statutory provisions
   C. Creation and organization
   D. De facto districts
   E. Unorganized territory
   F. Territorial extent and boundaries
   G. Alteration and creation of new districts
   H. Formation of districts and annexation and detachment of territory for school purposes
   I. Enumeration of children for school purposes
   J. Dissolution

4. Government, Officers, and District Meetings
   A. Administration of school affairs in general
   B. Constitutional and statutory provisions
   C. State boards and officers
   D. County boards and officers
   E. Officers of towns as school officers
   F. District meetings in general
   G. District boards
   H. District and local officers

TABLE A-1 (continued)

5. District Property, Contracts, and Liabilities
   A. Capacity to acquire and hold property
   B. Acquisition, use, and disposition of property
   C. School buildings
   D. School furniture, books, apparatus, and other appliances
   E. School libraries
   F. Contracts
   G. District expenses and charges
   H. Liabilities specially imposed by statute

6. District Debt, Securities, and Taxation
   A. Power to incur indebtedness and expenditures
   B. Constitutional and statutory provisions
   C. Administration of finances in general
   D. Appropriations
   E. Payment of indebtedness
   F. Warrants, orders, and certificates of indebtedness
   G. Bills and notes
   H. Bonds
   I. School taxes
   J. Assessments and special taxes for particular purposes
   K. Disposition of proceeds of taxes and other revenue
   M. Rights and remedies for taxpayers

7. Claims Against District and Actions
   A. Presentation and allowance of claims
   B. Actions by or against district

8. Teachers
   A. Eligibility in general
   B. Teachers' institutes
   C. Certificate or license
   D. Selection, appointment, and term of employment
   E. Contracts of employment
   F. Resignation or abandonment
   G. Suspension, removal, and reassignment
   H. Compensation
   I. Pensions
   J. Duties and liabilities

TABLE A-1 (continued)

9. Pupils, and Conduct and Discipline of Schools
   A. Nature of right to instruction in general
   B. Aid to indigent children
   C. Eligibility
   D. Proceedings to compel admission
   E. Health regulations
   F. Payment for tuition
   G. Transportation of pupils to and from schools
   H. Compulsory attendance
   I. Truants and truant officers and schools
   J. School terms, vacations, and holidays
   K. Grades or classes and departments
   L. Curriculum and courses of study
   M. Religious instruction and reading of Scriptures
   N. Textbooks
   O. Control of pupils and discipline
   P. Rules and regulations
   Q. Violations of rules and other offenses by pupils
   R. Punishment

ever, how important social questions were translated into lawyerly thinking since it is likely that the original West lawyer-editors sought to mirror existing ways of thinking among their peers. Historians and legal scholars may now wish to reclassify cases to match their own purposes—we find this essential in our own work—but the dominant taxonomy is itself an influence on the development of law.

Estimating the Volume and Character of Educational Litigation

We sought four types of evidence from the West digests: 1) the total number of cases litigated within a specified time interval; 2) the proportion of cases litigated in state courts and federal courts; 3) the distribution of cases in different areas of school law as defined by the West digestors (i.e., the nine major legal categories listed in table A-1); and 4) the number of cases dealing with specific social and educational issues such as the consolidation of school districts, teacher tenure, race, busing, and religion.

For the nineteenth century, we counted all cases reported in the *Century Digest* to calculate both the total number of appellate educational cases in a specified time interval (objective 1) and the number of cases of a particular type (objective 4). For the twentieth century, we employed a random sampling procedure (see below) to estimate the total number of educational cases (objective 1) and the number of cases in different areas of school law (objective 3). Finally, to derive the proportion of cases litigated in state and federal courts (objective 2), we independently calculated the number of federal educational cases from supplemental digests which treat only federal court cases and subtracted these figures from the total number of cases. Let us explain this series of procedures in greater detail.

We mentioned in the text one problem concerning the inaccurate number of cases listed in the last ten-year interval of the nineteenth century (1887–96). Although the *Century Digest*—published in 1897—intended to cover all cases up to and including the year 1896, publication deadlines forced it to underreport the number of cases litigated in 1895 and 1896. Consequently, many cases actually decided in those years are only reported in the first decennial edition (1897–1906). This means that the figures we report for the 1887–96 period are lower than they should be and those for the 1897–1906 period higher.

For the twentieth century we used a random sampling procedure to estimate the rapidly growing volume of cases—for example, between 1897 and 1906 American courts "rendered nearly half as many decisions as had been rendered in the 238 years preceeding."[7] For each decennial digest and for each of the nine major legal categories in the school law section, we took a random sample of at least 30 percent of the pages in the category and computed an average for the number of cases reported on each page. Then we multiplied the average number of entries per page by the number of pages of each legal category to derive the total number of cases falling within that legal category. This basic information enabled us to construct table 2.5 and its more comprehensive sequel, table A-2.

By summing the number of cases across all nine categories we deduced the total volume of court cases within a ten-year interval. We then proceeded to estimate the number of cases decided in state and federal courts. We began by independently counting federal educational cases reported in two other sources: the *Federal Digest* (covering the 1820–1939 period) and the *Federal Practice Digest* (covering the 1940–59 period) under the topic of "Schools." These counts were supplemented with estimates of the number of federal education cases decided between 1947–84 as reported by John Hogan in his book, *The Schools, The Courts and the Public Interest*. Once we had separate figures for the total number of education cases and for the number of cases decided in federal courts in each ten-year interval, we computed the number of cases litigated in state courts.[8]

We estimated the average rate of litigation in each ten-year interval by dividing each count of educational cases by the mean population during that period using population figures from the U.S. Statistical Abstract of 1984. We estimated mean population figures by summing population figures for the first and last years of the interval and dividing by two. The population figure used in the "Before 1836" interval is from the year 1830. Estimates for the most recent ten-year interval (1977–86) were found by multiplying the number of cases reported by Hogan for the 1977–84 period by 1.25 and dividing by the U.S. population in 1981. These estimates for the total volume of cases and for average rates of litigation provided the data for tables 2.4 and A-3 as well as figure 4.1.

In all the tables noted thus far, there is one basic problem that needs to be addressed. Because West editors cross-referenced some educational cases in more than one sub-category of the school law section, we are certain that our estimates of the number of educational cases are somewhat inflated. To address this problem we first cross-checked all cases decided in the 1870–1900 period and discovered that our figures over-estimated the number of actual cases by about 15 percent. It also came to our

TABLE A-2

Percent Distribution of Appellate Cases in School Law by Major Legal Categories for the Nineteenth Century and for Ten-Year Intervals in the Twentieth Century (1810–1981)[a]

	1810–1896	1897–1906	1907–1916	1917–1926	1927–1936	1937–1946	1947–1956	1957–1966	1967–1976	1977–1981
1. Cases Concerning Private Schools	2.0	1.1	1.0	0.8	0.7	0.7	1.5	1.3	3.3	1.9
Public School Cases:										
2. Establishment & Regulation of School Lands & Funds	7.0	8.2	6.1	3.7	5.4	4.4	6.3	7.6	17.8	14.1
3. Creation, Alteration, & Dissolution of School Districts	15.2	14.6	20.5	27.7	18.9	11.6	22.0	21.0	7.3	2.4
4. Government, Officers, and District Meetings	19.4	14.5	12.8	9.9	12.8	11.0	11.1	13.1	9.9	10.2
5. District Property, Contracts, and Liabilities	10.8	12.9	14.0	14.2	15.5	14.1	11.0	13.0	7.3	6.7
6. District Debt, Securities, and Taxation	23.8	23.4	25.5	26.4	25.2	25.5	19.7	12.0	6.3	4.4
7. Claims and Actions against School Districts	3.9	2.7	2.2	1.8	2.4	4.2	3.8	4.3	2.7	4.7

TABLE A-2 (continued)

	1810–1896	1897–1906	1907–1916	1917–1926	1927–1936	1937–1946	1947–1956	1957–1966	1967–1976	1977–1981
8. Teachers: Employment, Tenure, Discharge & Compensation	11.8	15.1	10.8	8.3	13.6	23.2	20.3	17.2	29.3	44.6
9. Pupils, Conduct, & Discipline of Schools	6.0	7.5	7.1	7.2	5.5	5.2	4.4	10.4	16.1	11.1
Totals	99.9	100.0	100.0	100.0	100.0	99.9	100.1	99.9	100.0	100.1
Estimated Number of Cases	(3,286)	(2,496)	(1,905)	(3,343)	(4,889)	(4,832)	(4,638)	(5,330)	(10,503)	(9,550)

ªBecause percentages were rounded off to the nearest tenth, not all columns summed to 100 percent.

attention that not all appeals of education-related cases were referenced under the topic "Schools and School Districts." So for the same 1870–1900 period we looked under other major topics of the West digests—constitutional law, for example—to discover how many additional cases involving schools or school districts had for whatever reason not been referenced under the school law category. This exercise resulted in our isolating a small number of cases, approximately 10 percent of the total, not cited in the "Schools and School District" category and meant that our original estimates slightly undercounting the actual volume of education-related cases. These two findings lead us to conclude that our figures for the total number of educational cases, while slightly on the high side, are probably quite close to the actual number of educational cases litigated during each interval.

Despite the caution needed in using this kind of evidence, we are convinced that historical patterns which emerge from the educational cases reported in the West digests provide a significant map of the nature and volume of educational litigation. They provide a valuable perspective on school law from which to raise new questions and puzzles. Certain social and educational conflicts and disputes found their way into the court system, and others did not, and that is an issue we have found worth pursuing. The volume and types of cases in school law changed over time, and those transitions clearly call for historical interpretation.

TABLE A-3

Volume of Educational Cases and Litigation Rates in State Appellate and Federal Courts during the Nineteenth and Twentieth Centuries Estimated in Ten-Year Intervals

| TEN-YEAR INTERVAL | *Estimated Volume of Educational Cases Litigated in Each Court System* | | | *Average Annual Rate of Educational Litigation per Million Population* | | |
	STATE APPELLATE	FEDERAL	TOTAL	STATE APPELLATE	FEDERAL	TOTAL
Before 1836	112	0	112	.83	.000	.83
1837–46	187	0	187	1.03	.000	1.03
1847–56	263	1	264	1.07	.004	1.07
1857–66	365	2	367	1.13	.006	1.14
1867–76	518	3	521	1.25	.007	1.26
1877–86	787	12	799	1.51	.021	1.53
1887–96	1.020	16	1,036	1.58	.025	1.61
1897–1906	2,481	15	2,496	3.18	.019	3.20
1907–16	1,883	22	1,905	2.01	.023	2.03
1917–26	3,299	44	3,343	3.01	.040	3.05
1927–36	4,822	67	4,889	3.93	.055	3.98
1937–46	4,743	89	4,832	3.53	.066	3.60
1947–56	4,526	112	4,638	2.93	.073	3.00
1957–66	4,601	729	5,330	2.53	.402	2.93
1967–76	7,017	3,486	10,503	3.15	1.936	5.09
1977–86 (est.)	(6,945)	(2,605)	(9,550)	(3.02)	(1.130)	(4.15)

SOURCES AND NOTES: See text of Appendix.

TABLE A-4

Distribution of Federal Education Cases by Substantive Legal Issues and by Historical Periods (1850–1955)

	1850–1899	1900–1919	1920–1939	1940–1955	TOTALS	PERCENT OF TOTAL
1. Constitutional Law/ Civil Rights/Equal Protection	3	0	11	15	29	13.3
2. Race—Separate Schools	1	1	0	6	8	3.7
3. School Lands/ School Funds	6	0	3	6	15	6.9
4. District Creation and Alteration	1	3	3	1	8	3.7
5. Board Meetings/ Officers	1	0	3	2	6	2.8
6. District Property/ Contracts	2	2	17	10	31	14.2
7. Debts/ Liabilities	3	2	6	5	16	7.3
8. Bonds	12	3	15	3	33	15.1
9. Taxes	7	3	5	12	27	12.4
10. Claims against Districts	1	1	2	1	5	2.3
11. Teachers: Tenure, Discharge	1	0	3	10	14	6.4
12. Transportation of Pupils	0	0	1	5	6	2.8
13. Compulsory Attendance	0	0	3	0	3	1.4
14. Curriculum/Religion	0	0	2	3	5	2.3
15. Textbooks	1	0	6	0	7	3.2
16. Rules & Regulations/Health	0	0	2	2	4	1.8
17. Eligibility	0	0	1	0	1	0.5
Totals	39	15	83	81	218	100.1

TABLE A-5
**Percent Distribution of Federal Education Cases by Type of Plaintiff
and Defendant (1850–1955)**

	PLAINTIFFS	DEFENDANTS
Individual: Business Representative	5.5	2.8
Individual: Citizen, Taxpayer	22.5	3.7
School Official	—	5.0
School District Board	9.6	57.8
City, County Board of Education	0.5	11.0
Company, Corporation	26.1	11.0
Class Action	10.1	—
State or State Official	1.4	3.7
Teacher	5.5	0.9
Multiple Parties	3.2	2.3
P.T.A.	—	0.5
Private School Official	0.5	—
Relator	0.9	—
Township	0.9	—
Black—"Negro"	7.8	—
Trustee in Bankruptcy	0.9	—
Non-Profit Organization	1.4	—
U.S. Government	3.2	0.9
Totals	100.0	99.6

SOURCE: *Federal Digest* and *Federal Practice Digest;* see text of Appendix.

TABLE A-6

Estimated Number of Appellate Cases Involving Issues of Race, Language, Ethnicity, and Religion (1810–1981)[a]

(Litigation rates per million population in parentheses)

	1810–1896	1897–1906	1907–1916	1917–1926	1927–1936	1937–1946	1947–1956	1957–1966	1967–1976	1977–1981
Ethnicity/Language										
1. Curriculum and Courses of Study (e.g., bilingual education)	3	1	0	3	0	0	1	0	6	5
	([a])	([a])	([a])	(.03)	([a])	([a])	([a])	([a])	(.03)	(.04)
Religion										
2. Religious Instruction/ Prayer	13	10	3	5	3	5	10	16	6	15
	(.05)	(.13)	(.03)	(.05)	(.02)	(.04)	(.06)	(.09)	(.03)	(.07)
Race										
3. Separate Schools for "Colored" Pupils; Desegregation	13	9	8	5	13	7	21	151	*1,457*	*644*
	(.05)	(.12)	(.09)	(.05)	(.11)	(.05)	(.14)	(.83)	(7.05)	(5.60)
4. Race or Color; Separate Taxation	47	11	11	11	7	4	3	28	6	0
	(.19)	(.14)	(.12)	(.10)	(.06)	(.03)	(.02)	(.15)	(.03)	([a])

[a]Rates less than .01 are not reported. Italicized figures are estimates of cases based upon a 30 percent sample of entries per page in the sub-category. Sources: West's Century Digest (1897) and the 1st through 9th decennial Digests. Peterson (1935) reports 42 separate taxation cases between 1870 and 1934 which were not reported in the West decennial digests; these are included in category #4.

NOTES

Introduction

1 W. H. Auden, "Law, Say the Gardeners, Is the Sun," in *Another Time* (New York, 1940), 5. Copyright 1940 and renewed 1968, W. H. Auden. Reprinted by permission of Random House, Inc.

2 Lawrence M. Friedman, *The Legal System: A Social Science Perspective* (New York, 1975), 15; Lawrence M. Friedman, *A History of American Law* (New York, 1973); J. Willard Hurst, *Law and Social Order in the United States* (Ithaca, 1977); David L. Kirp and Mark G. Yudof, *Educational Policy and the Law: Cases and Materials* (Berkeley, 1974); Harry N. Scheiber, "American Constitutional History and the New Legal History: Complementary Themes in Two Modes," *Journal of American History* 68 (1981): 337–50.

3 David L. Kirp, *Just Schools: The Idea of Racial Equality in American Education* (Berkeley, 1982); Morton J. Horwitz, *The Transformation of American Law, 1780–1860* (Cambridge, Mass., 1977).

4 Historians of quite different ideological persuasions have questioned this "nonpolitical" view of public schools. See, for example, Diane Ravitch, *The Great School Wars, New York City, 1805–1973: A History of the Public Schools as Battlefield of Social Change* (New York, 1979); Ira Katznelson and Margaret Weir, *Schooling for All* (New York, 1985); Carl F. Kaestle, *Pillars of the Republic: Common Schools and American Society, 1780–1860* (New York, 1983).

5 Michael A. Rebell and Arthur R. Block, *Educational Policy Making and the Courts: An Empirical Study of Judicial Activism* (Chicago, 1982), 16; Jethro K. Lieberman, *The Litigious Society* (New York, 1981); Nathan Glazer, "Toward an Imperial Judiciary?" *The Public Interest*, no. 41 (1975): 104–23.

6 Jesse K. Flanders, *Legislative Control of the Elementary School Curriculum* (New York, 1925).

7 Jerold S. Auerbach, *Unequal Justice: Lawyers and Social Change in Modern America* (New York, 1976); for a review of literature on the relation between law and behavior, see Henry S. Lufler, Jr., "Compliance and the Courts," David C. Berliner, ed., *Review of Research in Education* 8 (Washington, D.C., 1980), 336–59.

8 Joel F. Handler, *Social Movements and the Legal System: A Theory of Law Reform and Social Change* (New York, 1979).

9 David Tyack and Elisabeth Hansot, "Conflict and Consensus in American Public Education," *Daedalus* 110 (1981): 1–25; Carl F. Kaestle, "Conflict and Consensus: Toward a Reinterpretation of American Educational History," *Harvard Educational Review* 46 (1976): 390–96; Stephen Arons, *Compelling Belief: The Culture of American Schooling* (New York, 1983).

10 Alexis de Tocqueville, *Democracy in America*, ed. Phillips Bradley (New York, 1945).

219

11 James G. March and Johan P. Olsen, "The New Institutionalism: Organizational Factors in Political Life," *American Political Science Review* 78 (1984): 738, 734–49; as they indicate, scholars of many ideological persuasions are finding it useful to reexamine the role of institutions.

12 James Willard Hurst, "The State of Legal History," *Reviews in American History* 10 (1982): 294, 292–305; in chapter 2 we discuss how our approach to case law differs from traditional approaches, and in the Epilogue we use and cite a number of recent social science studies of school law, most of which deal with the period since 1954.

13 Hurst, "Legal History," 297–98.

Prologue: Exploring the "Primeval Forest"

1 James Bryce, *The American Commonwealth* (New York, 1888), II: 2–3.

2 Ellwood P. Cubberley, *Public Education in the United States: A Study and Interpretation of American Educational History* (Boston, 1934) and the early state histories; Lawrence A. Cremin, *The Wonderful World of Ellwood Patterson Cubberley: An Essay on the Historiography of American Education* (New York, 1965); Carl F. Kaestle, *Pillars of the Republic: Common Schools and American Society, 1780–1860* (New York, 1983).

3 Daniel J. Elazar, *The American Partnership: Intergovernmental Cooperation in the Nineteenth-Century United States* (Chicago, 1962); Fletcher H. Swift, *A History of Public Permanent School Funds in the United States, 1795–1905* (New York, 1911); John D. Hicks, "The Constitutions of the Northwest States," University of Nebraska, *University Studies* 23 (1923): 82–83.

4 Daniel Webster, *Works* (Boston, 1854), I: 41–42; Edward Everett, *Orations and Speeches on Various Occasions* (Boston, 1878), II: 316–21; Per Siljestrom, *The Educational Institutions of the United States: Their Character and Organization* (London, 1853).

5 "Report of Committee on Public Lands, February 24, 1826," as published in *Barnard's American Journal of Education* 28 (1878): 944, 939–45; Pierce, "Report of the Superintendent of Public Instruction of the State of Michigan," in Michigan Senate, *Senate Journal*, 1837, Documents no. 7, pp. 28–84, as quoted in Floyd R. Dain, *Education in the Wilderness* (Lansing, 1968), 232.

6 Kaestle, *Pillars* gives rich detail on the conflicts between those who wanted to centralize schooling and those who distrusted state control.

7 Letter of Stephen Arons to David Tyack, October 28, 1985.

8 For the story of such developments in one state, see Daniel Putnam, *The Development of Primary and Secondary Public Education in Michigan* (Ann Arbor, Mich., 1904); David Tyack and Elisabeth Hansot, *Managers of Virtue: Public School Leadership in America, 1820–1980* (New York, 1982), ch. 6.

9 *Ottawa v. Tinnon* 26 Kan. 19 (1881); Derrick A. Bell, *Race, Racism, and American Law* (Boston, 1980), 368–71.

10 *Roberts v. City of Boston* 59 Mass. (5 Cush.) 198, 201–4 (1850); Bell, *Race*, 365–68; for cases in California, see Charles M. Wollenberg, *All Deliberate Speed: Segregation and Exclusion in California Schools, 1855–1975* (Berkeley, 1976); and Irving G. Hendrick, *The Education of Non-Whites in California, 1849–1970* (San Francisco, 1977).

11 For some pertinent developments in the literature on constitutionalism, see Her-

man Belz, "New Left Reverberation in the Academy: The Antipluralist Critique of Constitutionalism," *Review of Politics* 36 (1974): 265-83; Michael Parenti, *Democracy for the Few* (New York, 1980); Herman Belz, "The Realist Critique of Constitutionalism in the Era of Reform," *American Journal of Legal History* 15 (1971): 288-306; Michigan offers a useful case study of how constitutional, statutory, and case law interacted—see, for example, John D. Pierce, "Origin and Progress of the Michigan School System," *Report of the Pioneer Society of the State of Michigan* 1 (1874-76): 37-45; Thomas M. Cooley, *Michigan: A History of Governments* (Boston, 1888).

Chapter 1: Federal Influence on the Spread of Public Education, 1785-1912

1 William M. Wiecek, *The Guarantee Clause of the U.S. Constitution* (Ithaca, 1972); Fletcher H. Swift, *A History of Public Permanent School Funds in the United States, 1795-1905* (New York, 1911); Harry N. Scheiber provides a critical review of concepts of federalism in "Federalism and Legal Process: Historical and Contemporary Analysis of the American System," *Law and Society Review* 14 (1980): 663-722.

2 For illuminating discussion of constitutions in recent nation-states, corresponding in some functions with educational provisions in the separate American states, see John Boli-Bennet and John W. Meyer, "The Ideology of Childhood and the State: Rules Distinguishing Children in National Constitutions, 1870-1970," *American Sociological Review* 43 (1978): 797-812; John Boli-Bennett, "The Ideology of Expanding State Authority in National Constitutions, 1870-1970," in John W. Meyer and Michael T. Hannan, eds., *National Development and the World System* (Chicago, 1979), 222-37.

3 "A Statement of the Theory of Education in the United States of America as Approved by Many Leading Educators" (Washington, D.C., 1874); the statement was signed by 77 college presidents and city and state superintendents of schools; see David B. Tyack, ed., *Turning Points in American Educational History* (Waltham, Mass., 1967), 325.

4 Roy J. Honeywell, *The Educational Work of Thomas Jefferson* (Cambridge, Mass., 1931); Howard C. Taylor, *The Educational Significance of the Early Federal Land Ordinances* (New York, 1922), chs. 2-5; in sharp contrast to the lack of mention of education in the U.S. Constitution, almost all new nations formed since World War II have elaborate provisions on schooling.

5 U.S. Department of the Interior, Bureau of Land Management, *Public Land Statistics 1983* (Washington, D.C., 1984), 5; Swift, *School Funds;* Richard L McCormick, "The Party Period and Public Policy: An Exploratory Hypothesis," *Journal of American History* 66 (1979): 279-98; on the distributive functions of state and federal government, see Theodore J. Lowi, "American Business, Public Policy, Case Studies, and Political Theory," *World Politics* 1 (1964): 677-715; and Gerald N. Grob, "The Political System and Social Policy in the Nineteenth Century: Legacy of the Revolution," *Mid-America* 58 (1976): 11-13.

6 On the failed hopes of reformers for a stronger federal role in education: Donald R. Warren, *To Enforce Education: A History of the Founding Years of the United States Office of Education* (Detroit, 1974); and Gordan C. Lee, *The Struggle for Federal Aid: First Phase* (New York, 1949).

7 Jefferson quotations from Gordon C. Lee, ed., *Crusade against Ignorance: Thomas*

Jefferson on Education (New York, 1961), 17, 100; for an illuminating discussion of how Washington and other early national leaders viewed education as essential to civility in a republican society, see Lawrence A. Cremin, *American Education: the National Experience, 1783–1876* (New York, 1980), Washington quoted on 103.

8 L. H. Butterfield, ed., *The Letters of Benjamin Rush* (Princeton, 1951), I: lxviii; Frederick Rudolph, ed., *Essays on Education in the Early Republic* (Cambridge, Mass., 1965).

9 David B. Tyack, "Forming the National Character: Paradox in the Educational Thought of the Revolutionary Generation," *Harvard Educational Review* 36 (1966): 29–41.

10 Donald S. Lutz, "The Theory of Consent in the Early State Constitutions," *Publius* 9 (1979): 17, 30, 11–42; on qualifications for leaders, see Willi Paul Adams, *The First American Constitutions: Republican Ideology and the Making of the State Constitutions in the Revolutionary Era* (Chapel Hill, 1980), 176–80.

11 Charles Z. Lincoln, ed., *State of New York: Messages from the Governors, Comprising Executive Communications to the Legislature and Other Papers Relating to Legislation from the Organization of the First Colonial Assembly in 1683 to and Including the Year 1906* (Albany, 1909), II:1100; Rush Welter, *Popular Education and Democratic Thought in America* (New York, 1962), ch. 2. For one attempt to popularize knowledge of the laws, see William B. Wedgewood, *The Constitution and Revised Statutes . . . Reduced to Questions and Answers for the Use of Schools and Families* (Philadelphia, 1844). On debate among scholars regarding the bias of constitutional rules, see Herman Belz, "New Left Reverberations."

12 Tyack, "Paradox."

13 Joseph Story, "On the Science of Government as a Branch of Popular Education," in *The Introductory Discourse and the Lectures Delivered before the American Institute of Instruction in Boston, August, 1834* (Boston, 1835), 260, 264, 265, 249–75; Theodore Frelinghuysen, "Study of Our Political Institutions, *American Annals Of Education and Instruction* 2 (1832): 505–9; James McClellan, *Joseph Story and the American Constitution: A Study in Political and Legal Thought* (Norman, Okla., 1971); Jean V. Matthews, *Rufus Choate: The Law and Civic Virtue* (Philadelphia, 1980).

14 On the limited impact of the American Revolution on education, see Bernard Bailyn, *Education in the Forming of American Society* (New York, 1972), 45–49.

15 Carl Kaestle, *Pillars of the Republic: Common Schools and American Society, 1780–1860* (New York, 1983), chs. 1–3.

16 Massachusetts provisions and commentary on Adams' authorship in Franklin B. Hough, "Constitutional Provisions in Regard to Education in the Several States of the American Union," Bureau of Education, *Circular of Information*, no. 7 (Washington, 1875), 49–51; full texts of constitutions and enabling acts in Francis N. Thorpe, ed., *The Federal and State Constitutions, Colonial Charters, and Other Organic Laws of the States, Territories, and Colonies Now or Heretofore Forming the United States of America* (Washington, 1909).

17 Adams, *The First American Constitutions*, 218, 223, 224.

18 Robert H. Wiebe, *The Opening of American Society: From the Adoption of the Constitution to the Eve of Disunion* (New York, 1984), xiv, 7–20, 37.

19 U.S. House of Representatives, Committee on Public Lands, "Report on Educational Land Policy," Feb. 24, 1826, as published in *Barnard's American Journal of Education* 28 (1878): 939; 942, 944.

20 J. Ross Browne, comp., *Report of the Debates in the Convention of California, on the Formation of the State Constitutional Convention in September and October, 1849* (Washington, 1850), 207.

21 See, for example, Browne, *Convention of California*, 203–11, 346–53; *Debates and Proceedings of the Constitutional Convention of the State of Michigan, 1867*, I (Lansing, 1867), 301–309, 398–419, 467–72 on cleavages over finances and control within a general consensus on the value of schools; *Proceedings of the Constitutional Convention of South Carolina, Held at Charleston, S.C., beginning January 14th and ending March 17th, 1868*, II (Charleston, 1868), 690 and passim.

22 Enabling act in Thorpe, *Constitutions*, IV:2291. Shifts in constitutional language reflected changing conceptions of how to delimit and properly govern education as a common good. An example is the shift from "may" to "shall" in the educational provisions of state constitutions, from empowering the legislature to establish schools to actually requiring as a positive duty the creation of a uniform and free school system, and then subsequently also requiring the attendance of individuals within a specified age span in the state.

23 Thorpe, *Constitutions*, V:2910–12; it is important to note, however, that the common good could be sought under private as well as public auspices; school funds sometimes flowed to institutions not under state control. For an interpretation of the evolution of notions of "public" and "private" in American education, see Thomas James, "Questions About Educational Choice: An Argument from History," in Thomas James and Henry M. Levin, eds., *Public Dollars for Private Schools* (Philadelphia, 1983), 55–70.

24 North Dakota, Constitution of 1889, Article 8.

25 Washington, Constitution of 1889, Article IX, Section 1; the states with clauses on diffusion of knowledge or similar language of broad social purpose were: Massachusetts, 1780; New Hampshire, 1784; Ohio, 1802; Indiana, 1816; Mississippi, 1817; Maine, 1820; Tennessee, 1834; Arkansas, 1836; Rhode Island, 1842; Texas, 1845; Minnesota, 1858; Missouri, 1865; Arkansas, 1868; North Carolina, 1868; Idaho, 1889; North Dakota, 1889; South Dakota, 1889; "paramount duty" in Florida, 1868, and Washington, 1889; phrases on "promotion of arts, literature, and the sciences" or equivalent statements occur in these constitutions: Delaware, 1792; Alabama, 1819; Missouri, 1820; Arkansas, 1836; Michigan, 1837; Iowa, 1846; California, 1849; Kansas, 1859; West Virginia, 1861; Nevada, 1864.

26 "An Ordinance for ascertaining the Mode of Disposing Lands in the Western Territory," May 20, 1785, *Journals of the American Congress, 1785* (Washington, 1823), 520–22, quote on 520.

27 *U.S. Statutes at Large*, I (Boston, 1845) 51–53, quote on 52. The educational provision of the ordinance also appears in Thorpe, *Constitutions*, II:961.

28 Honeywell, *Jefferson;* Taylor, *Land Ordinances,* chs. 2–5.

29 Joseph Schafer, *The Origin of the System of Land Grants for Education,* University of Wisconsin, *Bulletin No. 63* (Madison, 1902), 5–53.

30 Payson J. Treat, *The National Land System, 1785–1820* (New York, 1910), 268–70; Mathias N. Orfield, *Federal Land Grants to the States with Special Reference to Minnesota* (Minneapolis, 1915).

31 Enabling acts and constitutions in Thorpe, *Constitutions;* Swift, *School Funds,* 54–65.

32 Daniel Feller, *The Public Lands in Jacksonian Politics* (Madison, 1984), 5–6, 48.

33 Harry N. Scheiber, "Land Reform, Speculation, and Government Failure: The Administration of Ohio's State Canal Lands, 1836–60," *Prologue* 7 (1975): 85–98; Allan C. Bogue, "Land Policies and Sales," in *Encyclopedia of American Economic History* ed. Glenn Porter (New York, 1980), II:598; Malcolm J. Rohrbough, *The Public Land Office Business: The Settlement and Administration of American Public Lands, 1789–1837* (New York, 1968); Vernon Carstensen, ed., *The Public Lands: Studies in the History of the Public Domain* (Madison, 1963).

34 Swift, *School Funds,* 54–65; enabling acts and constitutions in Thorpe, *Constitutions.*

35 Ibid.

36 Feller, *The Public Lands,* 40–48.

37 Committee on Public Lands, "Report," 939, 945.

38 George B. Germann, *National Legislation Concerning Education: Its Influence and Effect in the Public Land States East of the Mississippi Admitted Prior to 1820,* (New York, 1899), 35–36; *Register of Debates in Congress,* 21st Congress, 1st Session, House of Representatives, December 16, 1829 (Washington, D.C., 1830), 475–77; Daniel J. Elazar, *The American Partnership: Intergovernmental Cooperation in the Nineteenth-Century United States* (Chicago, 1962), 142–43.

39 Swift, *School Funds,* 69–78; Germann, *National Legislation,* 36–37; the bill backed by Clay and the controversy that its veto sparked are discussed in the *Register of Debates in Congress,* 23rd Congress, 1st Session, Senate, December 5, 1833 (Washington, D.C., 1834), 14–18; Elazar, *Partnership,* 200–202. On the debate over internal improvements and democratic development, see Oscar Handlin and Mary Flug Handlin, *Commonwealth: A Study of the Role of Government in the American Economy: Massachusetts, 1774–1861* (Cambridge, 1947); Louis Hartz, *Economic Policy and Democratic Thought: Pennsylvania, 1776–1860* (Cambridge, 1948); Gerald D. Nash, *State Government and Economic Development: Administrative Policies in California, 1849–1933* (Berkeley, 1964); and Harry N. Scheiber, "Government and the Economy: Studies of the 'Commonwealth Policy' in Nineteenth-Century America," *Journal of Interdisciplinary History* 3 (1972): 135–51.

40 Elazar, *Partnership,* 100–102; Swift, *School Funds,* 78–80.

41 Swift, *School Funds,* 98–106.

42 U.S. Commissioner of Education, *Report for 1886–87* (Washington, D.C., 1888), 79–80.

43 Taylor, *Educational Significance,* 86–89; George W. Knight, *History and Management of Land Grants for Education in the Northwestern Territory,* American

Historical Association, *Papers*, vol. I, no. 3 (New York, 1885), 43–116, 157–60; Carl F. Kaestle, *Pillars of the Republic: Common Schools and American Society, 1780–1860* (New York, 1983), 183–84; John D. Hicks, "The Constitutions of the Northwest States," University of Nebraska, *University Studies*, vol. 23 (Lincoln, 1923): 82–83.

44 Swift, *School Funds*, part II, documents what happened to the common school funds in individual states.

45 Hicks, "Constitutions of the Northwest States," 82–83.

46 Knight, *History and Management of Land Grants*, 43–63.

47 *Fifth Annual Report of the Superintendent of Schools of the State of Missouri, 1870* (Jefferson City, 1871), xii–xiv; Swift, *School Funds*, 129–38.

48 Swift, *School Funds*, 108–18. On the development of public authority over education in Michigan, see George W. Knight, "History of the Land Grants for Education in Michigan," *Report of the Pioneer Society of the State of Michigan*, vol. 7, 1884 (Lansing, 1886): 17–35; Daniel Putnam, *The Development of Primary and Secondary Education in Michigan* (Ann Arbor, 1904); Arthur Mead, *The Development of Free Schools in the United States as Illustrated by Connecticut and Michigan* (New York, 1918); James B. Edmonson, *The Legal and Constitutional Basis of a State School System* (Bloomington, Ill., 1926); Jackson, *Development of State Control;* Floyd R. Dain, *Education in the Wilderness* (Lansing, 1968). See also Samuel G. Iverson, "The Public Lands and School Funds of Minnesota," Minnesota Historical Society *Collections* 15 (1915): 287–314.

49 Knight, *History and Management of Land Grants*, 82–85.

50 Taylor, *Educational Significance*, ch. 8.

51 Hicks, "Northwest," 82–83; Knight, *History and Management of Land Grants*, 157–60, on waste and mismanagement generally, see note 33.

52 See references in note 48 on the development of public education in Michigan.

53 U.S. Commissioner of Education, *Report for 1867–68*, 73; Iverson, "Public Lands and School Fund"; Hicks, "Northwest," 77–80; John M. Matzen, *State Constitutional Provisions for Education* (New York, 1931), 101.

54 James C. Zabriskie, *The Public Land Laws of the United States* (San Francisco, 1870), 396–411; Hicks, "Northwest,"; Elazar, *Partnership*, 186–88.

55 Thorpe, *Constitutions*, I:473; IV:2293; Elazar, *Partnership*, 190–91; Orfield, *Federal Land Grants*, 50–52; Swift, *School Funds*, 173–74, 177–79; on controversies and achievements in state centralization, see chapter 2 below; see also a useful set of essays by John G. Richardson on the governance and bureaucratization of state school systems: "Settlement Patterns and the Governing Structures of Nineteenth-Century School Systems," *American Journal of Education* 92 (1984): 178–206; "The American States and the Age of School Systems," *American Journal of Education* 92 (1984): 473–502; and "Variation in Date of Enactment of Compulsory School Attendance Laws: An Empirical Inquiry," *Sociology of Education* 53 (1980): 153–63; a good index of the increasing complexity of state school systems, and of their increasing legalization, is the "Summary of Constitutional and Legal Provisions Relating to Education in the Several States and Territories," in U.S. Commissioner of Education, *Report for 1885–86* (Washington, D.C., 1887), 47–214.

Chapter 2: Education as a Fourth Branch of State Government: Nineteenth Century

1 Alexis de Tocqueville, *Democracy in America*, ed. Phillips Bradley (New York, 1945), I:59–60; Stephen Skowronek, *Building a New American State: The Expansion of National Administrative Capacities, 1877–1920* (Cambridge, England, 1982), chs. 1–2.

2 Tocqueville, *Democracy*, 59ff, 260.

3 Gregory G. Schmidt, "Republican Visions: Constitutional Thought and Constitutional Revision in the Eastern United States, 1815–1830" (Ph.D. diss., University of Illinois at Urbana-Champaign, 1981); Fletcher M. Green, "Cycles of American Democracy," *Mississippi Valley Historical Review* 48 (1961): 3–23; Ronald P. Formisano, "Deferential-Participant Politics: The Early Republic's Political Culture, 1789–1840," *American Political Science Review* 68 (1974): 473–87; on political parties as private organizations mediating collective activity in the public sphere, see Perry M. Goldman, "Political Virtue in the Age of Jackson," *Political Science Quarterly* 87 (1972): 46–62.

4 George P. Parkinson, Jr., "Antebellum State Constitution-Making: Retention, Circumvention, Revision," (Ph.D. diss., University of Wisconsin, 1972), 219–29; Merrill D. Peterson, ed., *Democracy, Liberty, and Property: The State Constitutional Conventions of the 1820's* (Indianapolis, 1966).

5 Gerald N. Grob, "The Political System and Social Policy in the Nineteenth Century: Legacy of the Revolution," *Mid-America* 58 (1976): 8, 11–13, 14.

6 Arnold J. Heidenheimer, "Education and Social Security: Entitlements in Europe and America," in Peter Flora and Arnold J. Heidenheimer, eds., *The Development of Welfare States in Europe and America* (New Brunswick, N.J., 1981), 269–304; Wallace D. Farnham, "The Weakened Spring of Government: A Study in Nineteenth Century American History," *American Historical Review* 68 (1963): 662–80.

7 David Tyack and Elisabeth Hansot, *Managers of Virtue: Public School Leadership in America, 1820–1980* (New York, 1982), Part 1.

8 Donald S. Lutz, "The Theory of Consent in the Early State Constitutions," *Publius* 9 (1979): 11–42; James Q. Dealey, "General Tendencies in State Constitutions," *American Political Science Review* 1 (1907): 203–4; J. Willard Hurst, *The Growth of American Law: The Lawmakers* (Boston, 1950), ch. 2; Lawrence M. Friedman, *A History of American Law* (New York, 1973), 100–109.

9 James Bryce, *The American Commonwealth* (New York, 1888), II:138–41; Bayrd Still, "An Interpretation of the Statehood Process, 1800 to 1850," *Mississippi Valley Historical Review* 23 (1936): 189–204; Arthur A. Ekirch, Jr., "Democracy and Laissez Faire: The New York State Constitution of 1846," *Journal of Libertarian Studies* 1 (1977): 319–23.

10 Ibid.; Thomas M. Cooley, *A Treatise on the Constitutional Limitations Which Rest Upon the Legislative Power of the States of the American Union*, 4th ed. (Boston, 1878), 266.

11 Bryce, *Commonwealth*, II:138; for angry denunciations of corporations by members of the Workingmen's Party, see *Debates and Proceedings of the Constitutional Convention of the State of California . . . 1878–79*, 3 vols. (Sacramento, 1880);

Carl B. Swisher, *Motivation and Political Technique in the California Constitutional Convention, 1878–79* (Claremont, Calif., 1930); on the role of courts in economic development, see Morton H. Horwitz, *The Transformation of American Law, 1780–1860* (Cambridge, Mass., 1977).

12 West Virginia report quoted in Bryce, *Commonwealth*, II:131, n. 1; Morton Keller, *Affairs of State: Public Life in Nineteenth Century America* (Cambridge, Mass., 1977), 323–26; Frank L. McVey, "Past and Present Sticking Points in Taxation," Mississippi Valley Historical Association, *Proceedings, 1909–10* 3 (1911): 348–60.

13 Ballard C. Campbell, *Representative Democracy: Public Policy and Midwestern Legislatures in the Late Nineteenth Century* (Cambridge, Mass., 1980), 167; Carl V. Harris, "Spotlight on State Legislatures," *Reviews in American History* 10 (1982): 78–83; Bryce, *Commonwealth*, 128–32, 138, 156, 161; *Report of the Proceedings and Debates in the Convention to Revise the Constitution of the State of Michigan* (Lansing, 1850), 803, passim; *Debates California, 1878–79*; Southern constitutions in Frances N. Thorpe, ed., *The Federal and State Constitutions, Colonial Charters, and Other Organic Laws of the States, Territories, and Colonies Now or Heretofore Forming the United States of America* (Washington, D.C., 1909).

14 Friedman, *American Law*, 302–18; Keller, *Affairs of State*, 319–30.

15 Ibid.; Cynthia E. Brown, *State Constitutional Conventions: From Independence to the Completion of the Present Union, 1776–1959* (Westport, Conn., 1973), introduction by Richard H. Leach.

16 Noel Sargent, "The California Constitutional Convention of 1878–79," *California Law Review* 6 (1917): 12; Swisher, *Convention*, 96.

17 Bryce, *Commonwealth*, 167.

18 Bryce, *Commonwealth*, 149.

19 Kaestle, *Pillars*, 114–15; James P. Wickersham, *A History of Education in Pennsylvania* (Lancaster, Penn., 1886), chs. 17–18; George L. Jackson, *The Development of State Control of Public Instruction in Michigan* (Lansing, 1926), chs. 2–4; James J. Burns, *Educational History of Ohio* (Columbus, 1905), ch. 14.

20 Grob, "Social Policy" 14 n. 16; Hurst, *Lawmakers*, 48–49, 97; Bryce, *Commonwealth*, II, ch. 44.

21 Ann S. Orlov and Theda Skocpol, "Why Not Equal Protection? Explaining the Politics of Public Social Spending in Britain, 1900–1911, and the United States, 1880s–1920s," *American Sociological Review* 49 (1984): 726–50; Flora and Heidenheimer, *Welfare States*.

22 Theda Skocpol and John Ikenberry, "The Political Formation of the American Welfare State in Historical and Comparative Perspective," *Comparative Social Research* 8 (1983): 87–148; William L. Riordan, *Plunkitt of Tammany Hall* (New York, 1905); on private relief and charitable organizations performing public functions and exercising official powers, see Robert H. Bremner, ed., *Children and Youth in America: A Documentary History*, II, 1866–1932 (Cambridge, Mass., 1971).

23 We are indebted to Professor George Frederickson for calling to our attention the contrast between private and public power in a talk at Stanford University; on educational contrasts, see Arnold J. Heidenheimer, "Education and Social Security."

24 Campbell, *Representative Democracy*, 200.

25 Bryce, *Commonwealth*, 154–55; Richard L. McCormick, "The Party Period and Public Policy: An Exploratory Hypothesis," *Journal of American History* 66 (1979): 279–98; J. Willard Hurst, *Law and the Conditions of Freedom in the Nineteenth Century United States* (Madison, 1956), ch. 1; Oscar and Mary Flug Handlin, *Commonwealth: A Study of the Role of Government in the American Economy: Massachusetts, 1774-1861*, rev. ed. (Cambridge, Mass., 1969); Louis Hartz: *Economic Policy and Democratic Thought: Pennsylvania, 1776–1860* (Cambridge, Mass., 1948); Gerald D. Nash, *State Government and Economic Development: A History of Administrative Policies in California, 1849–1933* (Berkeley, 1964).

26 Grob, "Policy," 8, 11–12, 13; Michigan committee quoted in Jackson, *State Control*, 216.

27 Grob, "Policy," 16, 18.

28 Albert Fishlow, "Levels of Nineteenth-Century Investment in Education," *Journal of Economic History* 26 (1966): 435; Heidenheimer, "Entitlements."

29 Fishlow, "Investment," 420–21; James H. Blodgett, *Report on Education in the United States at the Eleventh Census: 1890*, Census Office Monograph (Washington, D.C., 1893), introduction; Samuel W. Brown, *The Secularization of American Education as Shown by State Legislation, State Constitutional Provisions and State Supreme Court Decisions* (New York, 1912); Kaestle, *Pillars*, documents the shift from private to public education before the Civil War, 116–21.

30 In the table and text commenting on the table we analyze the educational provisions of state constitutions given in Thorpe, ed., *Constitutions:* up to 1875 these have been conveniently summarized in Franklin B. Hough, "Constitutional Provisions in Regard to Education in the Several States of the American Union," U.S. Bureau of Education, *Circular of Information*, no. 7 (Washington, D.C., 1875); see also John M. Matzen, *State Constitutional Provisions for Education: Fundamental Attitude of the American People Regarding Education as Revealed by State Constitutional Provisions, 1776–1929* (New York, 1931) and Frank S. White, *Constitutional Provisions for Differentiated Education* (Parkersburg, West Virginia, 1950).

31 George W. Knight, *History and Management of Land Grants for Education in the Northwest Territory* (New York, 1885); Samuel G. Iverson, "The Public Lands and School Fund of Minnesota," Minnesota Historical Society, *Collections* 15 (1915): 287–314; Daniel J. Elazar, *The American Partnership: Intergovernmental Cooperation in the Nineteenth-Century United States* 142–43; *Register of Debates in Congress*, 21st Congress, 1st Session, House of Representatives, December 16, 1829, 475–77.

32 *Report of Proceedings, Michigan, 1850*, 548; Illinois delegate quoted in Arthur C. Cole, ed., *The Constitutional Debates of 1847* (Springfield, Ill., 1919), 901; for an illuminating discussion of how children encountered republican ideology in schools, see Jean H. Baker, *Affairs of Party: The Political Culture of Northern Democrats in the Mid-Nineteenth Century* (Ithaca, N.Y., 1983), ch. 2; see also Carl F. Kaestle, "Conflict and Consensus Revisited: Notes Toward a Reinterpretation of American Educational History," *Harvard Educational Review* 46 (1976):

390–96; Kaestle, *Pillars*, 148–58 discusses localist opposition to centralization.

33 A fascinating example of borrowing from Northern states, particularly Massachusetts, in the Reconstruction conventions occurred in South Carolina in 1868; see *Proceedings of the Constitutional Convention of South Carolina, Held at Charleston, S.C., Beginning January 14th and Ending March 17th, 1868* (Charleston, 1868), II:690, 692, 706, 707, 747; Edwin S. Lide, *Constitutional Basis of Public School Education*, U.S. Office of Education, Leaflet no. 40, July 1931 (Washington, D.C., 1931).

34 On regional differences and timing of institutionalization see John G. Richardson, "Settlement Patterns and the Governing Structures of Nineteenth-Century School Systems," *American Journal of Education* 92 (1984): 178–206 and ibid., "The American States and the Age of School Systems," 473–502; "Variation in Date of Enactment of Compulsory School Attendance Laws: An Empirical Inquiry," *Sociology of Education* 53 (1980): 153–63.

35 David Tyack, *The One Best System: A History of American Urban Education* (Cambridge, Mass., 1974).

36 Kaestle, *Pillars*, 113–16; Matzen, *Constitutional Provisions*, chs. 2–4.

37 Matzen, *Constitutional Provisions*, ch. 3; National Education Association, *Studies in State Educational Administration*, no. 9 (Washington, D.C., 1931), 5–6.

38 Keller, *Affairs of State*, 110–14, 319–45, 473–80; Ulman S. Alexander, *Special Legislation Affecting Public Schools* (New York, 1929).

39 A rich study of decision-making at the local level in rural districts is Wayne E. Fuller, *The Old Country School: The Story of Rural Education in the Middle West* (Chicago, 1982); on regulation in one city system, see David Tyack, "Bureaucracy and the Common School: The Example of Portland, Oregon, 1851–1913," *American Quarterly* 19 (1967): 475–98.

40 James B. Edmondson, *The Legal and Constitutional Basis of a School System* (Bloomington, Ill., 1926); Roger Wyman, "Wisconsin Ethnic Groups and the Election of 1890," *Wisconsin Magazine of History* 51 (1968): 269–93.

41 Andrew Gulliford, *Country School Legacy: Humanities on the Frontier* (Silt, Colo., 1981), 7.

42 For a perceptive review of the literature on federalism, see Harry N. Scheiber, "Federalism and Legal Process: Historical and Contemporary Analysis of the American System," *Law and Society Review* 14 (1980): 663–722.

43 *Plessy v. Ferguson*, 163 U.S. 537 (1896); *Brown v. Board of Education*, 347 U.S. 483 (1954); Clark Spurlock, *Education and the Supreme Court* (Urbana, Ill., 1955); Henry S. Lufler, Jr., "Compliance and the Courts," in David C. Berliner, ed., *Review of Research in Education* 8 (Washington, D.C.: AERA, 1980), 336–58. For historical examples of school law textbooks, see C. W. Bardeen, *A Manual of Common School Law* (Syracuse, 1900); Harvey C. Voorhees, *The Law of the Public School System of the United States* (Boston, 1916); Harry R. Trusler, *Essentials of School Law* (Milwaukee, 1927); Robert L. Drury, *Law and the School Superintendent* (Cincinnati, 1958).

44 David Tyack and Aaron Benavot, "Courts and Public Schools: Educational Litigation in Historical Perspective," *Law and Society Review* 19 (1985): 339–80. On the West digests, see: West Publishing Company, *Century Edition of the American*

Digest (St. Paul, Minn., 1897) and subsequent decennial digests; Newton Lamson, "For Lawyers, West Isn't a Direction—It's a Way of Life," *Juris Doctor* 4 (1974): 28–33; Jill Abramson, John Kennedy, and Ellen Joan Pollock, "Inside the West Empire," *The American Lawyer* V (1983): 90–95; Martin Mayer, *The Lawyers* (New York, 1967), ch. 12. For quantitative articles on court cases, using a variety of methodologies, see Robert Kagan *et al.*, "The Business of State Courts," *Stanford Law Review* 30 (1977): 121–56 and Joel B. Grossman and Austin Sarat, "Litigation in the Federal Courts: A Comparative Perspective," *Law and Society Review* 9 (1975): 321–46; for a description of the court structure, see Henry Glick, *Courts, Politics, and Justice* (New York, 1983), ch. 2.

45 "Summary of Constitutional and Legal Provisions relating to Education in the Several States and Territories," U.S. Commissioner of Education, *Report for 1885–86* (Washington, D.C.: GPO, 1887), 47–217; David Tyack and Elisabeth Hansot, "Conflict and Consensus in American Public Education," *Daedalus* 110 (1981): 1–25; For general approaches to the social history of the law, see Lawrence M. Friedman, *The Legal System: A Social Science Perspective* (New York, 1975), 15; J. Willard Hurst, *Law and Social Order in the United States* (Ithaca, 1977); Harry H. Scheiber, "American Constitutional History and the New Legal History: Complementary Themes in Two Modes" *Journal of American History* 67 (1981): 337–50; Robert W. Gordon, "J. Willard Hurst and the Common Law Tradition in American Legal Historiography," *Law and Society* (1975): 9–55.

46 Lawrence M. Friedman, "Notes toward a History of American Justice," in Friedman and Harry Schieber, eds., *American Law and the Constitutional Order: Historical Perspectives* (Cambridge, Mass., 1978), 19–20; Nevada official quoted in John F. Bender, *The Functions of Courts in Enforcing Compulsory School Attendance Laws* (New York, 1927), 10.

47 Tyack and Hansot, *Managers*, part 1; "Constitutional Provisions in regard to Education in the Several States of the American Union," Bureau of Education, *Circular of Information*, no. 7, 1875 (Washington, D.C., 1875); Timothy Smith, "Protestant Schooling and American Nationality," *Journal of American History* 53 (1967): 679–95; Robert Michaelson, *Piety in the Public School* (New York, 1970).

48 B. E. Packard, "The Lawyer in the School-room," *Maine Law Review* 7 (1913–14): 176–96; B. B. Bassett, "The Jurisdiction of the Teacher and the School Board, *Case and Comment* 20 (1913) 227–32; "Recent Cases," *Washington Law Review* 6 (1931): 39; and school law textbooks cited in note 43.

49 Thomas E. Finegan, *Judicial Decisions of the State Superintendent of Common Schools* (Albany, N. Y., 1914), 5–6; Lawrence M. Friedman, "Courts over Time; A Survey of Theories and Research," in Keith O. Boyum and Lynn Mather, eds., *Empirical Theories about Courts* (New York, 1983), 7–50.

50 Uhlman S. Alexander, *Special Legislation Affecting Public Schools* (New York, 1929), 5–6, 10, 15, 17, 26, 45, 52, 110–12; Roger Wyman, "Wisconsin Ethnic Groups and the Election of 1890," *Wisconsin Magazine of History* 51 (1968): 271, 269–93; J. J. Mapel, "The Repeal of the Compulsory Education Laws in Wisconsin and Illinois," *Educational Review* 1 (1891): 52–57.

51 Fuller, *Country School.*

52 Kaestle, *Pillars*, 161–71.

53 James H. Blodgett, *Report on Education in the United States at the Eleventh Census: 1890* (Washington, D.C., 1893), 51, 52, 113, 114; James W. Saunders, *The Education of an Urban Minority: Catholics in Chicago, 1833-1965* (New York, 1977).

54 George W. Knight, *History and Management of Land Grants for Education in the Northwest Territory,* American Historical Association, *Papers,* vol. I, no. 3 (New York, 1885); Fletcher H. Swift, *A History of Public Permanent Common School Funds in the United States, 1795-1905* (New York, 1911).

55 Bryce, *Commonwealth,* vol. II; Keller, *Affairs of State;* McElvey, "Sticking Points."

56 *Davis v. Indiana,* 94 U.S. 792 (1876); *School District v. Insurance Company,* 103 U.S. 707 (1880); *Kelly v. Pittsburg,* 104 U.S. 78 (1881); *Doon Township v. Cummins,* 142 U.S. 366 (1891); *State of Indiana v. Glover,* 155 U.S. 513 (1894).

57 "Summary of Constitutional and Legal Provisions."

58 Fuller, *Country School;* Warren Burton, *The District School as It Was by One Who Went to It* [1833] ed. Clifton Johnson (New York, 1928); H. Leroy Jackson, "Agent of the Law: The Town Board of Education," *Connecticut Bar Journal* 23 (1949): 248-67.

59 "Summary of Constitutional and Legal Provisions," 59, passim; Fuller, *Country School,* ch. 3; Kaestle, *Pillars,* chs. 6-7.

60 S. R. Thompson, comp. *The School Laws of Nebraska* (Lincoln, Neb., 1877), back cover, preface.

61 Edward D. Mansfield, *American Education, Its Principles and Elements* (New York, 1851), 271-22; the cases treated in the West Century Digest often revolve on the kinds of technical procedures mentioned in the text.

62 Blodgett, *Education,* introduction; Jorgensen, *Wisconsin,* 146-48; Morgan Kousser, "Separate But Not Equal: The Supreme Court's First Decision on Racial Discrimination in Schools," *Journal of Southern History* 46 (1980): 17-44.

63 *Stuart v. School District no. 1,* 30 Mich. 69 (1874); Otto T. Hamilton, *The Courts and the Curriculum* (New York, 1927), ch. 2.

64 Blodgett's introduction to *Education* gives rich evidence on the actual diversity of school-formation in different states and territories; see also essays by Richardson cites in note 34 above.

Chapter 3: Law and State School Policy: Case Studies of Michigan and California, 1835-1900

1 John D. Pierce, "Origin and Progress of the Michigan School System," *Report of the Pioneer Society of the State of Michigan* 1 (1874-76): 37-45; Charles O. Hoyt and R. Clyde Ford, *John D. Pierce, Founder of the Michigan School System* (Ypsilanti, 1905).

2 J. Ross Browne, *Report of the Debates in the Convention of California on the Formation of the State Constitution in September and October, 1848* (Washington, D.C., 1850), 18, 210.

3 Pierce, "Origin," 38; James B. Edmondson, *The Legal and Constitutional Basis of a School System* (Bloomington, Ill., 1926).

4 Willis F. Dunbar, *The Michigan Record in Higher Education* (Detroit, 1963), 25-27; Lucy Salmon, "Education in Michigan during the Territorial Period,"

Report of the Pioneer Society of the State of Michigan 7 (1884): 36–51; Thomas
M. Cooley, *Michigan: A History of Governments* (Boston, 1888), Cass quoted
on 315; Floyd R. Dain, *Education in the Wilderness* (Lansing, 1968), 120–31.

5 Pierce, "Origins," 41.

6 Cooley, *Michigan*, 316–17; Daniel Putnam, *The Development of Primary and
Secondary Public Education in Michigan* (Ann Arbor, 1904), 12–18.

7 Harold M. Dorr, ed., *The Michigan Constitutional Conventions of 1835–36:
Debates and Proceedings* (Ann Arbor, 1940), 28–29, introduction; Hezekiah G.
Wells, "A Sketch of the Members of the Constitutional Conventions of 1835 and
1850," *Report of the Pioneer Society of the State of Michigan* 3 (1877–80): 37–40.

8 Dorr, *Conventions*, 338–43; Dain, *Education*, 205–13; Putnam, *Michigan*.

9 Pierce, "Origin," 39–40.

10 "Report of the Superintendent of Public Instruction of the State of Michigan,"
in Michigan Senate, *Senate Journal*, 1837, Documents, no. 7, 28–84; quoted in
Dain, *Education*, 230–32.

11 Pierce, "Report"; Dain, *Education*, 229–39.

12 W. O. Hedrick, "The Financial and Tax History of Michigan," *Michigan History
Magazine* 21 (1937): 35–36; Michigan, *Acts of the Legislature* (1837), LV:102–6;
LXIII:116–26; CIV:209–14.

13 Dain *Education*, 241–52; Hoyt and Ford, *Pierce*, 124–29.

14 Hedrick, "Tax History," 45–46; George W. Knight, "History of the Land Grants
for Education in Michigan," *Report of the Pioneer Society of the State of Michigan*
7 (1884): 17–35.

15 Dain *Education*, 256–59.

16 Articles XIII and IX, "Education" and "Finance and Taxation," Michigan Constitution of 1850, Thorpe, ed., *Constitutions*, IV:1961–64; *Report of the Proceedings and Debates in the Convention to Revise the Constitution of the State
of Michigan* (Lansing, 1850), 803, passim; the table of members indicates that
almost half were farmers and the next largest group were lawyers.

17 *Report of Proceedings*, 541–42.

18 Ibid., 548.

19 Ibid., 273, 535.

20 Ibid., 267–69, 272–73, 274–75, 551.

21 Constitution of 1908, Article XI, Section 1; *Debates and Proceedings of the Constitutional Convention of the State of Michigan, 1867* (Lansing, 1869), I:304–5,
307–8, 402, 418–19, 515, 797; this constitution was turned down by the people;
Henry A. Ford, "A Quarter Century of Education in Michigan," *Report of the
Pioneer and Historical Society of the State of Michigan* 9 (1886): 92–99; D. C.
Shilling, "The Michigan Constitution of 1908: Or Constitution Making Since
1850," *Michigan History Magazine* 18 (1934): 33–47; Citizens Research Council
of Michigan, *A Comparative Analysis of the Michigan Constitution*, I, Article
XI (Detroit, 1961).

22 John Swett, "The Elementary Schools of California: A Monograph," San Francisco Department of Education, California Louisiana Purchase Exposition Commission, 1904, 6–7.

23 On constraints limiting governmental power, see Wallace D. Farnham, "The

Weakened Spring of Government: A Study in Nineteenth Century American History," *American Historical Review* 68 (1963): 662–80; see also Gerald N. Grob, "The Political System and Social Policy in the Nineteenth Century: Legacy of the Revolution," *Mid-America* 58 (1976): 5–19.

24 Browne, *Report of Debates*, 205–215.

25 California Constitution of 1849, Article IX; Roy W. Cloud, *Education in California: Leaders, Organizations and Accomplishments of the First Hundred Years* (Stanford, 1952).

26 David Frederick Ferris, *Judge Marvin and the Founding of the California Public School System* (Berkeley, 1962).

27 Ferris, *Judge Marvin;* A. D. Mayo, "The Development of the Common School in the Western States from 1830 to 1865," U.S. Bureau of Education, *Report of the Commissioner of Education 1898–99*, 445, San Francisco figures on 446— Mayo notes that in 1858 the city of San Francisco spent four times as much on its schools as the state distributed for all the schools in California (p. 447); Cloud, *California*, 26.

28 John G. Marvin, Superintendent of Public Instruction, "An Act to Establish a System of Common Schools in the State of California; and Other Acts Providing for Revenue of the Same, with Explanatory Forms" (Sacramento, 1852).

29 John Swett, *History of the Public School System in California* (San Francisco, 1876), part I.

30 Marvin, "Act to Establish Common Schools (1852)."

31 Ferris, *Marvin;* Paul Goda, "The Historical Background of California's Constitutional Provisions Prohibiting Aid to Sectarian Schools," *California Historical Society Quarterly* 46 (1967): 149–71.

32 William E. North, "Catholic Education in Southern California" (Ph.D. diss., Catholic University of America, 1936), 124.

33 William Gleeson, *History of the Catholic Church in California* (San Francisco, 1872), 273–76; on the development of ward schools, flexible language policies for immigrant groups, and other local forms of ethnic diversity in San Francisco after the restriction on public funding for private schools, see Lee S. Dolson, "The Administration of the San Francisco Public Schools, 1847–1947" (Ph.D. diss., University of California, Berkeley, 1964); and Victor L. Shradar, "Ethnic Politics, Religion and the Public Schools of San Francisco, 1849–1933" (Ph.D. diss., Stanford University, 1974).

34 In addition to the *Revised School Law*, published each year by the state printer in Sacramento, the annual and biennial reports of the state superintendents trace the development of statutes; for a succinct review of yearly changes, see Swett, *History*, part I.

35 *Revised School Law;* Swett, *History*, part I; Leighton H. Johnson, "Development of the Central State Agency for Public Education in California, 1949–1949" (Ph.D. diss., University of California, Berkeley, 1951) I.

36 Swett, *History*, part I; Cloud, *Education in California.*

37 State of California, Superintendent of Public Instruction, *Second Biennial Report*, 1866–67; Swett, *History*, part I.

38 Falk, *The Development and Organization of Education in California* (New York,

1968); William G. Carr, *John Swett: The Biography of an Educational Pioneer* (Santa Ana, Calif., 1933); Nicholas C. Polos, *John Swett: California's Frontier Schoolmaster* (Washington, D.C., 1978); Morton Keller, *Affairs of State: Public Life in Late Nineteenth Century American* (Cambridge, Mass., 1977).

39 John Swett, "Address of the Superintendent of Public Instruction... before the State Teachers' Institute... May 7th, 1867" (San Francisco, 1867).

40 Swett, "Address, May 7th, 1867,"; cf. "Public Instruction in California," *American Journal of Education* 16, New Series (1866): 625–38.

41 Andrew J. Moulder, *Commentaries on the School Law with the Elements of School Architecture. Laws Relating to the School Lands. Forms and Instructions* (Sacramento, 1858), 11; *The California Teacher* 3 (July 1865): 19.

42 *The California Teacher* 3 (February 1866): 91.

43 Arthur B. Stout, "An Essay on Public Education in California" (San Francisco, 1866), 1.

44 State of California, Superintendent of Public Instruction, *Second Biennial Report*, 1866–67; reprinted in Swett, *History*, quote on 52.

45 "An Act to Enforce the Educational Rights of Children," March 28, 1874, *Statutes of California 1873–74*, ch. 516, 751; for the sequence of states passing compulsory attendance laws, see August W. Steinhilber and Carl J. Sokolowski, *State Law on Compulsory Attendance* (Washington, D.C., 1966), 3; on the fiscal impact of the seven dollar per pupil state apportionment, see Cloud, *Education in California*, 61.

46 State of California, Superintendent of Public Instruction, *Fifth Biennial Report*, 1872–73, 14.

47 "Annual Address of Superintendent Fitzgerald, State Teachers' Institute, November 7, 1871," *The California Teacher* 9 (December 1871): 162.

48 On the general history of compulsory attendance, see David Tyack, "Ways of Seeing: An Essay on the History of Compulsory Schooling," *Harvard Educational Review* 46 (1976): 355–89.

49 Swett, *History*, errata.

50 James M. Guinn, "The Beginnings of the School System of Los Angeles," An Address Delivered Before the History Section of the Southern California Teachers' Association, December 23, 1909, *Annual Publications of the Historical Society of Southern California*, vol. 8, part 3 (1911), 203; for a comparison with similar views in other states, see the compilation of quotes from superintendents on their inadequate compulsory attendance laws in U.S. Bureau of Education, *Report of the Commissioner of Education 1888–89*, 470–531.

51 Henry N. Bolander, "School Attendance," *The California Teacher* 13 (1875): 91; Cloud, *Education in California*, 104; for an analysis of the reach of compulsory attendance laws decade by decade, see Roy O. Moss, "Compulsory Attendance Legislation in California" (Masters thesis, University of California, Berkeley, 1924).

52 U.S. Commissioner of Education, *Report for 1888–89*, pp. 470–531; Jabez Franklin Cowdery, "The Word 'White' in the California School Laws," speech in the California Legislature by State Representative from San Francisco, January 30, 1874, reprinted for the Executive Committee of the California State Convention of Colored Citizens (San Francisco, 1874).

53 *Ward v. Flood*, 48 Cal. 42 (1874); see also Charles M. Wollenberg, *All Deliberate Speed: Segregation and Exclusion in California Schools, 1855–1975* (Berkeley, 1976); Irving G. Hendrick, *The Education of Non-Whites in California, 1849–1970* (San Francisco, 1977); and Victor Low, *The Unimpressible Race: A Century of Educational Struggle by the Chinese in San Francisco* (San Francisco, 1982).

54 Ibid.

55 For the views of Fitzgerald, see annual reports and circulars of the state superintendent of public instruction, along with concurrent issues of *The California Teacher*, during the late 1860s and early 1870s.

56 O. P. Fitzgerald, "Special Legislation in School Matters," *The California Teacher* 7 (1870): 253; "Annual Address of Superintendent Fitzgerald . . .", 153.

57 See Edward W. Harrington, "The Public School System and the Second Constitution of California" (Ph.D. diss., Stanford University, 1933), for a close account of the political machinations surrounding the controversy.

58 Ibid.

59 Carl B. Swisher, *Motivation and Political Technique in the California Constitutional Convention, 1878–79* (Claremont, Calif., 1930).

60 Swisher, *California*, 98; State of California, *Debates and Proceedings of the Constitutional Convention of the State of California*, 1878–79, 3 vols. (Sacramento, 1880–81).

61 Golden Gate Grange, San Francisco, *Public Education*, report of a Special Committee (San Francisco, 1877), 2–3.

62 Not all of these provisions remained central to state authority, however. That California's Constitution of 1879 was an inadequate instrument of government in the developing state was demonstrated by the hundreds of amendments adopted in the coming decades; see "California's Constitutional Amendomania," *Stanford Law Review* 1 (1949): 279–88.

63 *Pacific School and Home Journal* 3 (1879): 103, 172, 175, 177.

64 John Swett, *Methods of Teaching* (New York, 1880), 10–11; *Kennedy v. Miller* 97 Cal. 429, 432; 32 P.558 (1893).

65 On the opposition of teachers to the constitutional amendment on textbooks, see "Report Adopted by the State Teachers' Association, held in San Francisco, Dec. 26th, 27th and 28th, 1883," *California Teacher and Home Journal* 2 (1883–84): 492–95.

66 *The California Teacher and Home Journal* 2 (1883–84): 63–64.

67 For the broader agenda for reform among professionals, see Lawrence A. Cremin, *The Transformation of the School: Progressivism in American Education* (New York, 1961).

68 Daniel T. Rodgers, "In Search of Progressivism," *Reviews in American History* 10 (1982): 113–32.

69 David Tyack, *The One Best System: A History of American Urban Education* (Cambridge, Mass., 1974), part 3.

Chapter 4: Law and the Bureaucratization of Public Schools: Twentieth Century

1 James H. Blodgett, *Report on Education in the United States at the Eleventh Census: 1890* (Washington, D.C., 1893), 20.

2 David Tyack and Elisabeth Hansot, *Managers of Virtue: Public School Leadership in America, 1820–1980* (New York, 1982), part II.

3 For a view of rural schools by an administrative progressive, see Ellwood P. Cubberley, *Rural Life and Education: A Study of the Rural-School Problem as a Phase of the Rural-Life Problem* (Boston, 1914).

4 Joseph M. Cronin, *The Control of Urban Schools: Perspectives on the Power of Educational Reformers* (New York, 1973).

5 George D. Strayer, "Progress in School Administration during the Past Twenty-Five Years," *School and Society* 32 (1930): 375–78; Joel H. Spring, *Education and the Rise of the Corporate State* (Boston, 1972); Paul Violas, *The Training of the Urban Working Class* (Chicago, 1978).

6 Two of the key administrative progressives, Cubberley and George D. Strayer, wrote and lobbied extensively for better state school finance; for financial developments at the state level in the Great Depression, see David Tyack, Robert Lowe, and Elisabeth Hansot, *Public Schools in Hard Times: The Great Depression and Recent Years* (Cambridge, Mass., 1984), ch. 2; Larry Cuban, "Enduring Resiliency: Enacting and Implementing Federal Vocational Education Legislation," in Harvey Kantor and David Tyack, eds., *Work, Youth, and Schooling: Historical Perspectives on Vocationalism in American Education* (Stanford, Cal., 1982), 45–78.

7 Willard S. Elsbree, *The American Teacher: Evolution of a Profession in a Democracy* (New York, 1939).

8 Corinne Gilb, *Hidden Hierarchies: The Professions and Government* (New York, 1966), 36–37.

9 William G. Carr, "School Legislation as a Factor in Producing Good Schools," *American School Board Journal* 81 (1930): 37–38.

10 Daniel T. Rodgers, "In Search of Progressivism," *Reviews in American History* 10 (1982): 113–32; David Tyack, *The One Best System: A History of American Urban Education* (Cambridge, Mass., 1974), parts II–IV.

11 On alliance-building and networking, see Tyack, *One Best System*, 137–47; and Tyack and Hansot, *Managers*, 129–40.

12 Henry Pritchett, "Educational Surveys," in Carnegie Foundation for the Advancement of Teaching, *Ninth Annual Report of the President and Treasurer* (New York, 1914), 118–23; Charles Judd, "Summary of Typical School Surveys," *Thirteenth Yearbook of the National Society for the Study of Education* (Chicago, 1916), 72–78; Leonard Ayres, *A Comparative Study of the Public School Systems in the Forty-Eight States* (New York, 1912).

13 On conflicts between teachers and administrators, see Grace C. Strachan, *Equal Pay for Equal Work* (New York, 1910); Margaret A. Haley, "Why Teachers Should Organize," NEA, *Addresses and Proceedings, 1904*, 145–52; Wayne Urban, *Why Teachers Organized* (Detroit, 1982); with some exaggeration, but with more than a grain of truth, Arthur Bestor wrote of the "interlocking directorate" of "educationists" in *Educational Wastelands: The Retreat from Learning in our Public Schools* (Urbana, Ill., 1953).

14 On the campaign to change city charters see Tyack, *One Best System*, part 4;

Norton Grubb and Marvin Lazerson, *Education and Industrialism: Documents in Vocational Education, 1870–1970* (New York, 1975).

15 Lucien B. Kinney, *Certification in Education* (Englewood Cliffs, N.J., 1964).

16 See reports on school legislation in the reports of the United States Commissioner of Education in 1893–94, 2:1063–1300 and 1903–4, vol. 1:249–518; and the following USOE Bulletins: no. 3, 1906; no. 7, 1908; no. 2, 1910; no. 55, 1913; no. 47, 1915; no. 23, 1918; no. 30, 1920; and no. 20, 1922; Madaline K. Remmlein, "Statutory Problems," *Law and Contemporary Problems* 2 (1955): 125–37; Ward W. Keesecker, "A Review of Educational Legislation, 1935 and 1936," USOE *Bulletin,* no. 2, 1937 (Washington, D.C.: GPO, 1937).

17 Ellwood P. Cubberley, *State and County Educational Organization: The Revised Constitution and School Code of the State of Osceola* (New York, 1922); Glenn W. Caulkins, "A Proposed Criterion for Evaluating State School Laws," *Nation's Schools* 14 (1934): 27–29.

18 Gilb, *Hierarchies,* ch. 6; Bestor, *Educational Wastelands;* Jesse Sears and Adin Henderson, *Cubberley of Stanford and His Contribution to American Education* (Stanford, Cal., 1957); Stephen K. Bailey, Richard D. Frost, Paul E. Marsh, Robert Wood, *Schoolmen and Power: A Study of State Aid to Education in the Northeast* (Syracuse, 1962); James D. Koerner, *Who Controls American Education? A Guide for Laymen* (Boston, 1968), 95–103.

19 For sample school law textbooks, see: C. W. Bardeen, *A Manual of Common School Law* (Syracuse, 1900); Harry Trusler, *Essentials of School Law* (Milwaukee, 1927); Harvey Voorhees, *The Law of the Public School System in the United States* (Boston, 1916).

20 Ellwood P. Cubberley, *Public School Administration: A Statement of the Fundamental Principles Underlying the Organization and Administration of American Education* (Boston, 1916); "Proceedings of the First National Conference on Rural School Consolidation," *Bulletin of the Iowa State Teachers College* 25 (1920): 1–83.

21 Tyack, *One Best System,* part 5; Sister M. Bernard Loughery, *Parental Rights in American Educational Law: Their Basis and Implementation* (Washington, D.C., 1952), 122.

22 Whitney R. Harris, "Teachers' Tenure in California," *California Law Review* 24 (1936): 441–46; NEA, "The Problem of Teacher Tenure," *Research Bulletin* vol. 2, no. 5; NEA, "Teachers' Retirement Allowances," *Research Bulletin,* vol. 2, no. 3.

23 "First National Conference on Rural School Consolidation."

24 Charles G. Howard, "School Law in Illinois," *Illinois Law Quarterly* 5 (1923): 168–75; Wayne Fuller, *The Old Country School: The Story of Rural Education in the Middle West* (Chicago, 1982), chap. 11.

25 Marshall A. Barber, *The Schoolhouse at Prairie View* (Lawrence, Kan., 1953).

26 Edith Lathrop, *The Improvement of Rural Schools by Standardization* (Washington D.C., 1925); Jonathan Sher, ed., *Education in Rural America: A Reassessment of Conventional Wisdom* (Boulder, Colo., 1977); also see cases on school consolidation treated in the West decennial digests.

27 Harold H. Punke, *Law and Liability in Pupil Transportation* (Chicago, 1943).

28 Earl William Anderson, *The Teacher's Contract and Other Legal Phases of Teacher Status* (New York, 1927), 149.

29 Cubberley quoted in Anderson, *Contracts*, 140; Thomas M. Griffin and Donald N. Jensen, "The Legalization of State Educational Policymaking in California (Stanford, Cal.: Institute for Research in Educational Finance and Governance, 1982), 4.

30 Loughery *Parental Rights*, 105.

31 Daniel R. Hodgdon, "School Law—A Social Philosophy," *Junior-Senior High School Clearing House* 8 (1933): 229.

32 David Tyack and Michael Berkowitz, "The Man Nobody Liked: Towards a Social History of the Truant Officer, 1840–1940," *American Quarterly* 29 (1977): 31–54.

33 John Frederick Bender, *The Functions of Courts in Enforcing School Attendance Laws* (New York, 1927), 139, 142.

34 *State v. Bailey,* 157 Ind. 324, 61 N.E. 730 (1901); *Knox v. O'Brien* 7 N.J. Super. 608. 72 A. 2nd 389 (1950); *Byler v. State,* 26 Ohio App. 329, 157 N.E. 421 (1927); Bender, *Functions,* 11; we are indebted to Michael Schlessinger for a legal brief on 146 cases dealing with compulsory attendance and for discussions with him about these cases and other issues treated in this chapter.

35 John R. Sutton, "Social Structure, Institutions, and the Legal Status of Children in the United States," *American Journal of Sociology* 88 (1983): 915–47.

36 Aaron Benavot, "Federal Courts and Public Schooling: Historical and Legal Patterns before *Brown*"—paper delivered at the annual meeting of the Organization of American Historians, Minneapolis, Minn., April, 1984; for an interpretation of bureaucratization at the federal level as a defense of individual and minority rights against majoritarian rule, see William E. Nelson, *The Roots of American Bureaucracy, 1830–1900* (Cambridge, Mass., 1982).

Prologue: The Many Faces of Power

1 Peter Bachrach and Morton S. Baratz, "Two Faces of Power," *American Political Science Review* 56 (1962): 947–52.

2 Gender, like race, is a visible characteristic given great social meaning; unlike race, however, gender rarely was mentioned as an issue either in statutes or court cases. This relative invisibility of gender as an issue of official school policy is a puzzling question which Elisabeth Hansot and David Tyack are exploring in a forthcoming study of gender in schools.

3 Margaret Szasz, *Education and the American Indian: The Road to Self-determination* (Albuquerque, N.M., 1974).

4 *St. Louis School Report for 1875,* 111–15.

5 Stephen Arons, *Compelling Belief: The Culture of American Schooling* (New York, 1983), 137–39.

6 *West Virginia Board of Education v. Barnette* 319 U.S. 624 (1943).

7 *Meyer v. Nebraska* 262 U.S. 510 (1923); *Pierce v. Society of Sisters* 268 U.S. 510 (1925).

Chapter 5: The Constitutional Moment: Reconstruction and Black Education in the South, 1867–1954

1 *Proceedings of the Constitutional Convention of South Carolina . . . 1868* (Charleston, S.C., 1868), 707, 696.

2 *Congressional Globe,* 40th Congress, 1st Session, March 16, 1867, 166–67.

3 Ibid.; David Donald, *Charles Sumner and the Rights of Man* (New York, 1970), 424–26.

4 Eric Foner, "Reconstruction Revisited," *Reviews in American History* 10 (1982): 90, 94.

5 For Southern constitutional clauses on the virtue of diffusing knowledge, see Franklin B. Hough, comp., *Constitutional Provisions in Regard to Education in the Several States of the American Union,* U.S. Bureau of Education, *Circular of Information, No. 7, 1875* (Washington, D.C., 1875), 2, 22, 43, 57, 59, 70, 83, 84; Foner, "Reconstruction Revisited," 90.

6 William M. Wiecek, *The Guarantee Clause of the U.S. Constitution* (Ithaca, 1972), 136, 145, 173, 175, 181, 207.

7 W. E. B. Du Bois, *Black Reconstruction in America: An Essay towards the History of the Part which Black Folk Played in the Attempt to Reconstruct Democracy in America, 1860–1880* (reprint of 1935 ed., Cleveland and New York, 1962), ch. 15.

8 W. E. B. DuBois, *The Negro Common School* (Atlanta, 1901), 82, 79–83; John Blassingame, *Black New Orleans* (Chicago, 1973), ch. 5; Roger A. Fischer, *The Segregation Struggle in Louisiana, 1862–77* (Urbana, Ill., 1974), 44–52.

9 See chapters 1–3 *supra.*

10 Horace Mann Bond, *The Education of the Negro in the American Social Order* (New York, 1934).

11 Lawrence M. Friedman, *The Legal System: A Social Science Perspective* (New York, 1975), 15, passim; David L. Kirp, *Just Schools: The Idea of Racial Equality in American Education* (Berkeley, 1982); Richard Kluger, *Simple Justice: The History of Brown v. Board of Education and Black America's Struggle for Equality* (New York, 1977).

12 Man quoted in Jacqueline Jones, *Soldiers of Light and Love: Northern Teachers and Georgia Blacks, 1865–1873* (Chapel Hill, 1980), 63; John B. Alford, Bureau of Refugees, Freedmen, and Abandoned Lands, *Inspector's Report of Schools and Finances* (Washington, D.C., 1866); Roberta Sue Alexander, "Hostility and Hope: Black Education in North Carolina during Presidential Reconstruction, 1865–1867," *North Carolina Historical Review* 53 (1976): 113–32; Leon F. Litwak, *Been in the Storm So Long: The Aftermath of Slavery* (New York, 1979), 75, 499; John W. Blassingame, "Before the Ghetto: The Making of the Black Community in Savannah, Georgia, 1865–1880," *Journal of Social History* 6 (1973): 470–73; Peter Kolchin, *First Freedom: The Responses of Alabama's Blacks to Emancipation and Reconstruction* (Westport, Conn., 1972), 87–97.

13 James D. Anderson, "Ex-Slaves and the Rise of Universal Education in the New South, 1860–1880," in Ronald K. Goodenow and Arthur O. White, eds., *Education and the Rise of the New South* (Boston, 1981), 1–25; Herbert G. Gutman, "Observations on Selected Trends in American Working-Class Historiography Together with Some New Data that Might Affect Some of the Questions Asked by Historians of American Education Interested in the Relationship between 'Education and Work,' " unpublished paper presented at the Conference on Education and Work, Stanford University, August 17–18, 1979; Litwak, *Storm,* 474.

14 Robert Morris, *Reading, 'Riting, and Reconstruction: The Education of Freedmen in the South, 1861–1870* (Chicago, 1981), 33–53.

15 William S. McFeeley, *Yankee Stepfather: General O. O. Howard and the Freedmen* (New Haven, 1968), 49, 250.

16 William F. Messner, *Freedmen and the Ideology of Free Labor: Louisiana, 1862–1865* (Lafayette, Louisiana, 1978), 166.

17 Ibid., 164–83; after the war, the Freedmen's Bureau assisted and coordinated the schools for blacks; for a study of a contrasting state, where a private association took the white lead rather than the army, see Richard P. Fuke, "The Baltimore Association for the Moral and Educational Improvement of the Colored People 1864–1870," *Maryland Historical Magazine: A Quarterly* 66 (1971): 369–404.

18 Jones, *Soldiers;* Ronald E. Butchart, *Northern Schools, Southern Blacks, and Reconstruction: Freedmen's Education, 1862–1875* (Westwood, Conn., 1980); Litwak, *Storm,* 494–501.

19 Anderson, "Universal Education," 19–22; Du Bois, *Black Reconstruction,* ch. 15; Alexander, "Hostility and Hope"; Butchart, *Freedmen's Education.*

20 *Congressional Globe,* 39th Congress, 2nd Session, February 26, 28, pp. 1842–45, 1893, 1949–50; ibid., 40th Congress, 1st Session, March 16, 1867, p. 166; Fawn M. Brodie, *Thaddeus Stevens: Scourge of the South* (New York, 1959), 321; James M. McPherson, *The Struggle for Equality: Abolitionists and the Negro in the Civil War and Reconstruction* (Princeton, 1964), 370–75, 383; William Preston Vaughn, *Schools for All: The Blacks & Public Education in the South, 1865–1877* (Lexington, Ky., 1974), ch. 6.

21 Donnelly quoted in Donald R. Warren, *To Enforce Education: A History of the Founding Years of the United States Office of Education* (Detroit, 1974), 78— see also his chapter 3 on the legislative history of the agency.

22 *Congressional Globe,* 39th Congress, 1st Session, February 26, 1867, p. 1843; Vaughn, *Schools for All,* 120–22; on later Southern reaction to federal aid, see C. Vann Woodward, *Origins of the New South, 1877–1913* (Baton Rouge, La., 1951), 63–64.

23 *Congressional Globe,* 40th Congress, 1st Session, March 16, 1867, pp. 168, 166–170; for speeches on Congressional Reconstruction giving the larger context of this debate on schools, see ibid., 39th Congress, 2nd Session, Appendix, 83–108.

24 *Congressional Globe,* 40th Congress, 1st Session, March 16, 1867, 169.

25 Hough, comp., *Constitutional Provisions,* 90, footnote; Bertram Wyatt-Brown, "The Civil Rights Act of 1875," *Western Political Science Quarterly* 18 (1965): 763–75.

26 Alfred E. Kelly, "The Congressional Controversy over School Segregation, 1867–1875," *American Historical Review* 64 (1959): 539, 537–63.

27 Mobile *Nationalist,* January 23, 1868, as quoted in Malcolm C. McMillan, *Constitutional Development in Alabama, 1798–1901: A Study in Politics, the Negro, and Sectionalism* (Chapel Hill, 1955), 143.

28 Francis N. Thorpe, ed., *The Federal and State Constitutions, Colonial Charters and other Organic Laws of the States, Territories and Colonies Now or Heretofore Forming the United States of America* (Washington, D.C., 1909), I:149, 322; III:716, 868, 1465; V:2817; VI:3301; among Southern states between 1865 and 1870, Arkansas and Texas directed the legislature to make laws compelling

school attendance for children of school age; South Carolina made a similar provision, but it said that it was not binding until the school system was "thoroughly and completely organized"; constitutions in Missouri, and North Carolina gave the legislature power to compel school attendance, and in Virginia to do whatever was necessary to make parents prevent ignorance and vagrancy in their children, thus indicating that a policy of compulsory schooling had become a desirable goal but not requiring it absolutely.

29 Hough, *Constitutional Provisions*, 9, 12-13, 19, 22-23, 40-43, 57, 70, 80, 84-85, 90.

30 Hough, *Constitutional Provisions*, 21 and passim; Richard L. Hume, "The 'Black and Tan' Constitutional Conventions of 1867-69 in Ten Former Confederate States: A Study of Their Membership" (Ph.D. diss., University of Washington, 1969), 234; McMillan, *Alabama*, 144; Vaughn, *Schools for All*, 65-68.

31 Hough, *Constitutional Provisions*, 44, 82, Hume, "Constitutional Conventions," 28, 150, 358-59, 490-91, 656.

32 *Debates and Proceedings of the Convention . . . to Form a Constitution for the State of Arkansas* (Little Rock, 1868), 630-31.

33 *Carolina Convention Journal*, 342, as quoted in Hume, "Constitutional Conventions," 491.

34 *Proceedings of the Constitutional Convention of South Carolina, 1868*, 690-93, 747-48, 873, 901; Joel Williamson, *After Slavery: The Negro in South Carolina during Reconstruction, 1861-1877* (Chapel Hill, N.C., 1965), ch. 8.

35 Williamson, *After Slavery*, 221-23; Louis R. Harlan, "Desegregation in New Orleans during Reconstruction," *American Historical Review* 68 (1962): 663-75.

36 Du Bois, *Negro Common School*, 43, passim; Du Bois, *Black Reconstruction*, ch. 15; Bond, *Education of Negro*, 49 and passim.

37 Du Bois, *Black Reconstruction*, 667; Foner, "Reconstruction Revisited," 94; U.S. Bureau of the Census, *Historical Statistics of the United States* (Washington, D.C.: GPO, 1975), I:382; William R. Davis, *The Development and Present Status of Negro Education in East Texas* (New York, 1934), 11-16; Charles L. Coon, "The Beginnings of the North Carolina City Schools, 1867-1887," *South Atlantic Quarterly* 7 (1913): 235-47; a full accounting of the degree to which Reconstruction educational provisions were actually implemented is beyond the intent or scope of this chapter.

38 Woodward, *Origins*, 51; *Journal of the Constitutional Convention of the State of South Carolina . . . 1895* (Columbia, S.C.: State Printer, 1895), 2; Constitutions of Alabama (1875), Arkansas (1874), Florida (1885), Georgia (1877), Louisiana (1879), Mississippi (1890), North Carolina (1876), South Carolina (1895), Texas (1876), in Thorpe, ed., *Constitutions;* Bond, *Education of the Negro*, 80-97; Du Bois, *Negro Common School*, 38; Stuart G. Noble, *Forty Years of the Public Schools in Mississippi, with Special Reference to the Education of the Negro* (New York, 1918), 53-54.

39 Woodward, *Origins*, 62; Bond, *Education of the Negro*, 94-104; Noble, *Mississippi*, 54-75; Gladys Tignor Peterson, "The Present Status of the Negro Separate School as Defined by Court Decisions," *Journal of Negro Education* 4 (1935): 366-67.

40 Ibid.

41 Theodore R. Mitchell, "Oppositional Education in the Southern Farmers' Alliance, 1890–1900" (Ph.D. diss., Stanford University, 1983); Bond, *Education of the Negro*, 98–115; Thomas Jesse Jones, *Negro Education: A Study of the Private and Higher Schools for Colored People in the United States*, Bureau of Education, *Bulletin no. 38, 1916* (Washington, D.C., 1917), I:7.

42 Louis R. Harlan, *Separate and Unequal: Public School Campaigns and Racism in the Southern Seaboard States 1901–1915* (New York, 1969), 11, 8–18.

43 Charles H. Thompson, "Court Action the Only Reasonable Alternative to Remedy Immediate Abuses of the Negro Separate School," *Journal of Negro Education* 4 (1935): 421.

44 Ibid., 421–27; for a condescending version of the human relations approach, see William H. Kilpatrick, "Resort to Courts by Negroes to Improve their Schools a Conditional Alternative," *Journal of Negro Education* 4 (1935): 412–18.

45 *State ex rel. Farmers v. Board of School comm'rs.* 226 Ala. 62, 145 So. 575 (1933); Charles S. Mangum, *The Legal Status of the Negro* (Chapel Hill, 1940), ch. 4; Maurice L. Risen, *Legal Aspects of Separation of Races in the Public Schools* (Philadelphia, 1935); Franklin Johnson, *The Development of State Legislation Concerning the Free Negro* (New York, 1918).

46 Peterson, "Negro Separate School," 351–74; *Gong Lum v. Rice*, 275 U.S. 78 (1927); *Cumming v. Richmond County*, 175 U.S. 528 (1899); J. Morgan Kousser, "Separate But Not Equal: The Supreme Court's First Decision on Racial Discrimination in Schools," *Journal of Southern History* 46 (1980): 17–44; for a brilliant account of the cases leading to racial desegregation, see Kluger, *Simple Justice.*

47 Foner, "Reconstruction Revisited," 95.

Chapter 6: Moral Majorities and the School Curriculum: Making Virtue Mandatory, 1880–1930

1 NEA, *Addresses and Proceedings, 1891*, 298, 294–403; for a discussion of modern forms of control of curriculum see J. Myron Atkin, "Government in the Classroom," *Daedalus* 109 (1980): 85–97.

2 Robert Wiebe, "The Social Functions of Public Education," *American Quarterly* 21 (1969): 147–64; Ruth Elson, *Guardians of Tradition: American Schoolbooks of the Nineteenth Century* (Lincoln, 1964).

3 Lawrence M. Friedman describes the general phenomenon of "normative domination" in "Notes toward a History of American Justice," in Lawrence M. Friedman and Harry N. Scheiber, eds., *American Law and the Constitutional Order: Historical Perspectives* (Cambridge, Mass., 1978), 21–24; Walter Lippmann, *American Inquisitors: A Commentary on Dayton and Chicago* (New York, 1928); Bessie L. Pierce, *Public Opinion in the Teaching of History in the United States* (New York, 1926); Lewis P. Todd, *Wartime Relations of the Federal Government and the Public Schools, 1917–18* (New York, 1945).

4 John W. Meyer and James G. Roth, "A Reinterpretation of American Status Politics," *Pacific Sociological Review* 13 (1970): 95–102; Josiah Strong, *Our Country* (Cambridge, Mass., 1963).

5 Jesse K. Flanders, *Legislative Control of the Elementary Curriculum* (New York, 1925), 68, 79–81; Joseph R. Gusfield, *Symbolic Crusade: Status Politics and the American Temperance Movement* (Urbana, Ill., 1963); Norton Mezvinsky, "The White-Ribbon Reform, 1874–1920," (Ph.D. diss., University of Wisconsin, 1959), 154–55.

6 Elizabeth P. Gordon, *Women Torch-Bearers: The Story of the Women's Christian Temperance Union* (Evanston, Ill., 1924); Ruth Bordin, *Woman and Temperance: The Quest for Power and Liberty, 1973–1900* (Philadelphia, 1981), 55, 135–39, 163–75; Mezvinsky, "White Ribbon," 148–49, 153–55.

7 Map reproduced by an approving U.S. Commissioner of Education, William T. Harris, in *Report for 1894–95*, 1833; Bordin, *Temperance*, 135–36; Daniel J. Whitener, *Prohibition in North Carolina, 1715–1945* (Chapel Hill, 1945), 106–7.

8 U.S. Commissioner of Education, *Report for 1894–95*, p. 1830; Sara Phillips Thomas, "Temperance Teaching in Our Cities," *The Temperance Educational Quarterly* 5 (1921): 10–11; Augusta B. Bainbridge, "The Best Method of Teaching the Nature and Effects of Narcotics," *The Temperance Educational Quarterly* 4 (1920): 22; Willard Waller, *The Sociology of Teaching* (1932; reprint ed. New York, 1965); on the politics of the NEA, see H. E. Buchholz, "Pedagogues Leap to Save Us," *American Mercury* 26 (1932): 328–45.

9 Mezvinsky, "White Ribbon," 170; Flanders, *Curriculum*, 69–79; for the political strategies—aimed at adults—used by another temperance group, see Peter H. Odegard, *Pressure Politics: the Story of the Anti-Saloon League* (New York, 1928).

10 U.S. Commissioner of Education, *Report for 1889–90*, II:697–98; Mezvinsky, "White Ribbon," 158–66.

11 *The Temperance Educational Quarterly* 4 (1920, no. 3): 8; 7 (1923, no. 1): 35–36; passim.

12 Ernest P. Bowditch and Chester F. Hodge, "Report on the Present Instruction on the Physiological Action of Alcohol," in John F. Billings, *The Physiological Aspects of the Liquor Problem* (Boston, 1903), 44; George H. Martin, *Report on Scientific Temperance Teaching for the Massachusetts State Board of Education, 1887–88* (Boston, 1888), 731; Mezvinsky, "White Ribbon," 184, 187; Howard K. Beale, *A History of Freedom of Teaching in American Schools* (New York, 1941), 220–26.

13 Bordin, *Temperance*, ch. 9; Dinah Shelton, "Legislative Control over Public School Curriculum," *Willamette Law Review* 15 (1979): 485, n. 55.

14 Robert G. McCloskey, ed., *The Bible in the Public Schools: Arguments before the Superior Court of Cincinnati in the Case of Minor v. Board of Education of Cincinnati, 1870* (New York, 1967), 213; Francis Michael Perko, "A Time to Favor Zion; A Case Study of Religion as a Force in American Educational Development, 1830–1870," (Ph.D. diss., Stanford University, 1981); Raymond Culver, *Horace Mann and Religion in Massachusetts Public Schools* (New Haven, 1927); Ray Allen Billington, *The Protestant Crusade, 1800–1860* (New York, 1952).

15 Timothy Smith, "Protestant Schooling and American Nationality, 1800–1850," *Journal of American History* 53 (1967): 679–95; David Tyack, "The Kingdom of God and the Common School: Protestant Ministers and the Educational Awaken-

ing in the West," *Harvard Educational Review* 36 (1966): 447–69; Horace Mann, *Twelfth Annual Report* (Boston, 1849), 116–17; Culver, *Mann*, 252.

16 Robert Baird, *Religion in America* (New York, 1844), 148.

17 Otto T. Hamilton, *The Courts and the Curriculum* (New York, 1927), 113; Donald E. Boles, *The Two Swords: Commentaries and Cases in Religion and Education* (Ames, Iowa, 1967), 83–87.

18 *Donahue v. Richards*, 38 Me. 379 (1854), 381, 387.

19 Vincent P. Lannie, *Public Money and Parochial Education: Bishop Hughes, Governor Seward, and the New York School Controversy* (Cleveland, 1968); Daniel Dorchester, *Romanism Versus the Public School* (New York, 1888), 81ff.

20 National Teachers' Association, *Proceedings, 1869*, 19, 23; A. D. Mayo, "Object Lessons in Moral Instruction in the Common School," NEA, *Addresses and Proceedings, 1880*, 8–10; Robert Michaelson, *Piety in the Public Schools: Trends and Issues in the Relationship Between Religion and the Public School System in the United States* (New York, 1970), 168; U.S. Commissioner of Education, *Report for 1903*, II:2445.

21 Sources for table 6.2 are: Ward W. Keesecker, *Legal Status of Bible Reading and Religious Instruction in Public Schools*, U.S. Office of Education, *Bulletin no. 14, 1930* (Washington, D.C., 1930) and Alvin W. Johnson and Frank H. Yost, *Separation of Church and State in the United States* (Minneapolis, 1948), 33–34; Willard B. Gatewood, Jr., ed., *Controversy in the Twenties: Fundamentalism, Modernism, and Evolution* (Nashville, 1969), 169—an excellent selection of primary sources.

22 Keesecker, *Legal Status;* Johnson and Yost, *Separation*, 33–36; in Colorado the Ku Klux Klan feted a judge who had ruled in favor of Bible reading—see Frank Swancara, "The Colorado Bible Case," *Lawyer and Banker* 21 (1928): 165–67; for a concise discussion of legal issues and translations of the Bible, see Anson P. Stokes and Leo Pfeffer, *Church and State in the United States* (New York, 1964), 9, 371–78; *Constitution and Laws of the Knights of the Ku Klux Klan* (Atlanta, 1921), 87; John Higham, *Strangers in the Land: Patterns of American Nativism, 1860–1925* (New York, 1978), ch. x.

23 Gatewood, *Controversy*, 36; Norman F. Furniss, *The Fundamentalist Controversy* (New Haven, 1954), 83–95; Maynard Shipley, *The War on Modern Science: A Short History of the Fundamentalist Attacks on Evolution and Modernism* New York, 1927), 172; Dorothy Nelkin, *The Creation Controversy: Science of Scripture in the Schools* (New York, 1982), 33.

24 WCFA and Ferguson quotations from Furniss, *Controversy*, 44, 52; Oklahoma legislator's quotation from R. Halliburton, Jr., "The Nation's First Anti-Darwin Law: Passage and Repeal," *Southwestern Social Science Quarterly* 41 (1960): 126, 123–35.

25 Martin quoted in Shipley, *War*, 65; Furniss, *Controversy*, 56–75; Kenneth K. Bailey, "The Enactment of Tennessee's Antievolution Law," *Journal of Southern History* 16 (1950): 472–90; R. Halliburton, Jr., "The Adoption of Arkansas' Antievolution Law," *Arkansas Historical Quarterly* 23 (1964): 271–83.

26 George M. Marsden, *Fundamentalism and American Culture: The Shaping of Twentieth-Century Evangelicalism, 1870–1925* (New York, 1980), 184–85; L.

Sprague de Camp, *The Great Monkey Trial* (Garden City, N.Y., 1968), chs. 1–2; Jerry T. Thompkins, ed., *D-Days at Dayton: Reflections on the Scopes Trial* (Baton Rouge, 1965); Ray Ginger, *Six Days or Forever? Tennessee v. John Thomas Scopes* (Boston, 1958), ch. 1; Robert M. Miller, *American Protestantism and Social Issues, 1919–1939* (Chapel Hill, 1958), 155–160.

27 Lippmann, *Inquisitors*, 3–6, ch. 3.

28 William J. Reese, "The Public Schools and the Great Gates of Hell," *Educational Theory* 32 (1982): 9–17.

29 *Committee Reports and Resolutions Adopted at the First National Convention of the American Legion November 10, 11, and 12, 1919* (Minneapolis, 1919) as quoted in Bessie L. Pierce, *Citizens' Organizations and the Civic Training of Youth* (New York, 1933), 35, and Sentinels quotation ibid., 7.

30 Textbook law of Oregon, 1923, quoted in Flanders, *Control*, 35; Higham, *Strangers*, chaps. 8–10; William Preston, Jr., *Aliens and Dissenters: Federal Suppression of Radicals, 1903–1933* (New York, 1963); Robert K. Murray, *Red Scare: A Study of National Hysteria, 1919–1920* (Minneapolis, 1955); Howard K. Beale, *A History of Freedom of Teaching in American Schools* (New York, 1941), 235–36.

31 U.S. Bureau of Education, *Bulletin no. 14, 1924* (Washington, D.C.: GPO, 1925), 578–79; "German in the Schools," *School and Society* 7 (1918): 645; Flanders, *Control*, ch. 2; Bessie L. Pierce, *Public Opinion and the Teaching of History in the United States* (New York, 1926), 57, 84, 85, 99–102, 105, 189, and passim; Heinz Kloss, *The American Bilingual Tradition* (Rowley, Mass., 1977).

32 Sources for table 6.3: Flanders, *Legislative Control*, 62; certain figures for 1923 taken from NEA, "Facts on the Public School Curriculum," *Research Bulletin*, vol. I, no. 5 (Washington, D.C., 1923); "Summary of Constitutional and Legal Provisions Relating to Education in the Several States and Territories," U.S. Commissioner of Education, *Report for 1885–86*, 47–214.

33 Lem Dever, *Inside the Klan: Invisible Empire Revealed* (Portland, 1923), 29–30; Kenneth T. Jackson, *The Ku Klux Klan in the City, 1915–1930* (New York, 1967); Pierce, *Public Opinion;* Lippmann, *Inquisitors*, 67–72.

34 Mary R. Dearing, *Veterans in Politics: The Story of the G.A.R.* (Baton Rouge, 1952), 403–8; Pierce, *Opinion*, 45–46.

35 Dearing, *Veterans*, 403–8, 475, 472–76.

36 Dearing, *Veterans*, 403–8; Pierce, *Opinion*, 57, 94, ch. 3.

37 Pierce, *Citizens,* ch. 3; Pierce, *Opinion*, 270–72; Gellerman, *Legion.*

38 Committee on American Citizenship, "Program for Promoting American Ideals," *American Bar Association Journal* 8 (1922): 585, 587, 585–88; Martin J. Wade, "Teaching the Constitution in the Public Schools of the Nation," *Proceedings of the Iowa State Bar Association* (1924), 178–87.

39 Ibid., 587–89; *Report of the American Bar Association*, 48 (1923), 442–51; *Report of the American Bar Association*, 49 (1924), 255–69; Pierce, *Opinion*, 184–88.

40 "German in the Schools," *School and Society* 7 (1918): 645; "Teaching the Constitution in the Schools," *The Constitutional Review* 7 (1923): 255–58; Pierce, *Opinion*, 188–90; the board of directors of the League forced Professor William B. Otis to resign from the board because he dissented from their opinion that

there should be compulsory military training in colleges—"Professor Otis and Compulsory Military Training," *School and Society* 23 (1926): 107–8.

41 Quotations from Pierce, *Opinion*, 190–93.

42 "Loyalty Tests for School Teachers," *Law Notes* 26 (1922): 101; Beale, *Free*, preface, chaps. 5–8.

43 Hayes quoted in Lippman, *Inquisitors*, 33; Gellerman, *Legion*, ch. 9; Dean William Russell, quoted in Flanders, *Control*, iii; "Compulsory Training in Patriotism," *School Review* 29 (1921): 650–52; Beale, *Free*, 527–28; Lawrence H. Chamberlain, *Loyalty and Legislative Action: A Survey of Activity by the New York State Legislature, 1919–1949* (Ithaca, 1951).

44 On the wide zone of discretion allowed state legislatures by the courts, see Hamilton, *Courts*, 29–31; Theodore C. Sorensen, "Legislative Control of Loyalty in the School System," *Nebraska Law Review* 29 (1950): 485–505; Stephen Arons has raised critical questions about the implications of majority rule for legal and educational policy in *Compelling Belief: The Culture of American Schooling* (New York, 1983); for our response, see Thomas James, "The Tantalizing Case for Liberty," *Harvard Educational Review* 54 (1984): 201–7 and David Tyack, "Freedom of Thought and Majority Rule in the Public School: The Bankrupcy of Liberal Ideology?" *Teachers College Record* 85 (1984): 653–57; for the reply of Arons, see "Hemlock for Two: A Reply to Professor Tyack's Review of *Compelling Belief*," *Teachers College Record* 85 (1984): 658–62.

Chapter 7: Compulsory Public Schooling and the Perils of Pluralism: The Case of Oregon, 1922

1 Luther Powell, in preface to George Estes, *The Old Cedar School* (Troutdale, Ore., 1922), 9; Lloyd Jorgenson, "The Oregon School Law of 1922: Passage and Sequel," *Catholic Historical Review* 54 (1968): 455–66; David Tyack, "The Perils of Pluralism: The Background of the Pierce Case," *American Historical Review* 74 (1968): 74–98.

2 *Constitution and Laws of the Knights of the Ku Klux Klan* (Atlanta, 1931), 87; for examples of the KKK's faith in public education, see Lem Dever, *Inside the Klan: Invisible Empire Revealed* (Portland, Ore., 1923), 10, 20, 23 and Estes, *Old Cedar School*, 22–24, 32–39; John Higham, *Strangers in the Land: Patterns of American Nativism* (New York, 1966), ch. 10.

3 *Proposed Constitutional Amendments and Measures (with Arguments) to Be Submitted to the voters at the General Election, Tuesday, November 7, 1922* (Salem, Ore., 1922), 22; David Tyack, "Ways of Seeing"; Tyack and Berkowitz, "The Man Nobody Liked."

4 Portland *Telegram*, Oct. 26, 1922; Silverton *Appeal*, Oct. 13, 1922; *Telegram*, Nov. 2, 1922.

5 Ellwood P. Cubberley *et al.*, *Report of the Survey of the Public School System of School District No. 1, Multnomah County, Oregon* (Portland, 1913), 71–74; David Tyack, "The Kingdom of God and the Common School: Protestant Ministers and the Educational Awakening in the West," *Harvard Educational Review* 36 (1966): 459–67.

6 The Lutherans kept a close watch on the campaign of the KKK to abolish pri-

vate schools, and in Oregon the Lutheran Schools Committee kept a file on its efforts in Oregon and elsewhere which is deposited in the Oregon Historical Society (hereafter cited as LSC). On views of Oregon as precedent for similar laws in other states, see the Masonic *New Age* 28 (1920): 322; Dayton, Washington, *Dispatch,* Dec. 30, 1922; Portland *Journal,* June 10, 1922; and letter from Arthur Brohm to Rudolph Messerli, Sept. 15, 1922, in LSC, saying the petitions for a similar initiative had failed in California for lack of signatures.

7 *Proposed Constitutional Amendments,* 22–24; *New Age* 30 (1922): 549; Eugene *Guard,* Nov. 4, 1922; Baker City *Democrat,* Nov. 3, 1922; Portland *Telegram,* Nov. 2, 1922.

8 Salem *Journal,* Oct. 26, 1922; LaGrange *Observer,* Oct. 28, 1922; Portland *Oregonian,* Oct. 29 and Nov. 9, 1922; Dorothy O. Johansen and Charles M. Gates, *Empire of the Columbia: A History of the Pacific Northwest* (2nd ed., New York, 1967), 494–98.

9 David Chalmers, *Hooded Americanism: The First Century of the Ku Klux Klan, 1865–1965* (Garden City, N.Y., 1965), ch. 12; Eckard V. Toy, "The Ku Klux Klan in Tillamook, Oregon," *Pacific Northwest Quarterly* 53 (1962): 60–64; Lem Dever, *Confessions of an Imperial Klansman* (Portland, 1924); Kenneth T. Jackson, *The Ku Klux Klan in the City, 1915–1930* (New York, 1967), 242.

10 E. Haldemann-Julius, *The Kreed of the Klansmen* (Girard, Kansas, 1924), 30; Dever, *Inside the Klan,* 29–30; Jackson, *Ku Klux Klan,* 205.

11 Dever, *Inside the Klan,* 23, 25; for examples of the anti-Catholicism rampant in the press, see Glendale *News,* Oct. 12, 1922; Silverton *Appeal,* Oct. 13, 1922; and for Catholic reaction, Portland *Catholic Sentinel,* Oct. 12, 1922.

12 Estes, *Old Cedar School,* 5–7, 9, 40–43.

13 Glendale *News,* Oct. 12, 1922; Silverton *Appeal,* Oct. 13, 1922; Portland *Oregonian,* Oct. 24, Nov. 2, 1922.

14 Portland *Spectator,* Oct. 14, 1922; Catholic Civil Rights Association of Oregon, *Twenty-four Reasons Why You Should Vote 'No'* (Portland, 1922), 1.

15 Portland *Telegram,* Oct. 26, 1922; *Oregon Voter,* Oct. 7, 1922, 16–17 and files of LSC.

16 Portland *Scribe,* Nov. 3, 1922; Salem *Journal,* Oct. 28, 1922; Portland *Times,* n.d., clipping in LSC files; *Twenty-four Reasons,* 9; Martin Anderson, "A Study of Bills and Resolutions for Curriculum Prescriptions Introduced at the Oregon Legislature, 1901–1939," M.A. thesis, University of Oregon, 1939, 27–28.

17 *Proposed Constitutional Amendments,* 29–30; *Twenty-four Reasons,* 7; Astoria *Astorian,* Oct. 31, 1922; Portland *Telegram,* Oct. 21, 1922; many Protestant ministers, however, were among the bill's most enthusiastic supporters.

18 Clatskanie *Chief,* Oct. 22, 1922; in the December, 1922 issue of the journal the American Legion's campaign for prefervid Americanization won the hearty endorsement of the magazine; it is striking that in the hundreds of letters to newspapers on the compulsory education bill there were few, if any, from teachers or administrators.

19 University presidents quoted in an advertisement in Portland *News,* Nov. 1, 1922; see Jorgenson, "Oregon School Law," for national comments on the Oregon measure.

20 *Oregon Teacher's Monthly* 27 (1922), Oct., 12; Nov. 6.

21 Portland *Journal*, Oct. 27, 1922; Portland *Telegram*, Oct. 27, Nov. 6, 1922; *The Survey*, October 15, 1922, as quoted in Portland *Telegram*, Oct. 15, 1922; John Mecklin, *The Ku Klux Klan: A Study of the American Mind* (New York, 1963; first ed. 1924), 50.

22 Portland *Oregonian*, Oct. 29, Nov. 9, 1922; Portland *Catholic Sentinel*, Oct. 19, 1922; Rudolph Messerli to F. Pfotenhauer, Nov. 10, 1922, in LSC; in 1922 there were 238,444 registered Republicans as opposed to 89,477 Democrats in Oregon, and hence the victory of the Klan's candidate Pierce surprised many—see Jalmar Johnson, "When the Klan 'Took Over' Oregon," Portland *Oregonian*, Apr. 2, 1965.

23 Messerli to Pfotenhauer, Nov. 10, 1922, LSC; Seattle, Wash., *Times*, Jan. 21, 1923; Spokane, Wash., *Chronicle*, Feb. 14, 1922.

24 The lawyers' arguments and other information bearing on the case were collected in a book entitled *The Oregon School Fight: A True History* (Portland, 1924), esp. see 28, 40-41, 43-45, 66-69, 110-18; *Pierce v. Society of Sisters* 268 U.S. 510 (1925); Sam Duber, *The Public Schools and Religion: The Legal Context* (New York, 1966); Robert F. Drinan, *Religion, the Courts, and Public Policy* (New York, 1963), 122-27.

25 *Oregon School Fight*, 63, 118.

26 Ibid., 80-82, 88, 97-98.

27 *Society of Sisters of the Holy Names, Plaintiff, v. Pierce et al, Defendents*, nos. E8662 and 8660 cons. (D. Oregon, filed Mar. 31, 1924) in *Oregon School Cases: A Complete Record* (Baltimore, 1925), 54.

28 Portland *Catholic Sentinel*, Apr. 3, 1923; Portland *Oregonian*, Apr. 1, 1923; *Oregon School Fight*, 147-48.

29 *Oregon School Cases*, 102-3, 115-16.

30 Ibid., 275, 281, 285, 614.

31 *Pierce v. Society of Sisters*, 268 U.S. 510.

32 Ibid., for an intriguing First Amendment reading of *Pierce*, see Stephen Arons, "The Separation of School and State: *Pierce* Reconsidered," *Harvard Educational Review* 46 (1976): 76-104; also see Joel S. Moskowitz, "Parental Rights and State Education," *Washington Law Review* 50 (1975): 623-51.

33 *Meyer v. Nebraska*, 262 U.S. 390 (1923).

34 *Minersville School District v. Gobitis*, 310 U.S. 586 (1940); Evelyn R. Fulbright and Edward C. Bolmeier, *Courts and the Curriculum* (Cincinnati, 1964).

35 *West Virginia State Board of Education v. Barnette*, 319 U.S. 624 (1943).

Epilogue

1 *Brown v. Board of Education* 347 U.S. 483 (1954); *Abington School District v. Schempp* 374 U.S. 203 (1963); *Tinker v. Des Moines Independent Community School Dist.* 393 U.S. 503 (1969); *Serrano v. Priest* 5 Cal. 3rd. 584, 96 Cal. Rptr. 601, 487 P.2d 1241 (1971); David L. Kirp, *Just Schools: The Idea of Racial Equality in American Education* (Berkeley, 1982); a rich source on the thinking of legal activists is the set of pamphlets issued by the Harvard Center for Law and Education, *Inequality in Education*—eg. "Discipline and Student Rights,"

20 (July 1975); "Testing and Tracking: Bias in the Classroom," 14 (July 1973); "Sex Discrimination," 18 (October 1974).

2 Donald L. Horowitz, *The Courts and Social Policy* (Washington, D.C., 1977), 10; Diane Ravitch, *The Uncertain Crusade* (New York, 1983); John C. Hogan, *The Schools, the Courts, and the Public Interest* (Lexington, Mass., 1974).

3 Nathan Glazer, "Towards an Imperial Judiciary," *Public Interest*, no. 41 (1975), 104–7; Michael A. Rebell and Arthur R. Block, *Educational Policy Making and the Courts* (Chicago, 1982), chap. 1; W. Hazard, "Courts in the Saddle: School Boards Out," *Phi Delta Kappan* 56 (1974): 259–61; Allen D. Schwartz, "Have Federal Courts Become Super School Boards?" *Illinois Bar Journal* 60 (1971): 104–12 (his answer is NO, but he indicates widespread dissatisfaction with the courts); Alexander M. Bickel, *The Supreme Court and the Idea of Progress* (New York, 1970); for discussion of the notion that America has become "litigious" and the positive functions of litigation, see Marc Galanter, "Reading the Landscape of Disputes: What We Know and Don't Know (and Think We Know) about Our Allegedly Contentious and Litigious Society," *UCLA Law Review* 31 (1983): 4–71, and Jethro K. Lieberman, *The Litigious Society* (New York, 1981). chs. 5, 7.

4 Keith Goldhammer, "Roles of the American School Superintendent," in Luvern L. Cunningham, Walter G. Hack, and Raphael O. Nystrand, eds., *Educational Administration: The Developing Decades* (Berkeley, 1977), 148–51; James S. Coleman, "The Struggle for Control of Education," ERIC Report Resume ED 015 158, October 7, 1967; for changes in the scope and nature of school law see David L. Kirp and Mark G. Yudof, *Educational Policy and the Law: Cases and Materials* (Berkeley, 1974); on the conservatism of lawyers in the 1950s, see Jerold S. Auerbach, *Unequal Justice: Lawyers and Social Change in Modern America* (New York, 1976), ch. 8.

5 For reviews of recent scholarship on legal changes in education see Paul W. Thurston, "Is Good Law Good Education?" and Henry S. Lufler, "Compliance and the Courts," in *Review of Research in Education 8*, David Berliner, ed. (Washington, D.C., 1980), 296–358.

6 Gunnar Myrdal, *An American Dilemma: The Negro Problem and Modern Democracy* (New York, 1972 ed.).

7 See Appendix for sources and estimation procedures for these figures on litigation in education; Lawrence M. Friedman, "Courts over Time: A Survey of Theories and Research," in Keith O. Boyum and Lynn Mather, eds., *Empirical Theories about Courts* (New York, 1983), 24–32.

8 Figures on pupil discipline cases from Lawrence M. Friedman, "Limited Monarchy: The Rise and Fall of Student Rights," table 1, in David L. Kirp. ed., *School Days, Rule Days*, forthcoming; Thomas Griffin and Donald N. Jensen, "The Legalization of State Educational Policymaking in California," Project Report No. 82-A2, Stanford University, Institute for Research on Educational Finance and Governance, January 1982, 9; Thomas Marvell, "The Rationales for Federal Question Jurisdiction: An Empirical Examination of Student Rights," *Wisconsin Law Review* 5 (1984): 1315–72.

9 David L. Kirp, "Law, Politics, and Equal Educational Opportunity: The Limits of Judicial Involvement," *Harvard Educational Review* 47 (1977): 117–36; Diane

C. Donohue, "Emerging First and Fourth Amendment Rights of the Student," *Journal of Law and Education* 1 (1972): 449-67; J. Michael Brown, "Hair, the Constitution and the Public Schools," *Journal of Law and Education* 1 (1972): 371-82; Kenneth Mott and Stephen Edelstein, "Church, State and Education: The Supreme Court and its Critics," *Journal of Law and Education* 2 (1973): 535-91; Kirp and Yudof, *Educational Policy.*

10 Joel F. Handler, *Social Movements and the Legal System: A Theory of Law Reform and Social Change* (New York, 1979); David Tyack and Elisabeth Hansot, *Managers of Virtue: Public School Leadership in America, 1820-1980* (New York, 1982), part 3. Richard Kluger, *Simple Justice: The History of Brown v. Board of Education and Black America's Struggle for Equality* (New York, 1977); Edith K. Mosher, Anne H. Hastings, and Jennings L. Wagoner, Jr., *Pursuing Equal Educational Opportunity: School Politics and the New Activists* (New York, 1979); for an excellent study of the interaction of social movements and law see Henry M. Levin, "Education and Earnings of Blacks and the *Brown* Decision," in N. Namorato, ed., *Have We Overcome?* (Jackson, Miss., 1979), 79-119.

11 Friedman, "Courts over Time," 31; John E. Coons, William H. Clune, and Stephen D. Sugarman, *Private Wealth and Public Education* (Cambridge, Mass., 1970); Michael W. Kirst, "The New Politics of State Education Finance," *Phi Delta Kappan* 60 (1979): 428.

12 On public interest lawyers see Auerbach, *Unequal Justice,* ch. 9; on the relation of the supreme court and legislature in California see the rich case study by Richard F. Elmore and Milbrey W. McLaughlin, *Reform and Retrenchment: The Politics of California School Finance* (Cambridge, Mass., 1983).

13 Horowitz, *Courts,* 10-11, footnote 41; see sources cited in note 3 above.

14 Horowitz, *Courts,* 34-56; Peter D. Roos, "Litigation: A Necessary Tool for Educational Reform," *Phi Delta Kappan* 64 (1983): 417-19; Ray C. Rist and Ronald J. Anson, eds., *Education, Social Science, and the Judicial Process* (New York, 1977); Judith Areen, "The Judiciary and Education Reform: A Reassessment," *Georgetown Law Journal* 61B (1973): 1009-24; for detailed accounts of unsuccessful attempts at judge-directed reform of an urban school system, see Larry Cuban, "Hobson v. Hansen: A Study in Organizational Response," *Educational Administration Quarterly* 2 (1975): 15-37, and Joan C. Baratz, "Court Decisions and Educational Change: A Case History of the D.C. Public Schools, 1954-1974," *Journal of Law and Education* 4 (1975): 63-80; for a perceptive discussion of courts and race, see Stephen Arons, "Constitutional Litigation and Educational Reform: Canada's Opportunity," forthcoming in *Courts in the Classroom.*

15 Kirp, "Judicial Involvement," 121, 117-36; Betsy Levin, "The Making (and Unmaking) of a Civil Rights Regulation: Language Minority children and Bilingual Education," Project Report No. 82-A4, Stanford University, Institute for Research on Finance and Governance, March 1982; *San Antonio Independent School District v. Rodriquez,* 411 U.S. 1 (1973).

16 Kluger, *Simple Justice;* Eve Cary and Kathleen Willert Peratis, *Woman and the Law* (Skokie, Ill., 1977), ch. 4; David L. Kirp and Donald N. Jensen, "What Does Due Process Do?" *Public Interest* 73 (1983): 75-89.

17 John Higham, "Integration v. Pluralism: Another American Dilemma," *The*

Center Magazine July/August 1974: 67–73; Kirp, *Just Schools*, chs. 2, 3, 9; William Greenbaum, "America in Search of a New Ideal: An Essay on the Rise of Pluralism," *Harvard Educational Review* 44 (1974): 411–40.

18 The separation of church and state creates special claims for certain religious groups vis-a-vis public education—see, for example, the case of the Amish and compulsory secondary education: *Wisconsin v. Yoder,* 406 U.S. 205 (1972).

19 Kenneth M. Dolbeare and Phillip E. Hammond, *The School Prayer Decision* (Chicago, 1971); William K. Muir, Jr., *Prayer in the Public Schools: Law and Attitude Change* (Chicago, 1967).

20 Stephen Arons, *Compelling Belief: The Culture of American Schooling* New York, 1983); Levin, "Bilingual Education"; Frances Fitzgerald, "A Disagreement in Baileyville," *The New Yorker,* January 16, 1984, 47–90.

21 William L. Boyd, "The Public, the Professionals, and Educational Policy Making," *Teachers College Record* 77 (1976): 539–77; Thomas B. Marvell, Armand Galfo, and John Rockwell, "Court Selection: Student Litigation in State and Federal Courts" (Report and Background Material), National Center for State Courts, March 1982, 27–28 and passim; Gerald Grant, "The Character of Education and the Education of Character," *Daedalus* 110 (1981): 135–49.

22 John H. Meyer, "Organizational Facts Affecting the Legalization of Education," in David L. Kirp, ed., *School Days, Rule Days,* in press; Julius Menacker and Ernest Pascarella, "How Aware Are Educators of Supreme Court Decisions that Affect Them?" *Phi Delta Kappan* 64 (1983): 424–26; Paul Wrubel, "An Assessment of the Impact of the Courts on Local School Boards," Stanford University, Institute for Research on Educational Finance and Governance, Program Report No. 79-B10, March 1979.

23 Tyack and Hansot, *Managers,* part 2; Kirp, *Just Schools,* ch. 3.

24 In the process of implementing reforms, a new concept of equality emerged almost unnoticed as analysts sought to evaluate what educators were accomplishing. Some reformers became convinced that the *results* of schooling should be, on balance, equivalent for different groups—as James Coleman put it, an equality of output as well as input. This notion of equality of results introduced a challenge for educators expected to achieve parity between groups, so uncertain were the means to accomplish that goal and so great were the handicaps of poverty and discrimination that children faced in their everyday lives. For a critical appraisal of the attempts of legislatures, courts, and administrative agencies to regulate instruction, see Arthur E. Wise, *Legislated Learning: The Bureaucratization of the American Classroom* (Berkeley, 1979)—he believes these attempts on the whole were unsuccessful.

Appendix

1 For studies of the Supreme Court, see Gerhard Casper and Richard Posner, *The Workload of the Supreme Court* (Chicago, 1976); Lawrence Baum, *The Supreme Court* (Washington, 1981). For studies of the U.S. Courts of Appeal, see Woodford Howard, Jr., "Litigation Flows in Three U.S. Courts of Appeals," *Law and Society Review* 9 (1973): 223–40; Lawrence Baum, Sheldon Goldman, and Austin Sarat, "Research Note: The Evolution of Litigation in the Federal Courts of Appeals,

1895–1975," *Law and Society Review* 16 (1981–82): 291–310. For federal district courts, see American Law Institute, *A Study of the Business of Federal Courts* (Philadelphia, 1934); Joel Grossman and Austin Sarat, "Litigation in the Federal Courts: A Comparative Perspective," *Law and Society Review* 9 (1975): 321–46; David Clark, "Adjudication to Administration: A Statistical Analysis of Federal District Courts in the Twentieth Century," *Southern California Law Review* 55 (1981): 65–152.

2 Victor Flango and Mary Elsner, "Advance Report: The Latest State Court Caseload Data," *State Court Journal* 7 (1983): 16–22; Thomas Marvell and Sue Lindgren, "The Growth of Appeals: 1973–1983 Trends," *Bureau of Justice Statistics Bulletin* (Washington, D.C., 1985).

3 Wayne McIntosh, "A State Court's Clientele: Exploring the Strategy of Trial Litigation," *Law and Society Review* 19 (1985): 421–47; Lawrence Friedman and Robert Percival, "A Tale of Two Courts: Litigation in Alameda and San Benito Counties," *Law and Society Review* 10 (1976): 267–302; Arthur Young and Company, *An Empirical Study of the Judicial Role of Family and Commercial Disputes* (Sacramento, 1981); Stephen Daniels, "Continuity and Change in Patterns of Case Handling: A Case Study of Two Rural Counties," *Law and Society Review* 19 (1985): 381–420. See also Marc Galanter "Reading the Landscapes of Disputes," *UCLA Law Review* 31 (1983): 4–71.

4 Robert Kagan, Bliss Cartwright, Lawrence Friedman, and Stanton Wheeler, "The Business of State Supreme Courts, 1870–1970," *Stanford Law Review* 30 (1977): 121–56; Thomas Marvell, "Appellate Court Caseloads: Historical Trends," *Appellate Court Administrative Review* 4 (1983): 3–9.

5 Shortly after the publication of the Century Digest, the American Bar Association called the West classification the "standard" and urged its general adoption. Numerous states began using the American Digest System in their own digests of cases. Thus the West digests helped to standardize legal categories, became a common point of entry into published caselaw, and were an important reference tool in helping to professionalize the work of lawyers by providing them with a perspective that went beyond the limits of their state and region. See Newton Lamson, "For Lawyers, West Isn't a Direction—It's a Way of Life," *Juris Doctor* 4 (1974): 28–33; Jill Abramson, John Kennedy, and Ellen Pollack, "Inside the West Empire," *The American Lawyer* 5 (1983): 90–99.

6 See J. Morgan Kousser, "Dead End: The Development of Nineteenth Century Litigation on Racial Discrimination in School," California Institute of Technology, *Social Science Working Paper* no. 349 (1980); and Gladys Peterson, "The Present Status of the Negro Separate School as Defined by Court Decisions," *Journal of Negro Education* 4 (1935); 351–74.

7 West Publishing Company, *First Decennial of the American Digest System* (St. Paul, Minn., 1907) p. v.

8 John Hogan, *The Schools, The Courts and the Public Interest*, 2nd Edition (Lexington, Mass., 1985).

INDEX

DESIGNED BY IRVING PERKINS ASSOCIATES
COMPOSED BY MASTER TYPOGRAPHERS, INC., ST. LOUIS, MISSOURI
MANUFACTURED BY CUSHING MALLOY, INC., ANN ARBOR, MICHIGAN
TEXT AND DISPLAY LINES ARE SET IN CALIFORNIA

ᵂ

Library of Congress Cataloging-in-Publication Data
Tyack, David B.
Law and the shaping of public education, 1785–1954.
Includes bibliographical references and index.
1. Educational law and legislation—United States—
History. 2. Education and state—United States—History.
I. James, Thomas, 1948–   . II. Benavot, Aaron.
III. Title.
KF4119.T9   1986   344.73'07'09   86-40062
ISBN 0-299-10880-5   347.304709